Prophets and Patrons: The French University and the Emergence of the Social Sciences

Prophets and Patrons:
The French University
and the Emergence of
the Social Sciences

Terry Nichols Clark

Harvard University Press, Cambridge, Massachusetts
1973

To Alice Hardenbergh Clark
and Lincoln Harold Clark,
Social Scientists

Acknowledgments

The present study originated in a concern to understand the intellectual outlooks associated with different university systems. This concern developed during the summers of 1958 and 1959 which I spent studying in Paris, Hamburg, and Cologne, and grew sharper during 1960–61 when I studied in Paris, and the next year in Frankfurt, Berlin, and Munich. That fall I enrolled at Columbia in sociology, working especially with Daniel Bell, Juan Linz, Robert Merton, and Paul Lazarsfeld.

The spring and summer of 1965 were spent in Paris collecting documentation, reminiscences, and advice, especially from Raymond Aron, Raymond Boudon, Pierre Bourdieu, Marcel Cohen, Armand Cuvillier, Eric de Dampierre, Georges Davy, François-André Isambert, Claude Lévi-Strauss, and Alain Touraine.

The next year was devoted to teaching and writing at Columbia, and the results were defended as a Ph.D. thesis in the fall of 1966. The thesis was a preliminary working paper for the present study. (Only two of the present chapters even build on it.)

At the University of Chicago, I have been fortunate in having stimulating colleagues, especially William Kruskal, Nathan Leites, George Stigler, and George Stocking, and as temporary colleagues, Louis Dumont, Annie Kriegel, and Georges Dumézil. Morris Janowitz made room for a volume on Gabriel Tarde in his Heritage of Sociology Series.

I returned to Paris in September and December 1966, July and September 1967, June 1968 (the last days of the barricades), August 1968, and the summer of 1969. During these visits, interpretations of the changing French university were productively discussed with Pierre Bourdieu, Lucien Karpik, Bernard Lécuyer, Michelle Perrot, Jesse Pitts, and Antoine Prost. Others have also been helpful: Steven Lukes at Oxford, Henri Peyre at Yale, Melvin Richter at Hunter, Fritz Ringer at Boston University, and Eugen Weber at the University of California, Los Angeles.

Whether gauged in terms of intellectual challenge or hours of convivial company, however, my greatest debts are clearly to Edward Shils and Joseph Ben-David.

Institutions that made available their various facilities were the Bureau of Applied Social Research at Columbia University and the Centre Universitaire International, the Centre d'Etudes Sociologiques, the Centre de Sociologie Européenne, and the Ministère de l'Education Nationale in Paris.

Along the way, generous financial support was provided by Columbia University, the National Institutes of Mental Health, the American Council of Learned Societies, and the Social Science Research Committee of the University of Chicago. Research assistance of different varieties was skillfully performed by Robert Mauri at Columbia, Rainald von Gizycki and Sandra Caillens in Paris, and Robert Buroker, Satya Pabuwal, and David Taylor in Chicago.

Ann Orlov of Harvard University Press had the footnotes placed where they belong.

An earlier version of Chapter 3 was published as "Le patron et son cercle: clef de l'Université française," *Revue française de sociologie,* XXII (January–March 1971), 19–39 (with the assistance of Priscilla P. Clark) and appears here with permission of the Editions du Centre National de la Recherche Scientifique, Paris. Chapter 6 draws, with permission, on two articles which appeared in the *European Journal of Sociology,* IX (1968), 37–71, 72–91.

T.N.C.

Contents

Contents

Appendixes
Social Recruitment and
Traditions of Research

x

Prologue

Perspectives on the Emergence of the Social Sciences

How are ideas affected by the social arrangements within which they develop? This basic question of studies in the sociology of knowledge is also central to the present work. While similar to certain studies in the history and sociology of natural science, the approach used here emphasizes more than do they differences in type of knowledge. Many philosophers of science — those whom one would expect to explore these issues — have ostensibly rejected the neo-Kantian distinction between the natural and cultural sciences, but have hardly developed any viable substitutes. If they have generally implied that their results apply to all sciences, their empirical attention has turned primarily to contemporary physics and chemistry. Several fields may share certain common elements, but they also diverge on many points. Rather than generalize about an arbitrarily defined and delimited "science," and imply that "paradigms" are central only to modern natural science, more attention should be focused on variations among paradigms and on their relative acceptance. Paradigms need to be carefully distinguished, according to their explanatory power, level of formalization, and type of empirical support. These and other characteristics require elaboration in and of themselves; they must also be carefully related to social arrangements in particular fields, countries, and time periods.

Like philosophers of science, sociologists and psychologists of science have largely concentrated on identifying reasonably constant patterns (values of the scientific community, principles of creativity) rather than identifying and explaining differences across fields. On the other hand, the focus of most historians of science has remained too narrow to admit systematic comparisons of this sort. Broad generalizations and specialized monographs are doubtless both useful. Still, more attention to mapping and analyzing differences currently seems in order.

This work examines variations in social scientific knowledge in France and relates them to the structural arrangements within which social scientists worked. The major focus is on sociology. But if sociology overlaps with other social sciences in the mid-twentieth century, as one moves back in time the diversity of antecedents and the overlap with other social sciences is still larger. In France, much of anthropology, segments of statistics and political science, and sizable elements of history, economics, and geography emerged from identical sources. Segmentation and reconsolidation of subfields have been continuous. Advocates for young fields tend to announce ambitious programs, and the social sciences in France proved no exception; many were about as modest as Marcel Mauss, who once declared, "J'entends par sociologie toute science bien faite." Others, however, were not always so scrupulous about the "bien faite." General labels even changed substantially over quite brief periods. For example, before 1914 many Le Playists, who today would be considered sociologists, rejected Comte's eponym and referred to their work as *la science sociale*. In the interwar years some of them adopted *sociologie expérimentale* to stress their empirical concerns while recognizing similarities with the Durkheimians. Terms like anthropology and statistics also continually shifted in content. The vagueness of such newer appellations as the behavioral sciences, *sciences humaines,* or *sciences de l'homme* testifies to the continuity of such change.

To circumscribe the subject, emphasis is focused primarily on three social and intellectual groupings: the social statisticians, the "international sociologists," and the Durkheimians, which, though they by no means constituted the whole of French social science near the turn of the century, make strong claims for attention. Their intellectual contributions were all significant, but they varied considerably in both type and quality. Second, each entertained very different relationships to institutional structures. The social statisticians grew out of the governmental ministries, the Durkheimians were consistently housed in the university, and although the international sociologists were associated with the institutions created by René Worms, they generally graced neither ministries nor the university. Comparison of the three thus illuminates the processes and consequences of institutionalization within different settings.

In the early years of work on this volume, more consideration was planned for the various non-Durkheimians and for specific substantive research. These plans were founded on the assumption that the Durkheimians' exceptional success in the university had unjustly obscured the ideas of their early competitors. The quantities of ore processed following this plan unfortunately yielded more dross than gold. A few nuggets merit concern and have been discussed elsewhere.[1] But seven years of panning the rivers of French social science have increasingly convinced this prospector that the success of the Durkheimians was thoroughly justified.

It may be an historiographic banality that people, and especially scientists, tend to perceive as most central those elements of the past that bear on their present activities. Consequently, some may argue, an American sociologist of the mid-twentieth century naturally exaggerates the role of the Durkheimians. However, the few efforts to demonstrate the importance of non-Durkheimians have not been particularly convincing.[2] If the Durkheimians play a central part in the pages that follow, it should be recalled that in an earlier scenario they were only part of the chorus.

The low quality of most ore also led to a shift away from the ideas themselves and toward the social sources of the rare but striking intellectual achievements. In considering the French social scientific past, if nothing else one cannot help but be convinced of the fallaciousness of what might be termed the null hypothesis of the sociology of knowledge: good ideas develop from the continued activity of qualified individuals. Institutions, alas, do matter. And in France they were absolutely central in

1. For example, "Jacques Bertillon," "Gabriel Tarde," "Henri de Tourville," and "René Worms," all in *International Encyclopedia of the Social Sciences* (New York: Macmillan and Free Press, 1968); "Discontinuities in Social Research: The Case of the *Cours élémentaire de statistique administrative,*" *Journal of the History of the Behavioral Sciences,* Vol. III (January 1967), 3–16; "Marginality, Eclecticism, and Innovation," *Revue Internationale de Sociologie,* Series II, Vol. III (1967), 12–27; *Gabriel Tarde on Communication and Social Influence* (Chicago: The University of Chicago Press, 1969).
2. See the accounts cited at the beginning of Chapter 7.

3

encouraging the development of certain ideas and individuals while discouraging others. Consequently the importance of such patterns for more general intellectual history led to a more sustained focus on specific institutional arrangements.

It soon becomes obvious that the core of such an institutional analysis is the university — or more precisely the complex of state institutions comprising French higher education. So much did the university dominate French intellectual life outside its confines that many such activities, especially in the social sciences, were oriented toward what went on inside. However, just what in fact did go on — in terms of day-to-day decision-making — was no simple tale. In contrast to German or American universities, which have benefited from a good deal of research, the French university exists in relatively solitary and relatively unexamined splendor.

Hence not the least of the concerns here is to present a sociological analysis of the French university system. In this task the social sciences have served as a sort of litmus paper for study of the formal and informal structure of the university and related institutions. The cluster model has been formulated as the core of the system in writing (mainly in Chapter 3) for the first time — although it must have figured in informal discussions for many decades.

Since institutionalization is the fundamental social process involved in the development of a new field, this work focuses on the entry of the social sciences into the university, which is to say the period from about 1880 to 1914.

With the partial exception of the Durkheimians, that usual luxury of sociologists looking to the past — secondary sources prepared by historians — was seldom available. Much of the information about social backgrounds, professional organizations, and courses has been assembled here for the first time. For this reason more such descriptive materials have been included than if well-charted terrain was being covered. Owing to greater knowledge of the more recent past, however, much less detail has been included concerning the social sciences after World War I. Indeed developments after 1914 are considered primarily in terms of the continuities and discontinuities of the three basic groupings: they illustrate the problems of less than complete institutionalization and the recurrent cycles of change associated with the cluster pattern.

Although many subjects considered here belong as much to the present as to the past, given the rapidity of recent changes in France, discretion has dictated the use of the past tense throughout even if the present might still be appropriate.

Part I

*Organization and Innovation in the
French System of Higher Education*

Introduction

Although the major focus is on institutions of higher education, these were immeshed in the national educational system in
a manner that demands analysis. The outlines of the system were
formed during the late Middle Ages in conjunction with the
Church, but most specific institutions were created, or re-created,
by the Revolutionary governments and Napoleon. Changes from
Napoleon through the 1960's are considered in subsequent pages,
but many basic characteristics remained constant for a century
and a half. Perhaps most important of these was the predominance of the lycée, the lynchpin that held the system together.
Some twentieth-century observers have suggested that to obtain
an ideal education a student should attend a French lycée, a
British university, and an American graduate school. Clearly, the
achievements of the lycée have been numerous and impressive.
But documenting its excellence is not the present task; the concern here is more with the extent to which its achievements were
made at the expense of the rest of the system.

From the early nineteenth century, the lycée was the raison
d'être of the Faculties of Letters and Sciences; the Faculties served
largely as examination committees for lycée teachers. This conception of professional training in the narrow sense was essentially similar in Faculties of Law, Medicine, Theology, and Pharmacy, and the specialized Grandes Ecoles. The one Grande Ecole
which served as a source of scholars was the Ecole Normale Supérieure, although, as its name indicates, it was created to train
schoolteachers. The three years of financial support provided for
normaliens was repaid by the student's contractual agreement to
serve the state for at least ten years. Although others attended
lectures at the Faculties of Letters and Sciences, the national system of examinations (in the Faculties of Letters and Sciences)
was structured around this elite core of Ecole Normale students.
The examinations, established by the Ministry of Education, in

turn constrained the types of professors appointed to Faculty chairs and the types of courses they would offer.

Initially the licence and agrégation degrees were offered in just two subjects, letters and sciences. Although a few more subjects were added during the nineteenth century, differentiation was curtailed as there was no demand for more specialized secondary schoolteachers. Correspondingly, there was no systemic need for university professors or lectures in more specialized subjects. The social sciences, therefore, could enter the system only by infiltrating philosophy or history, or a marginal field like pedagogy. Traditions of social philosophy, social scientific history, and educational psychology and sociology correspondingly emerged within the Faculties of Letters.

But this was not an easy process. Ambitious lycée teachers could prepare the two theses for the Doctorat d'Etat required of Faculty professors. As the thesis had to be completed under a Faculty professor, however, and as he often encouraged candidates to work on subjects of interest to him, differentiation at the thesis stage was difficult. With the Doctorat, a man could be named professor in a provincial university. But as the City of Light attracted most eminent professors, and they would normally advise the Ministry about examinations and promotions in their particular field, students would tend to complete theses under Parisian professors. Clusters of doctoral candidates, provincial university professors, and, later, research institute staff members consequently emerged around the few holders of chairs at the Sorbonne who served as patrons. Each follower would vie for the patron's favors by contributing to his journal, extending his ideas in publications, and sending him good students.

Institutionalization of innovations thus took place largely when old clusters were displaced by new ones; this generally occurred when the leader of an insurgent cluster was named to a Parisian chair. To achieve such a coup, nascent social scientists had to argue their merits to professors in the Faculty, who would vote on candidates when a chair became vacant; or they had to create public pressures on the Ministry, which could create a new chair and name its first incumbent.

Extensive preparation was generally necessary because of the system's resistance to piecemeal change. Recognition of a new discipline implied not simply budgetary commitment for one new chair but, generally, provision for a national system of examinations in the subject, and a staff to prepare students for the new examination in many if not all the universities. Hence the necessity for institutionalizing not one man, but an entire cluster.

Structural differentiation and expansion of the system in accordance with the growth of knowledge was thus clearly retarded by such grounding in the secondary schools. Although it was traditional that university professors would be appointed and promoted for their original research, there was little provision for training research workers as opposed to teachers. Or, more exactly, the knowledge disseminated in conjunction with the licence-agrégation sequence was of the sort essential for a secondary schoolteacher, or as a foundation for research *in the traditional fields* (those institutionalized at the secondary level). The aggregate of this learning — and the ability, reinforced by oral examinations, to present it with appropriate style — was referred to with no little provincialism as *la culture générale*. Traditionalists would correspondingly invoke the specter of the decline of French civilization whenever creation of a new university chair was discussed. But in a sense they were correct: since the French system (unlike the American, for example) was not internally differentiated sufficiently to provide separate preparation for secondary schoolteachers and advanced research, to emphasize one implied neglecting the other. Committed to training the young, the system could not legitimately introduce subjects irrelevant to this basic concern.

The usual solution was to construct appendages for research: thus were added the Ecole Pratique des Hautes Etudes and the Centre National de la Recherche Scientifique. Outstanding scholars were named to these institutions without the constraints of training schoolteachers, and a few social scientists joined the mathematicians, historians, and other scholars here. But although one could prepare a Doctorat d'Etat, or more abbreviated theses such as a Diplôme d'Etudes Supérieures, Doctorat de l'Université, or in later years, a Doctorat du Troisième Cycle at these more research-oriented institutions, this training complemented, but in no way replaced, the traditional secondary school-oriented sequence from licence to agrégation. Prior to the 1950's, when career alternatives to the lycée began to become significant, very few students worked with scholars in these institutions. In principle the research sequence could have replaced the teaching sequence; but it never did. The reasons are many and complex — the traditional prestige of general culture; the importance of the lycée as a career base; the continued requirement of the teaching sequence for the most prestigious students, the *normaliens;* and so forth — but the result was the same: the licence-agrégation sequence remained most central to the system, but for structural and cultural reasons was subject to only minimal change. In most cases, the "vicious circle of anti-innovation" operated effectively: only less qualified persons would leave traditional careers to specialize in an innovation; critics would point to their work as inferior; and without serious candidates, creating a new chair would remain out of the question.

For these many reasons, Ministry officials were most cautious about committing themselves to any new central chair. Then, because an itemized ministerial budget had to be approved by parliament, parliamentary support was generally essential for establishing new disciplines.[1]

Influence could be brought to bear on the Ministry and parliament in several ways, but one possible source was opinion in the Latin Quarter. Supported by the generalizing intellectuals of the Latin Quarter, a particular set of ideas, a group of scholars, or a particular individual could attract a popular following. Resulting competition with the official structures might force them to change. Once a field was institutionalized inside the university, the Latin Quarter climate also helped attract or repel talented students, and thus exercised considerable indirect influence on developing lines of thought.

1. See the reports on ministerial budgets in the *Revue internationale de l'enseignement* from 1881 to 1914 and the associated discussions of parliamentary attitudes.

Chapter 1

The French System of Higher Education: Basic Institutional Structures

L'Ecole des hautes études est un germe que je dépose dans les murs lézardés de la vielle Sorbonne; en se développant, il les fera crouler. — Victor Duruy to Gabriel Monod in 1868. Gabriel Monod, *Portraits et souvenirs* (Paris: Calmann-Lévy, 1897), p. 129.

The Latin Quarter

The leading structures of French higher education have long been located in the *Quartier Latin*. Although under Church supervision, the institutions that grew up here in the late Middle Ages originated as small boarding schools of one or more scholars. Robert de Sorbonne was one of the best known, and his establishment grew so considerably that certain structures of later centuries continued to bear his name.[1] Scholars and students were united in corporations and Facultés which, under the ancien régime, comprised the University of Paris. After the Revolutionaries abolished the traditional universities, Napoleon sought to replace them with structures that discouraged organized dissent. He was apparently successful. Individual dissatisfactions were not easily channeled into institutional expression.

Most students and many faculty members were only loosely attached to any social or intellectual institutions. Writers, artists, publishers, journalists, streetcorner philosophers, and would-be poets worked and resided in the same area, forming a constantly

---

1. In the pages that follow the term will be employed, as in current usage, to refer to the building, the activities in the building, and the Paris Faculty of Letters. The specific referent will be clear from the context.

arguing, gesticulating, criticizing audience that would float in and out of cafés, cabarets, bookstores, and lectures. With no dormitories, hostels, *Studentenheime*, fraternities, or residential colleges, minimal involvement in sports, clubs, or extracurricular activities as in other countries, the student arriving from the provinces could easily become anomic. And most students were from the provinces: one-third to one-half of all students in France enrolled in Parisian institutions after 1800, although only about 10 percent of the French population resided in Paris. The new student might arrive with no more plan than to enroll in an advanced lycée or a particular Faculty. There were certain established tracks — such as from the Faculty of Letters to lycée professor, or from the Faculty of Law to the bar. But even inside a Faculty and particular examination sequence, there was still room for choice. Further, if a student failed — and about half of the candidates for examinations regularly did — he might well consider changing fields. In addition, young *agrégés* in philosophy or history, recent *licenciés* in law, or Sciences Politiques graduates — all likely converts for the social sciences — had remarkably few guides for subsequent specialization. The climate of the Latin Quarter, at such turning points in a career, could exert a significant influence.

A constant throughout most of the nineteenth and early twentieth centuries was the leading role of the literary intellectual. An appeal to general ideas and some literary accomplishments were sufficient qualification to speak on almost any issue. Prior to 1870, political repression and censorship restricted the range and intensity of activities somewhat, but the last years of the nineteenth century made up for lost time. Individual statements and criticisms reached a crescendo in the collective furor of the Dreyfus Affair. Indeed it was to characterize these persons that the term "intellectual" was first coined during the affair. Emile Zola's *J'accuse* and the 1898 Manifesto of the Intellectuals were only two of the most famous examples of their ideological proclamations. Intellectual reviews and newspapers were continually founded that carried statements such as these along with short stories and poetry, discussions of recent books, plays, art shows, and essays on recent political issues and ideas — as well as, in many periods, the emerging social sciences. The *Revue de Paris*, the early socialist *Humanité,* Charles Péguy's *Cahiers de la Quinzaine,* the *Action Française,* the Catholic *Esprit,* and Jean-Paul Sartre's *Les temps modernes* have had longer and more successful careers than most such journals, but were similar in the leading role they accorded to contributions from generalizing literary intellectuals. Such journals dominated the cultural landscape, especially that of the Latin Quarter, far more than their analogues in Germany or the United States.

Although some observers might have exaggerated the prestige of the artist or literary man, and minimized that of the scientist,[2] there remain famous supporting cases from many periods, such as that of Claude Bernard, who turned to medicine only after failing as a playwright. Student heroes over the last century have certainly included more names like Maurice Barrès, André Gide, and Sartre than those of natural scientists.[3] With few and fragile structures to direct them, potential social scientists were particularly susceptible to drawing intellectual inspiration, possible research questions, and self-images from generalizing intellectuals of the Latin Quarter.

Role models were adopted by professors not just from their field of specialization, or traditions of a teaching institution, but also by acceptance of or reaction against the climate of the Latin Quarter. The role of generalizing rhetorical stylist dominated the Faculty of Letters in the days of Victor Cousin and François Guizot, who could draw sizable audiences from the boulevards. One reaction against the dominant literary ethos was that of the austere scholar at the Ecole Pratique des Hautes Etudes and often the Collège de France; such men attracted few students. During the Dreyfus Affair many professors assumed strong ideological positions, inside and outside classrooms. With professors declaiming on political issues, students in turn organized to support their favorites and harass their enemies. Latin Quarter spokesmen for

2. The preliminary results of a survey questionnaire on occupational prestige administered in 1967 tend to indicate that literary men ranked considerably lower than earlier accounts have suggested. Precisely how much the occupational prestige structure has changed over the years is of course open to question.

3. Historical changes in literary and intellectual heroes are analyzed in Priscilla P. Clark and Terry N. Clark, "Writers, Literature, and Student Movements in France," *Sociology of Education,* XLII (Fall 1969), 293–314.

positions unrepresented in the University could still mobilize student listeners to carry disruptions into classrooms.[4] An extreme case, but one that demonstrated the involvement of the university in the Latin Quarter, was the "Thalamas Affair" of the fall of 1908.[5] It concerned a *cours libre* at the Faculty of Letters by Thalamas, a lycée professor critical of Joan of Arc. For eleven successive Wednesdays, riotous mobs of increasing size battled with the police until they finally forced their way into the lecture hall, manhandled and then ejected Thalamas, whereupon the university terminated the course.

The decade preceding each of the two World Wars witnessed some of the most continuous student demonstrations, where literally thousands of students would clash with one another and with the police in street fights. If such outbursts of militancy did not lead to physical intrusion into university buildings on a regular basis, the penetration of political ideology, literary fads, and rhetorical concerns from nearby streets was an all too constant phenomenon. In the early nineteenth century chairs in the ancient languages were substituted for those in history to avoid intrusion of ideology; later the concern that social science chairs would excite further demonstrations was a very real factor associated with their creation or abolition. But the specific reaction to a new chair almost always depended on the momentary climate of the Latin Quarter.

Cartesianism and Spontaneity

More than one axis of variation in Latin Quarter climate will be discussed below, but an especially important one is that of

4. For example, after 1894, Anatole Leroy-Beaulieu organized lectures at the Comité de Défense et de Progrès Social in which he would blast forth against "toute espèce de petits socialismes édulcorés." The crowds would respond, according to Mlle. Jeanne Weill, "par des cris de bataille, par des cris d'émeute, et souvent par des cris d'animaux." Concerned about the impact of such activities on the university, Mlle. Weill asked if Leroy-Beaulieu's "plan primitif" was not "l'érection du tapage en système d'éducation à l'usage de l'enseignement supérieur." See Dick May, *L'enseignement social à Paris* (Paris: Arthur Rousseau, 1896), pp. 46–47.

5. See Louis Dimier, *Vingt ans d'Action Française* (Paris: Nouvelle Librairie Nationale, 1926), pp. 111–114.

cartesianism and spontaneity.[6] The two configurations complemented and reinforced one another. At certain periods, in certain
institutions, one might dominate the other; but as deeply rooted
elements of French culture, strong emphasis on one generated a
reaction toward the other.

Cartesianism was identified with order, hierarchy, authority,
and the bureaucratic institutions exemplifying the *esprit de géo-
métrie:* the state, the military, and the university. Laying claim
to the Enlightenment heritage, seeking to realize the ideal of
raison, the bourgeoisie was the social group most identified with
cartesianism. In the late eighteenth and the nineteenth centuries,
it was the bourgeoisie that opposed aristocratic excesses of arbi-
trariness, irrationality, and corruption. In the Revolutionary
edicts abolishing traditional structures and creating uniform arrangements throughout the land, it was the bourgeoisie that
sought to institutionalize values of reason and order. What the
Revolutionaries began, Napoleon continued in seeking to establish uniform administrative structures and to eliminate all uncon-
trolled private activities — that might grow into political parties
or interest groups — separating the state from the individual citizen. In the realm of ideas, cartesianism was most compatible with
the scientific mentality. It sought to replace the richness of individual cases with the precision of general laws. In philosophy and
the study of man, cartesianism in the nineteenth century was most
directly linked with positivism.

The efforts of realizing these cartesian programs, however,
strengthened opposing tendencies toward spontaneity. Imposition
of order and hierarchy from above created resistance and irre-
sponsibility below: with centralized, comprehensive institutions
the sole legitimate agents of the collectivity, individuals could re-
linquish responsibility and concern for order. This was a frequent

6. These concepts build on studies in cultural anthropology, organization
theory, intellectual history, and French national character, and are presented
here with only minimal supporting documentation. They are discussed in Terry
N. Clark, ed., *Gabriel Tarde on Communication and Social Influence* (Chicago:
University of Chicago Press, 1969); Priscilla P. Clark and Terry N. Clark,
"Writers, Literature, and Student Movements"; and especially in "Culture, Social Structure, and Intellectual Currents in Nineteenth Century France," unpublished manuscript.

traditional reaction of peasants and workers, as well as of others subordinated to the bureaucracies — students, taxpayers, foot soldiers, and so forth. However, a similar tendency toward glorification of personal invention and romantic subjectivism could be found in the highest social strata: from the prowess of medieval battle, to the romance of courtly love, to the indulgences of the salons ran a tradition which sneered at the cartesianism of the bourgeoisie. With rationality and order identified with the bourgeois state, the spontaneous reaction could become anti-institutional, anticollective, and destructively revolutionary. Aesthetic, political, and economic criticisms combined in various antibourgeois ideologies put forth by the heirs of the traditional nobility as well as the peasantry and proletariat. The romantic nationalism of a Chateaubriand, by the end of the nineteenth century, could merge with the anarchistic tendencies of students in street fights of the Action Française. The cultural similarities of both right and left opponents to bourgeois republicanism were clearly illustrated by the ease with which Georges Sorel and his followers could move from one to the other.

Although rooted in different sectors throughout French society, these antagonisms between cartesianism and spontaneity found particularly sharp expression in the bookstores, lecture halls, and streets of the Latin Quarter. Political upheavals, economic crises, and other societal developments were thus linked with intellectual movements. But more specific activities of scholars and students were still channeled by the more constant structures of the national educational system.

The National Educational System

After Napoleon, the term *université* was not restricted to individual institutions of higher education, but referred to most of the national system of higher and secondary education. There was only one university: *l'Université de France*. This official designation was abolished in 1850, but its informal usage continued.

The Napoleonic structure was rigidly hierarchical. It was a mixture of an ecclesiastical control of ideas, governmental bureaucracy, and the military style of the Emperor. A *Grand Maître* was the center of all formal control, and although his title soon changed to Minister,[7] centralization of authority was modified little. Under the Ministry of Education were some sixteen *Recteurs,* one for each *Académie* in France, although the exact number varied over the next century and a half with wars and territorial readjustments. The Académie was the basic administrative unit of the system, and generally included the Faculties (Letters, Sciences, Medicine, Law, Pharmacy, and at one time Theology) which together would comprise a reasonably complete "university." [8] Below the Faculties were the lycées. Parallel to them, in Paris, were the Grandes Ecoles. The Rector was the formal link between the Parisian Ministry and the Faculties and state secondary schools of the Academy. Under the Rector was a *Doyen* for each Faculty.[9]

To maintain uniform standards and enforce regulations, a corps of *Inspecteurs* traveled to secondary schools throughout the country. They not only questioned local officials and attended classes, they sought out talented teachers and students. On their recommendation, promising students were transferred to more demanding schools. Teachers of outstanding ability would also be likely to move to better institutions. Constant mobility of personnel in the secondary institutions as well as the Faculties thus maintained a clearly stratified system.

The unified administrative structure of the system was evident in all aspects of instruction and examination. Traditionally, at the secondary level all subjects were required, as were the hours of each class and recess, methods of teaching, and passages to translate or memorize. Under the Second Empire, a Minister could even draw out his watch and exclaim with satisfaction, "At this very time, in such a class, all the scholars of the Empire are studying a certain page in Virgil." [10] Family life was not to diminish

7. The name and jurisdiction shifted slightly from the nineteenth to the twentieth century as the Ministère de l'Instruction Publique et des Beaux-Arts became the Ministère de l'Education Nationale.

8. This narrower meaning of the term was officially reintroduced in 1896.

9. See J. B. Piobetta, *Les institutions universitaires* (Paris: Presses Universitaires de France, 1951), and Georges Amestoy, "Les universités françaises," special issue of *Education et gestion,* 1968, for useful compilations of legal and administrative information.

10. Hippolyte A. Taine, *The Modern Regime* (New York: Henry Holt, 1894), II, 162. For thorough documentation on how little things had changed more than a century after Napoleon, see Carlton J. H. Hayes, *France, A Nation of Patriots* (New York: Columbia University Press, 1930), pp. 35–63.

19

the commitment of teachers: celibacy and common housing were the general rule in the nineteenth century.[11] Standardized clothing was obligatory for teachers at all levels; the individual's rank in the hierarchy was made obvious by insignias, epaulettes, and similar quasi-military decorations. (Students of the Ecole Polytechnique could still be observed in the 1960's walking about Paris in Napoleonic military dress — including black riding boots, full cape, rapier, and two-cornered hat.) Classes began and ended not at the sound of a bell, but to the roll of a military drum.

The possibilities for indoctrination refined by the Jesuits under the ancien régime were not relinquished by nineteenth-century governments, Bonapartist, royalist, or republican.[12] The temptations of the educational system as a well-oiled propaganda machine were simply too great to resist.

This consistent domination of the educational system by national politics contrasted with England or the United States, where leading institutions had long been under private control, as well as Germany, where, although state-controlled, the universities won considerable autonomy from politics in the early nineteenth century.[13] The whole conception of academic freedom, implying freedom from state repression in Germany, or the absence of religious or other private controls in the United States, had no French analogue. This conception derived from a more general view of responsible citizenship that was largely absent in France. As a result, the system was more deeply influenced by political and governmental changes than the traditional German universities, and has resembled the state universities more than leading private institutions in the United States.[14] On the other

11. A. Aulard, *Napoléon Ier et le monopole universitaire* (Paris: Armand Colin, 1911), pp. 177ff. The most thorough study to date of secondary schoolteachers is Paul Gerbod, *La condition universitaire en France au XIXe siècle* (Paris: Presses Universitaires de France, 1965). Unfortunately, nothing analogous exists for higher education.

12. Cf. Roger Henry Soltau, *French Political Thought in the 19th Century* (London: E. Benn, 1931; New York: Russell and Russell, 1959); and Hayes, *France*.

13. See Fritz K. Ringer, *The Decline of the German Mandarins* (Cambridge: Harvard University Press, 1969) for a reconstruction of this process.

14. Cf. Malcolm Moos and Francis E. Rourke, *The Campus and the State* (Baltimore: Johns Hopkins, 1959), for a collection of incidents involving campus intervention by American states which go beyond their French analogues.

hand, there were fewer fundamental strains between professors and the society around them than in many other countries. Throughout much of the nineteenth century a liberal consensus in political matters was accepted by many. Basic research (by the individual professor) and traditional cultural values were supported without question by parliament and much of the general public. The shared ideology of many academics and political leaders during the Third Republic led to university-generated efforts to further national cultural and political goals. These became especially evident during World War I when, for example, Sorbonne professors discussed how best to draw the Americans into the war.[15] Clearly this sort of political involvement only came into play at certain times and in certain fields, but for appointments and instruction in the social sciences it could be especially important.

The fundamental resistance to social science, however, was found in the examination system. Professors were selected for their positions through an elaborate pyramid of examinations. These began with the baccalaureate examination, for which the lycées prepared students. Serving as both a terminal secondary school diploma and an entrance examination for the five Faculties, it was passed by only about half of all lycée students. (Those seeking entrance to a Grande Ecole had to pass more demanding examinations.) In the nineteenth century, most post-baccalaureate students attended the Faculties of Law, Medicine, or Theology, preparing for one of the professions (see Figure 2). Students at Faculties of Letters or Science generally planned to become lycée professors. For the most part of modest background, they normally worked full-time at such jobs as lycée monitor while completing their studies.[16] Holding such jobs, they very seldom attended lectures; most studying was done alone, and the normal pattern was to register at the Faculty only a day or two before a degree examination.

15. In addition to posts for Literature and Civilization of the United States, a chair in the History of Christianity was created, as some felt that Americans would consider any university without such instruction a heathen institution. Minutes of the Conseil de la Faculté des Lettres, Sorbonne archives, 1914–1918.

16. Cf. Gerbod, *La Condition;* Gerard Vincent, "Les professeurs du second degré au début du XXe siècle," *Le mouvement social,* 55 (April–June 1966), 47–74.

Prior to 1880, there was just one licence in letters, which focused largely on the classics. In 1880 moderate specialization in letters, philosophy, and history was permitted, but a common section was still required, including written examinations in French and Latin, and oral French, Latin, and Greek "explications." [17] There was further gradual differentiation, and in 1920 a system of *certificats* was introduced, four of which were necessary for a licence.

Most *licenciés* would then teach in lycées, but some would prepare the agrégation. The Ministry would decide each year how many advanced positions (with higher pay and reduced hours) could be supported in the lycées, and award the agrégation to that number of persons in order of their ranking in the competition. Agrégation examinations were held initially in just letters and science, but gradually philosophy (1828), history (1830), grammar, geography, and modern languages were added to letters, and science was divided into mathematics and physical and natural science. Many candidates were eliminated in the written part of the examination. It was also considered essential for a lycée professor to be able to work up a lecture topic rapidly and to present it with style. Hence for the second, oral part of the examination, candidates would be given a lecture topic and just one day to prepare it for the jury of examiners (usually Parisian Faculty professors). In this way, superficial but polished articulateness was rewarded and came to be seen as distinctive to the agrégé.[18] Since specific subject areas changed each year, if a candidate failed, and about half consistently did, he would have to prepare an entirely different subject area the following year. This discouraged many from continuing; but those who did, and passed, might undertake work for a Doctorat d'Etat, a prerequisite to a Faculty chair.

Before 1847, provincial Faculty professors were chosen from

17. Antoine Prost, *Histoire de l'enseignement en France 1800–1967* (Paris: Armand Colin, 1968), especially chap. 10, provides an excellent overview of the system.

18. On the role of the agrégation, especially in philosophy, see André Canivez, *Jules Lagneau, Professeur de philosophie: Essai sur la condition du professeur de philosophie jusqu'à la fin du XIXe siècle,* Publications de la Faculté des Lettres de l'Université de Strasbourg, 148 (Paris: Les Belles Lettres, 1965), 17–244.

the senior professors of nearby lycées; at the Paris Faculties of Letters and Sciences, professors simultaneously held positions at the Collège de France and a few other distinguished institutions.[19] The major function of the Faculty professors was to examine students, both for the baccalauréat and the licence, in the particular region. A Faculty thus included just enough professors to constitute an examination jury.

With almost no examination students attending classes, however, many professors presented polished lectures to appeal to the general public. This tradition continued, especially in the provinces, into the twentieth century, but after 1870 it was increasingly attacked by proponents of a more rigorous conception of scholarship. To provide a more serious audience, efforts were made to attract some of the many students from the Faculties of Law and Medicine; but their vocational concerns were too strong. The situation changed significantly only in 1877 when 300 fellowships were created for licence students in letters and science; 200 more were created for agrégation candidates in 1880. The presence of serious students led to creation of the subordinate faculty positions of *maître de conférence* and *chargé de cours,* both to provide more complete coverage of examination material and to permit more student contact with original research. Advanced lycée professors were generally named to these positions for one year; but appointments were often renewed until a chair became available. In 1885, the tenured position of *professeur adjoint* was created, to be replaced in 1921 by the title of *professeur sans chair;*[20] such *nontitulaires* were accorded all rights (of voting, courses, and so forth) of *professeurs titulaires* except the vote for incumbents of chairs.[21]

As the number of chairs gradually increased in the late nineteenth century, their incumbents were less often recruited from

19. Initially, in science there were two professors from the Collège de France, two from the Muséum, three from the Ecole Polytechnique, and two lycée professors of mathematics; in letters there were three professors from the Collège de France and three lycée professors in belles lettres. Louis Liard, *L'enseignement supérieur en France,* II (Paris: Armand Colin, 1894), 160ff.

20. See Jean Bonnerot, *La Sorbonne* (Paris: Presses Universitaires de France, 1935), p. 121.

21. This ignores the increasing number of junior faculty positions (chargé d'enseignement, maître-assistant, assistant, etc.) created after 1945. See Amestoy, "Les universités," for consideration of their legal rights and duties.

the lycées. Original research as reported in the two theses required for the Doctorat d'Etat became a more important criterion. In letters one thesis originally dealt with rhetoric and logic, and the other with ancient literature; the secondary thesis had to be written in Latin until 1903. The range of thesis topics was broadened after 1870 to include any subject taught in a Faculty. The possibility of theses moving toward the social sciences was correspondingly increased, in principle. But the structures of the system remained essentially constant, so although students could listen to professors lecture on problems of original research, and they could pursue such problems in their theses, the range of basic substantive fields remained constrained by the subjects taught in the lycées.

The Doctorat was necessary but not sufficient for a Faculty chair. Thus in competition for limited positions, the theses increased in proportions. By the twentieth century they were seldom completed before a man reached his late thirties, and what was initially to have been only his first serious work often became the capstone of his career. Theses had to be defended publicly for a minimum of two hours, where the candidate would summarize his work and all professors present would comment in order of seniority.

The Faculties of Law and Medicine required not a Doctorat, but a special agrégation. This examination restricted differentiation toward the social sciences in the Law Faculties as the same basic subjects were used for all candidates until 1896, when four separate competitions were inaugurated: civil law, political economy, history of law, and administrative and political sciences.[22] Even after this time, however, the custom prevailed of appointing agrégés to chairs in strict order of seniority, so that a would-be economist might be appointed to a chair in Roman Law. The undifferentiated character of appointments and curriculum in the Law Faculties was reinforced by the strong vocational emphasis and the absence of outside careers for potential social scientist-lawyers.

A Docteur could be named professor in a Faculty of Letters

22. See Ch. Turgeon, "L'utilité d'une agrégation ès science économique," *Revue internationale de l'enseignement*, XXX (July–December 1895), 209–229, and subsequent issues of the same journal.

or Sciences by assuming a chair left vacant through retirement or death of its incumbent, or by being named to a new chair. For much of the nineteenth century, selection of incumbents for chairs was controlled reasonably closely by the Ministry, complemented by a national advisory council. Although the specific composition and advisory powers of councils varied from government to government, they generally included representatives from the clergy, the judiciary, the Senate, and the Conseil d'Etat. Appointments to chairs, nominally for life tenure, were terminated on occasions when the incumbent became outspokenly critical of the Church or state. Under the Second Empire, control was so tight that ministerial approval of detailed course programs became obligatory. This was no empty formality; to assure that no *"développements intempestifs"* would trouble official instruction, a place was reserved in every lecture hall "for the rector or his representative, in charge of the surveillance of higher education." [23]

Under the Third Republic, much changed. The results were not immediate, for there was considerable resistance in parliament and among traditional *universitaires.* But enough had changed by the 1890's that many referred to the New University and in particular the New Sorbonne. Freedom of the individual professor increased considerably; the Ministry no longer sought to maintain supervision of classroom performance. Authority for selection and nominal supervision of professors was decentralized in 1885 when an assemblée and conseil were created in each Faculty.[24] The assemblée included all members of the teaching staff — professors, maîtres de conférences, chargés de cours, and other temporary appointments. It dealt with questions of library arrangements, student life, and so forth. The more important decisions about annual appointments of *Directeurs de Programme* (who supervised instruction and examinations in individual dis-

23. Decree of Rouland, Minister of Public Instruction, 15 March 1858, cited in Félix Ponteil, *Histoire de l'enseignement en France* (Paris: Sirey, 1966), p. 247.

24. But professorial opinion still favored considerably greater autonomy, especially from the tyranny of examinations. See du Mesnil, *L'enquête relative à l'enseignement supérieur* (Paris: Imprimerie Nationale, 1884), summarized in an article by the same title in *Revue internationale de l'enseignement,* 11 (January–June 1886), 2–19.

ciplines), maîtres de conférences, and chargés de cours, and permanent appointments to chairs, were reserved to the conseil, which included only the permanent members of the Faculty. The Doyen was selected from the titulary professors of the Faculty from a double list of names, one presented by the assemblée, the other by the conseil, although the two generally agreed. (Prior to 1885, the Dean had been named directly by the Ministry.) The several Faculties in the Académie were represented in the Conseil Général des Facultés, which included the Rector, Faculty Deans, and two professors elected from each Faculty by all members of the teaching staff. The Conseil Général des Facultés supervised course programs, authorized unreimbursed *cours libres,* and made recommendations about the budget for individual Faculties. Legal authority for virtually all fundamental decisions still remained in the hands of the Ministry, where the Directeur de l'Enseignement Supérieur played the key role. National councils of senior *universitaires,* largely from Parisian institutions, continued to advise the Ministry through the late nineteenth and twentieth centuries (Conseil de l'Université, Conseil Supérieur de l'Instruction Publique, Conseil de l'Enseignement Supérieur). Their approval was necessary for changes in the titles of chairs and the naming of all incumbents of chairs. As such advisory bodies based decisions on generally shared beliefs about the national system, their impact seems to have been to retard further possible structural and intellectual differentiation. After 1945 the Conseil de l'Enseignement Supérieur apparently became more important. It had to approve the first incumbent of a new chair (instead of leaving this to the Ministry as in earlier years), and it established national "pools" of names from which junior faculty for the entire system were drawn.[25] These new legal powers may nevertheless have done no more than formalize the patronal authority as it existed in earlier years.

For most of the nineteenth century, the number and titles of chairs varied little. As more and different chairs were created, however, the Faculty would first meet to recommend either that the chair be declared vacant or that its title be changed. The recommendation would be transmitted to the Ministry and the posi-

25. See Amestoy, "L'université," pp. 359ff.

tion announced in the *Bulletin officiel* for a minimum of twenty days, during which candidates could apply. Candidates had to be thirty years of age, possess a doctorate, have two years of teaching experience in an officially recognized institution, and normally be of French citizenship. Chairholders in the Faculty would then rank the candidates and present the ordering to the Ministry. All professorial appointments needed the signature of the President of the Republic; in fact, however, the Faculty's "first line" candidate was almost always approved. For newly created chairs, the first incumbent was named directly by the Ministry (before 1945), and although normally approval of the Faculty would be obtained, the freer hand of the Ministry made this an important vehicle for innovation. Specific legal arrangements such as these must nevertheless be considered in conjunction with the informal structures discussed in the next chapter.

Once appointed, professors held tenure until age seventy[26] and were subject to almost no legal constraints. Their major obligation was to present three weekly "leçons," generally one hour each, during the academic year. Salary increases were based almost entirely on seniority. Legally, all professors were to reside in the town of the Faculty, but with the construction of railroads, increasing numbers resided in Paris and went to the provincial Faculty only for a day or two each week. (The same pattern was followed by certain professeurs agrégés in lycées.) Commuting as far as Bordeaux was difficult, but in some Faculties estimates suggest that as many as half of the professors resided in Paris. It was said, not entirely in jest, that when a young man entered the Ecole Normale, if he planned properly he would never have to leave Paris for more than a few days at a time for the rest of his life.

Many of the administrative changes in the two last decades of the nineteenth century derived from two related factors. First was the creation of the Third Republic, whose successive governments, moving gradually to the left and deriving increasing support from the lower social strata, devoted more attention to public education. The immediate political concern was to expand the primary and secondary schools and to create more scholar-

26. For many years, members of the Institut de France were permitted to occupy Faculty chairs until age seventy-five.

ships; these in turn led to pressures for expansion and change in the Faculties. The second factor was the increasing salience of the German university. Whether gauged in numbers of professors and students, the range and quality of publications, or many other indicators, the German universities were clearly surpassing the French — as Hippolyte Taine, Ernest Renan, and other critics constantly pointed out. After 1870, in conjunction with general political pressures for change, the German university provided both an abstract ideal and a specific basis for comparison.

There remained the question of which specific elements of the German model should be borrowed, and how they should be grafted onto the French system. The Ministry of Education provided fellowships for promising future *universitaires* to study across the Rhine.[27] But the German sojourn was not solely to benefit the individual; he was expected to discuss possible reforms with the Ministry of Education and to publish his general observations.[28] It was following these personal recommendations of outstanding young men that a number of reforms were adopted.

An organization important in mediating these suggestions was the Société de l'Enseignement Supérieur. Created in 1880, it included mainly partisans of scientific research, republican secularism, and "modernists." Hippolyte Taine, Gabriel Monod, Emile Boutmy, Ernest Lavisse, and Louis Pasteur were active from an early date. Lavisse was secretary general for several years and Edmond Dreyfus-Brisac edited its journal, the *Revue internationale de l'enseignement* (*R.I.E.*). Conferences were held to discuss reorganization of the national system as well as modifications in individual disciplines. The *R.I.E.* became the leading forum for discussion of these issues: here appeared recommendations of fellowship students returning from Germany, demands for change in established fields, and discussions of recent developments in the emerging social sciences.

One point made repeatedly in the *R.I.E.* concerned the fragmentation of learning in France compared to Germany. In ad-

27. Charles Andler, *Vie de Lucien Herr* (Paris: Editions Rieder, 1932), p. 32.

28. See the accounts by Edmond Dreyfus-Brisac, Gabriel Monod, Emile Durkheim and others quoted in Claude Digeon, *La crise allemande de la pensée française.* (Paris: Presses Universitaires de France, 1959), pp. 371ff.

dition to the low degree of autonomy of the individual professor, such fragmentation posed barriers to intellectual communication. In earlier years subordination of each professor to the Ministry facilitated political control. The 1885 reforms establishing a conseil and assemblée for each Faculty constituted one result of these *R.I.E.* discussions. Then in 1896, the separate Faculties (Theology had been abolished in 1885) in each Académie merged in a single institution, called the University of Paris, of Bordeaux, and so forth. The Ecole Normale Supérieure, seat of much creative scholarship earlier in the century,[29] was also merged with the University of Paris in November 1903.[30] The direct organizational consequences, it was argued, were facilitated planning, less duplication, and a greater sense of community among the professors of the several Faculties, now represented in the Conseils de l'Université.

Symbolic of the administrative changes and rupture with the past was a major building program. In Paris it involved destroying or remodeling many of the older buildings and superimposing on them a mammoth structure (still called the Sorbonne), containing the Faculties of Letters and Sciences, administrative and faculty offices, and many of the laboratories, specialized libraries, and classrooms of the Ecole Pratique des Hautes Etudes.[31] Reflecting the new emphasis on local autonomy, buildings were also constructed in the provinces with considerable financial support from local citizens and governments. Into these new organizational structures and buildings was infused the philosophy of creative scholarship and original research. New professorships were established throughout the system in traditional fields as well as in new areas.

The exact amount of this expansion, however, is difficult to ascertain with precision. Meaningful historical statistics about

29. This frequently neglected point is stressed by Georges Davy in "L'Université comme corps et l'esprit propre à ce corps," *Année sociologique,* Third Series (1959), pp. 3–30.

30. See C. Bouglé, "The French Conception of the University," in Walter M. Kotschnig and Elined Prys, eds., *The University in a Changing World* (London: Oxford University Press, 1932), pp. 25–51.

31. Alexis Lemaistre, *L'Institut de France et nos grands établissements scientifiques: Collège de France, Muséum, Institut Pasteur, Sorbonne, Observatoire* (Paris: Hachette, 1896), pp. 243–398; Bonnerot, *La Sorbonne,* pp. 9–57.

students and faculty are sparse. Time series have been published for degrees awarded and the total number of chairs in the system. As pointed out, however, especially in the nineteenth century, many degree candidates were not students in residence. And after 1880 an increasing number of faculty positions were created in addition to the titulary chairs.[32]

With these qualifications, one can point out that from 1865 to 1928 the number of licences awarded annually in letters (throughout France) increased four times, from about 200 to 800, while the number of chairs in letters in the Paris and provincial Faculties of Letters, the Ecole Normale Supérieure, and the Collège de France just doubled, from 126 to 235 (see Figures 1 and 2). Then, from 1928 to 1966, the number of licences more than tripled, while the number of chairs doubled, from 235 to 488. These figures clearly understate the increase of actual students in residence and the size of the teaching staff, however, especially for the period after 1945, as near the turn of the century professeurs titulaires represented about half the teaching staff at the Paris Faculty of Letters, while in the 1960's they were less than a quarter of the total.[33] Most of this expansion took

32. The best unpublished historical statistics located in the Ministry of Education did not include breakdowns either for discipline or subordinate faculty positions. The most complete source for comparable data for the entire period was not even French, but the German *Minerva, Jahrbuch der Gelehrten Welt,* which lists the titles and names of incumbents of all chairs roughly every decade from 1865 to the present. Individual chairs for the entire system had to be counted and classified by field to generate most of the tables which follow. As positions at the EPHE were listed in *Minerva* only irregularly, they have been included only in the tables without breakdowns by field.

33. The distribution of positions at the Faculties of Letters was as follows:

	1905 *	1913 *	1949 †	1969 †
Professeurs titulaires	48	43	44	9
Professeurs adjoints	16	12		
Maîtres de conférences	13	14	30	19
Chargés de cours et de conférences	23	30	26 ‡	72 ‡
Total	100%	99%	100%	100%
(N)	(69)	(83)	(511)	(5,782)

　* Paris Faculty of Letters
　† All French Faculties of Letters
　‡ Maîtres-assistants and Assistants

Source: *Enquêtes et documents relatifs à l'enseignement supérieur,* LXXXVIII (Paris: Imprimerie Nationale, 1905), pp. 32ff; CVIII (Paris: Imprimerie Nationale, 1914), p. 9; Pierre Bourdieu, Luc Boltanski, Pascale Maldidier, "La défense du corps," *Social Science Information,* X (1971), 45–86.

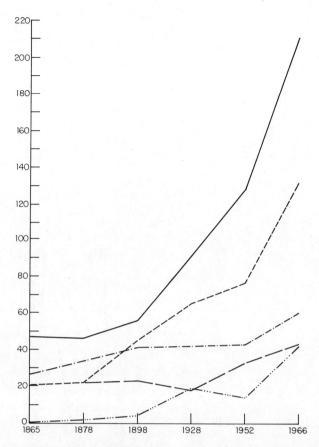

Figure 1. Number of chairs in Paris and provincial faculties, Ecole Normale Supérieure, Collège de France, 1865–1966. The five fields shown in the figure correspond to chairs numbered as follows in Tables 2, 3, and 4:

Philosophy: Tables 3 and 4, chairs coded 1, 2, and 3.

History: Tables 2 and 4, chairs coded 1 through 14, 33.

Classical Language and Literature: Tables 2 and 4, chairs coded 17, 18, 19.

Modern Languages and Literature: Tables 2 and 4, chairs coded 15, 16, 20 through 32, 34, 36.

Social Science: all chairs in Table 3 except those coded 1, 2, 3, 9, 10, 12, 13, 14.

Source: Minerva, Jahrbuch der Gelehrten Welt, issues from 1865 to 1966.

Modern Language and Literature ————
Classical Languages and Literature —·—·
History — — — — — — — — — — — —
Philosophy ——— ——— ——— ———
Social Science ——···—···—···—···—

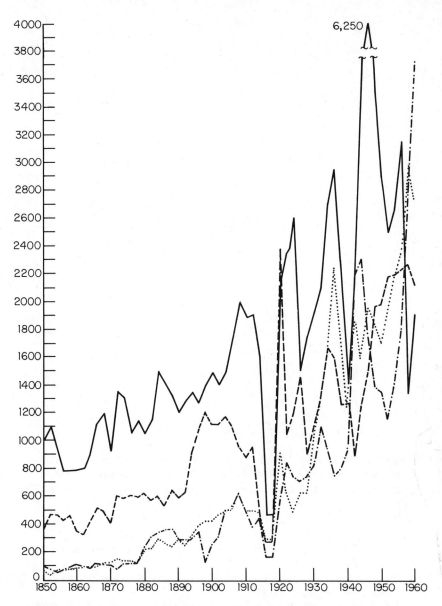

Figure 2. Degrees awarded by selected French faculties, 1850–1960.

Sources: Ministère de l'Economie Nationale et des Finances, *Annuaire Statistique,
1939* (Paris: 1941), pp. 30*–31*; Ministère de l'Economie et des Finances, *Annuaire
Statistique de la France 1966: Résumé rétrospectif* (Paris: 1966), p. 152.
Note: All *licences* are *licences d' enseignement.*

Licenses en droit ————————
Licences ès lettres ············
Licences ès sciences —·——·—
Docteurs en médecine — — —

place in the Paris and provincial Faculties of Letters rather than the Ecole Normale (where there were no chairs after 1898) or the Collège de France.

In terms of subject matter, the leading field in letters was consistently modern language and literature, claiming some 40 percent of all chairs from 1865 to 1966 (see Figure 1). Classical languages and literature was second with about one-fourth of the chairs in the nineteenth century, but it gradually declined. History and philosophy were the next most important fields from 1865 to 1878, each with about 18 percent of all chairs; but near the turn of the century, history moved ahead of philosophy. The place of philosophy was gradually taken over by the social sciences.

Breakdowns within the social sciences are presented in Table 3. Political economy was represented earliest at the Collège de France, where it was joined by a chair in geography in 1878. In the next twenty years social science chairs increased from two to four: a chair was added in social science at Bordeaux and another in pedagogy at the Sorbonne (held successively by Durkheim). By 1928 the number of chairs had jumped to twenty, including three in pedagogy, four in psychology, three in sociology and social science (in Bordeaux, Strasbourg and Paris), three in geography, and six in other fields (see Tables 2, 3, and 4 for the exact listings). In 1952 psychology and sociology still had four chairs each; but the other social sciences lost ground. By 1966, however, there had been considerable expansion, to forty-one chairs in the Paris and provincial Faculties of Letters and the Collège de France, and even more important increases in the social science sections of the Ecole Pratique des Hautes Etudes and the Centre National de la Recherche Scientifique (see Figure 3). Institutions and chairs outside Faculties of Letters will be considered in the rest of this chapter, and those inside the Faculties in subsequent chapters.

The Ecole Normale Supérieure

Despite changes in the central administration, the secondary schools and the Faculties had their counterparts under the ancien régime; this was not true of the Grandes Ecoles, creations of the

Convention and the Empire.[34] Each school had a particular mission of a reasonably applied nature. The Ecole Normale Supérieure was to train secondary school teachers. The Ecole Polytechnique was to train artillery officers and military technicians. Others were the Ecoles des Ponts et Chaussées for road and bridge engineers, Mines for mining engineers, and Centrale for industrial engineers and managers. The most important for the evolution of ideas, and the most eminent in their faculty and students,[35] were the Ecole Polytechnique and Ecole Normale Supérieure. The Polytechnique played a central role in diffusing cartesianism throughout French society. But in contrast to Polytechnique graduates only a very few Ecole Normale graduates went into government or industry; the world of the *normalien* was the national educational system. Students were drawn to the Ecole Normale from the national secondary system. Quality was emphasized, but politics could enter indirectly.

One of the deepest political conflicts of the Third Republic concerned the secularization of education. The battle was fought on the floor of parliament and in the Parisian press, but also in small towns and villages throughout France. There the leading spokesmen were the schoolteacher and the priest, each representative of opposing bureaucratic structures, political ideologies, and conceptions of the world.[36] Parents would side with one faction or another by entrusting their children either to the secular, state school or the clerically operated school — both groups took pains that an "appropriate" school was available.[37] A lukewarm

34. On the various Grandes Ecoles, see Mortimer d'Ocagne, *Les Grandes Ecoles de France* (Paris: J. Hetzel, 1879); F. A. Hayek's spirited and controversial *Counter-Revolution of Science* (Glencoe: The Free Press, 1955), Part II, chap. 1; Gaston Pinet, *Ecrivains et penseurs polytechniciens* (Paris: Paul Ollendorff, 1898); L. Pearce Williams, "Science, Education and Napoleon I," in Bruce Maslish, ed., *The Rise of Science in Relation to Society* (New York: Collier-Macmillan, 1964), pp. 84–90; and Frederick B. Artz. *The Development of Technical Education in France 1500–1850* (Cambridge: M.I.T. Press, 1966).

35. In *L'Inventeur* (Paris: Armand le Chevalier, 1867), chaps. 1–2, Yves Guyot argues that Polytechnique attracted the best French minds at the outset of the nineteenth century, but that they were more frequently found at the Ecole Normale by the middle of the century. Cf. Williams, "Science," for a more careful interpretation.

36. The many simplified interpretations of this polarity, and the changes in the twentieth century, should not obscure its importance for the early years of the Third Republic.

37. See André François-Poncet, *La vie et l'oeuvre de Robert Pinot* (Paris: Armand Colin, 1927), pp. 5ff.

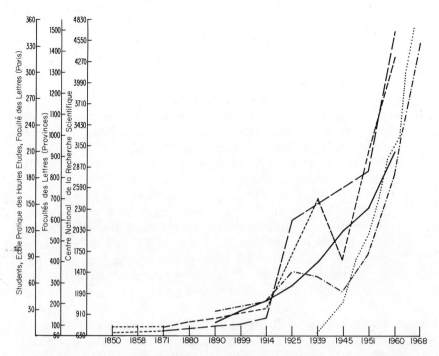

Figure 3. Number of positions at leading institutions, and number of students (in thousands), 1850–1968.

Sources: Minerva, Jahrbuch der Gelehrten Welt, issues from 1865 to 1966; Ministère de l'Economie Nationale et des Finances, *Annuaire Statistique, 1939* (Paris: 1941), pp. 30*–31*; Ministère de l'Economie et des Finances, *Annuaire Statistique de la France 1966: Résumé rétrospectif* (Paris: 1966), p. 152; Ministry of Education archives.

Université-Faculté des Lettres (Paris) — — — — — —
Université-Facultés des Lettres (Provinces) —— ——
Ecole Pratique des Hautes Etudes — · — · — · — · —
Students at All French Faculties ————————
Centre Nationale de la Recherche Scientifique · · · · · · · · ·

republican might send his child to a secular lycée. But once inside it was clear that the best students were not only the most intellectually gifted, they had also internalized the outlook of their teachers and could write enthusiastic papers on patriotic themes. Edouard Herriot, *normalien,* future national politician, already active in local politics as a lycée professor in Lyon, recounts his teaching experiences in a passage worth quoting at length:

35

On July 22, 1901, I had been entrusted with the initiation of an [advanced lycée] class . . . For the first time it was going to be possible to prepare for the Ecole Normale Supérieure in the provincial cities. I was excited by the work. If I had already had some personal successes, how much greater a joy it would be when my pupils brought home prizes or accessits from the General Competition! . . . My little group also included a young man in whom I was especially interested, Henri-Robert Laurent. Not only did he enter the Rue d'Ulm but he also won the honor prize in French composition, beating the Parisian champion. His subject was quite interesting, too: it was assumed that Rivarol, living in Hamm, near Hamburg, between 1795 and 1800, took in a refugee who told him of a French victory, and resumed his bitter jibing at the Revolution. The fugitive stressed the greatness of this idea of justice carried across Europe in the folds of the Tricolor and insisted that, despite the moment's destruction and suffering, the Revolution would give rise to a new France abounding in progress, even in the domain of the arts. Laurent had conceived an eloquent and brilliant dialogue on this theme, rich in information, astonishingly mature in spirit and full of enthusiasm for freedom, justice, right.[38]

The belief that intellectual prowess was synonymous with republican nationalism was hardly questioned. And Herriot's views seem hardly unique as his student won the national competition.

Committed professors such as Herriot sought out the most capable young men, whom they would encourage toward the Ecole Normale. Nevertheless some, and probably most, lycée professors were not as careful or enthusiastic in encouraging students, or did not maintain as firm intellectual standards, or were simply uninformed of the details of Normale preparation.[39] Because of such local differences, the traveling Inspectors played a crucial role. They would encourage promising students, especially those

38. Edouard Herriot, *In Those Days* (New York: Old and New World Publishing Company, n.d.), p. 149.
39. In 1842 there were 361 *normaliens* in the national secondary teaching corps, or 1 in 10 of the total corps; in 1865 there were 1 in 13. Cf. Prost, *Histoire*, p. 72. This proportion continued to decrease into the twentieth century.

with parents or professors not particularly inclined toward the Ecole Normale, to consider the possibility. Several *normaliens* of modest background report an Inspector asking them to translate a classical text, solve a mathematical problem, or perform some such task which they accomplished with distinction.[40]

Competition among individual students was intense, heightened by frequent posting of classroom rankings. Achievements on year end, and especially baccalaureate examinations, were traditionally rewarded with great solemnity. Representatives of the national system would honor the best students in public sessions of the lycée, with students, parents, and relatives in attendance.[41] Further awards were presented at the national level, and examination essays were often published.

Outstanding performance on such examinations could bring additional students to the attention of the Rector, who annually would transmit names of possible candidates for the Grandes Ecoles to the Ministry.[42] However, most outstanding candidates were shepherded to the leading Parisian lycées for one or two last years before attempting the Normale entrance examinations. Scholarships were available for boarders, and about half the

40. Here is Herriot's account, *In Those Days,* pp. 44–45:
"An incident in 1887 determined the new direction of this youth whose family intended him for a military school. The school inspector, Glachant, came to my rhetoric class, taught by an excellent man, M. Lambert . . . 'Herriot,' said M. Lambert, 'explain a passage from the *Pro Milone.* Start here . . .' When I had finished, M. Glachant offered me a scholarship in the Collège Ste-Barbe to prepare for the Ecole Normale Supérieure."

41. The importance of these sessions is indicated in their selection by a sociologist of French education, Mme. Viviane Isambert-Jamati, for a content analysis of the changing goals of secondary education. The results will appear shortly in her thesis; a preliminary report is "Permanence ou variations des objectifs poursuivis par les lycées dupuis cent ans," *Revue française de sociologie,* 8 (1967), 57–79. See Raoul Blanchard, *Ma jeunesse sous l'aile de Péguy* (Paris: Fayard, 1961), pp. 130–131, for the reactions of one student who won most of the prizes. Julien Luchaire, another, apparently chose the title of his book because he so dreaded placing second in any competition: *Confession d'un français moyen* (Florence: Leo S. Olschki, 1964); see especially Vol. 1.

42. Blanchard's career was advanced because he placed first in the history examination for all of France. Blanchard, *Ma jeunesse,* p. 130. Hubert Bourgin, among the Durkheimians, was first in philosophy. *Cinquante ans d'expérience démocratique, 1874–1924* (Paris: Nouvelle Librairie Nationale, 1925), p. 45. So was Paul Lapie. Albert Thomas won the prize in history; see B. W. Schaper, *Albert Thomas, Trente ans de réformisme social* (Paris: Presses Universitaires de France, n.d.), pp. 15ff.

normaliens near the end of the century were to benefit from such support.[43]

The two major lycées were Henri IV and Louis-le-Grand, which helped form the men who would later write and read essays with titles such as "Soyons durs."[44] The biographies from the period recount very similar experiences.[45] Boarders were roused to the beat of a drum at 6:30 A.M. in the winter, 6:00 in the summer, passed to unheated washrooms, study rooms, then breakfast at 7:30. Eleven hours of classes or supervised study followed, then dinner, and bed at 8:30 P.M.[46] Here the best students from throughout the country competed openly on a daily basis. Their success would be measured in four days of written entrance examinations for the Ecole Normale, followed by public oral examinations administered by the Ecole faculty. Many, including Emile Durkheim, would fail at least once before being admitted. Since only about twenty-five were accepted in letters and the same number in the sciences, the pressures were indeed intense: there were about ten applicants for each position. And all who applied were serious candidates, for, in addition to the special training, numerous documents had to be filed by the candidate's parents, the mayor, and the Rector of his Academy, including a signed promise to serve at least ten years in the national teaching corps.

43. Robert John Smith, "The Ecole Normale Supérieure in the Third Republic: A Study of the Classes of 1890–1904" (Ph.D. diss., University of Pennsylvania, 1967).

44. See Paul Lapie, "L'éducation morale dans les écoles françaises," *Enseignement public*, XC (1927), 103–112, and Pierre Bourdieu, Yvette Delsaut, Monique de Saint Martin, "Les fonctions du système d'enseignement," unpublished paper, Centre de Sociologie Européenne, 1970.

45. There are several impressive pages in the diary which Elie Halévy kept as a youth. For him to break away from the spontaneous elements from home, to which his brother Daniel gave such free reign, was particularly difficult. At eighteen, in the Lycée Condorcet, he agonized silently: "Je me suis appliqué à détruire en moi le feu des passions . . . Vous voyez que l'inspiration stoïcienne est à la source de ma conduite."

And then, in the fall of his first year at the Ecole Normale: "Il y a un vieux fond sémite et protestant en moi . . . il faut que Platon s'organise à l'intérieur des formes protestantes et kantiennes." "Extraits du journal d'Elie Halévy," in Alain, *Correspondance avec Elie et Florence Halévy* (Paris: Gallimard, 1958), pp. 21–23.

46. See Blanchard, *Ma jeunesse*, pp. 134–135, for the enthusiastic experience of a rough provincial, and Luchaire, *Confession d'un français moyen*, I, 23ff. for the snobbery of a Parisian.

For those accepted to the Ecole, the regime continued to be austere. The hours were about the same as those for boarders at the preparatory lycées. The basic curriculum in letters was built around the classics: each week included three hours of Latin and three of Greek, with sessions of two hours each in literature, philosophy, and history. (After 1870, one hour of modern language was added as a concession to the modernists.)[47] The major task in the first year was preparation of the licence examinations, which, after 1869, had to be passed by every first-year *normalien* if he was not to be dropped from the school—Léon Blum was a casualty of this law. An alternative was to be one of the first three in the class, a ranking based on papers and short examinations, as well as something unheard of at the Sorbonne, graded classroom performance. Indeed, with only about twenty students in a class, there was considerable discussion — and questioning of students by the professors. More freedom was available in the second year for courses inside and outside the Ecole, but the third year was devoted to preparation of the agrégation. As a "concours national," it brought the *normaliens* into competition with regular university students, as well as lycée professors preparing alone, who would come to Paris each year to try their luck. There was a concern to do well here again, as the inevitable prizes made their appearance: the one or two top agrégés would obtain traveling fellowships for a year or more before entering teaching.[48]

Although the student culture of the Normale retained many general contours throughout the nineteenth century — the stress on achievement, competition, a special vocabulary for statuses and activities at the Ecole, the classics, and two new suits of clothes from the state each year — there was progressive relaxation of the religious and social restrictions.[49] In 1881 the required high mass and hour of religious instruction were abolished; this step was important in attracting to the Ecole the Protestants and Jews who were central in remaking the educational system, and developing the social sciences, at the end of the century.

47. Smith, *The Ecole Normale*, pp. 95ff.

48. Julien Luchaire admitted that he even changed his agrégation topic to avoid the horror of placing second, and not winning a traveling fellowship. Luchaire, *Confessions d'un français moyen*, Vol. 1.

49. Pierre Jeannin, *Ecole Normale Supérieure* (Paris: Office Français de Diffusion Artistique et Littéraire, 1963), passim.

Directors Fustel de Coulanges (1881–1883) and Georges Perrot (1883–1904) were both classical scholars who sought to revitalize studies of the ancient world. They utilized not only the painstaking methods of the Germans, but by comparing family organization, myths, and rituals with those of other societies, they moved toward social scientific interpretations. This climate, especially as mediated by Fustel's *The Ancient City,* was particularly important in influencing Durkheim. An increasingly secular, republican, and scientific orientation was apparent in many other faculty members toward the end of the century. Gabriel Monod was seen as the apostle of Germanic historical scholarship. Gustav Bloch, historian and father of Marc Bloch, tended in the same direction. Charles Andler not only taught German language and literature, but edited the *Communist Manifesto* in French, taught a course on socialism at Sciences Po, and played a leading role in French socialist politics. Gustave Lanson, despite strong opposition from his colleague Ferdinand Brunetière, sought to make literary criticism into a science.

Continuing movement away from the classics — although more in research of the faculty than in examinations with professors outside the Ecole — crystallized in reorganizational efforts near the turn of the century. Louis Liard and Ernest Lavisse, both influential *universitaires,* were the leaders of the modernists.[50] We need not enter into the debates except to mention one dominant theme: the Ecole Normale should specialize in pedagogical theory.[51] These pressures led to abolishing the Ecole Normale as a separate teaching institution, and after 1904 its faculty was transferred to the Sorbonne. Lavisse became director of the new Ecole. *Normaliens* henceforth attended classes at the Sorbonne or other leading institutions. Still, recent Ecole graduates were retained as tutors, and individual professors, mainly from the Sorbonne, were invited to present short courses. Among the most emphasized were courses relating to pedagogical theory, and the leading lecturer on this subject was none other than Emile Durkheim, and in later years, his students.[52]

50. Pierre Nora, "Ernest Lavisse: son rôle dans la formation du sentiment national," *Revue historique,* 86 (1962), 73–106.

51. See the debates in the *R.I.E.* at the period.

52. An interesting discussion of cartesian "esprit" at the Ecole was included in an essay by an eminent professor and Director (1919–1927) of the Ecole,

The Ecole Normale may have inculcated a scientific and scholarly approach to life, and it may have attracted many of the best minds in France. But both with its own faculty before 1904, and afterward when students took courses elsewhere, it required its students to prepare for the standard secondary teaching degrees (licence and agrégation). Indeed a required course where students would present mock lectures was offered as preparation for both teaching and the oral section of the agrégation; in this way the distinctive verbal style of the *normalien,* and its identification with the agrégation, was maintained. This orientation toward the secondary schools was understandable in the early nineteenth century when most *normaliens* became and remained secondary school teachers; by the end of the century, however, the number of positions in higher education increased and after a few years of secondary school teaching many *normaliens* went into some branch of the university.[53] As research became increasingly specialized, the Ecole Normale training was no longer sufficient; it still produced generalists. Although certain specialized courses were available in Parisian institutions, especially in the second year, the bulk of the knowledge for a thesis had to be self-taught. And most thesis work was generally completed while carrying a heavy course load in a lycée far from the libraries and intellectual contacts of Paris. The best men would recognize their

---

Gustave Lanson. In its graduates, Lanson maintained, one finds "à travers les différences de tempéraments et des talents, le même besoin de clarté, d'ordre et d'enchaînement."

Further, "estime de l'intelligence, de la clarté, de la logique, développement de l'esprit critique, connaissance et pratique des méthodes: tout cela composerait un esprit solide et utile, un bon outil pour le travail scientifique et sociale, mais un esprit peut-être un peu sec, un peu acide, et insuffisamment orné de grâces, s'il ne s'enveloppait souvent d'ironie et de 'blague' . . . L'esprit que je viens de définir, essentiellement intellectuel et analytique, est par là même, essentiellement classique . . . Le classicisme des Normaliens a sa source d'une part dans le commerce familier et l'étude attentive des grandes oeuvres du XVIIe siècle, d'autre part dans ce besoin de clarté, de raison et de vérité que j'ai signalé tout à l'heure comme une des caractéristiques de l'esprit de l'Ecole."

Gustave Lanson, *L'Ecole Normale Supérieure* (Paris: Librairie Hachette, 1926), (republished from the *Revue des deux mondes,* February 1926). The quotations are from pp. 32–38.

53. About 40 to 50 percent near the turn of the century. See Smith, *The Ecole Normale Supérieure,* chap. 8. Bourdieu, Boltanski, and Maldidier, "La défense du corps," report that 25 percent of *normaliens* were teaching in Faculties in 1938 and 47 percent in 1969. The difference from the Smith figures seems due to treatment of nonrespondents (31 percent in 1938) and age of the *normaliens* sampled.

weak areas and fill in the gaps in one way or another. But an important systemic consequence of forcing the elite to be such autodidacts was generation of more of what had been learned at an earlier stage. To start on a topic outside the licence-agrégation curriculum implied not only more basic ground to cover, but possible fumbling for a workable thesis topic and sponsor. An almost certain consequence was lengthening the period of purgatory in the lycée. Doubtless the agrégation was considerably more demanding than an American or English B.A., but it was not the equivalent in research preparation of American postgraduate work or a German doctorate. Various solutions were attempted, such as the Ecole Pratique des Hautes Etudes; but, for various reasons, the French system never dealt adequately with the problem of training for advanced research on topics outside the established academic curriculum.

The Ecole Pratique des Hautes Etudes

Although major renovation of the university took place after the Franco-Prussian war, it was anticipated by several developments under the Second Empire. Probably the most important was creation of the Ecole Pratique des Hautes Etudes (EPHE). Minister of Education Victor Duruy was concerned with the weakening position of the French university in comparison with those in Germany. Sympathetic to the ideas of Renan and Taine concerning German scholarship, he initiated the custom of sending young agrégés for a year or two of study across the Rhine.[54] He also sought to encourage research training beyond that of existing institutions. Leading professors, whether at the Sorbonne, the Collège de France, or the Ecole Normale, were forced to lecture about their earlier work to general audiences, rather than focus on immediate problems of current research. The material facilities were especially scandalous — Pasteur's tiny laboratory under the stairs of the Collège de France became a famous case in point. There were almost no funds to support an outstanding

54. On Duruy, see Victor Duruy, *Notes et souvenirs, 1811–1894* (2 vols.; Paris: Hachette, 1902); Ernest Lavisse, *Un ministre: Victor Duruy* (Paris: Armand Colin, 1895).

agrégé as an apprentice for even a Pasteur or a Claude Bernard; agrégés had to teach in lycées far from Paris to support themselves.

The EPHE was conceived as a solution for these various problems. Created in 1868, it was essentially an administrative superstructure to dispense funds for advanced research and training, although the arrangements varied considerably in different fields.[55] It initially included four sections, one each for mathematics, physics and chemistry, natural history and physiology, and historical and philological sciences. The mathematicians needed funds mainly to support advanced training; the greatest demand of the natural scientists was for laboratory equipment and staffing. These the EPHE supplied. In all three of these sections, however, there was virtually no attempt to create new organizational structures: funds were merely distributed to a professor to expand existing facilities and support a few advanced students in his laboratory.

The history and philology section, however, did develop a distinctive identity, in large part, it appears, through the efforts of Gabriel Monod (1844–1912).[56] After the Ecole Normale, he had gone to Goettingen under the observation of Duruy to study German historical scholarship with George Waitz. In the spring of 1868 he returned to Paris, but at twenty-four he was still unknown and could legitimately do nothing on his own.[57] Hence, Duruy asked Michel Bréal and Alfred Maury, Collège de France professors, to assume responsibility for the history and philology section.[58] They met and talked, but it was Monod who pulled things together. He had shown organizational skill two years be-

55. See Liard, *L'Enseignement supérieur en France 1789–1893*, II, 271–297; Emile Durkheim et al., *La vie universitaire à Paris* (Paris: Armand Colin, 1918), pp. 182–193; and the *Bibliothèques* and *Annuaires* of the various sections of the EPHE.

56. On Monod, see Martin Siegel, "Science and the Historical Imagination: Patterns in French Historical Thought, 1866–1914" (Ph.D. diss., Columbia University, 1965); Digeon, *La crise allemande de la pensée française*, especially pp. 373–375, and the works cited immediately below.

57. Gabriel Monod, *Portraits et souvenirs* (Paris: Calmann-Lévy, 1897), pp. 129ff.

58. See the collection of articles in *Bibliothèque de l'Ecole Pratique des Hautes Etudes, IVe Section,* Vol. 231 (1922), especially those by Ferdinand Lot and Louis Havet.

fore in attracting Taine, Renan, Vidal de la Blache, Ernest Lavisse, and Fustel de Coulanges to launch the *Revue historique*. The school was to open in January 1869, and as late as December, Maury had not decided how instruction should be organized. He resisted the idea of actual collaboration between master and students; the authoritarian and rhetorical role of the French professor was not easily abandoned. Monod made numerous visits in this last crucial month, discussing specific plans, with the Goettingen seminars foremost in his mind. He brought enough pressure to bear on Maury so that the German model was largely followed in the section.

Léon Renier, professor at the Collège de France, became president of the section. Classroom and office space was scarce, but as Renier was also director of the Bibliothèque de l'Université, housed in the Sorbonne, he made available a few library rooms. Students were given small desks in the stacks. Renier's solution remained unsurpassed: the Fourth Section stayed in the back of the Sorbonne library for a full century.

At the outset there were only a few "Directeurs d'Etudes" (the title of professor was avoided), drawn mainly from the Collège de France and the Ecole Normale. Monod was charged with medieval history, and in subsequent years became professor at the Ecole Normale (1880), the Collège de France (1905), and president of the EPHE Fourth Section (1895–1912), as well as continuing as editor of the *Revue historique*. From these positions he organized a following of younger scholars who helped remake French historical scholarship.[59]

Another seminal grouping at the EPHE was that of the linguists: Ferdinand de Saussure participated in the section, as did Marcel Cohen, Sylvain Lévi, and Antoine Meillet, who served as president from 1936 to 1961. Adolph Landry was director of History of Economic Doctrines, and in turn was followed by François Simiand, who developed a select following in the interwar years.

59. See Gabriel Hanotaux's discussion of impressing a young faculty member while a student at the EPHE, and being invited, as an obvious consequence, to discuss his career with Monod. He collaborated with the *Revue historique* for a number of years. *Mon temps* (Paris: Plon, 1933), I, 230–237; II, 50–51.

EPHE salaries were quite modest compared to those at other institutions. In the 1890's they averaged between 2,000 and 3,000 francs annually in the Fourth and Fifth sections, while a professor at the Collège de France earned 10,000. By 1925 the EPHE paid about half the Collège de France salary of 25,000 francs (see Table 1). For directeurs cumulants holding lucrative posts elsewhere, this was reasonable; but for directeurs whose EPHE salary was their major support, it was meager indeed. In the 1920's this inequity was adjusted when directeurs and maîtres de conférences cumulants were paid about half of those holding no other position; the differential increased in subsequent years.[60] Salary scales and the budget for the Ecole were set in negotiations between the president of each section and the Director of Higher Education, referred to only half-humorously as "notre tsar."[61]

Through the 1880's the republican forces gained in the National Assembly, and in 1885 they abolished the Faculties of Catholic Theology. The stated reason was that they were superfluous as Church-operated seminaries trained sufficient clergy. (The Faculties of Protestant Theology, which did train ministers, were not abolished.) However, to maintain religious scholarship, and compete with the German theological faculties, it was felt essential to continue the tradition of Renan's *Life of Jesus* somewhere in France. The EPHE seemed the ideal solution, and the next year the Fifth Section, religious sciences, was created.[62] Initially housed in the former Faculty of Catholic Theology, seven years later it was moved into the back of the Sorbonne library, along with the Fourth Section. It remained about one-third

60. Thus, by 1939, when the average salary of professors at the Paris Faculty of Letters was 74,500 francs, in both the Fourth and Fifth sections the president was paid a 5,000 franc "préciput" for his services; directeurs noncumulants, 42,000 to 49,000 francs; maîtres de conférences, 30,000 francs; directeurs and maître de conférences cumulants, 11,375 francs.

61. "En fait, nous sommes sous son sceptre une petite dominion, heureuse de lui exprimer un parfait loyalisme," as Louis Havet, president of the Fourth Section, put it. "Discours," *Bibliothèque de l'Ecole Pratique des Hautes Etudes, IVe Section*, 231 (1922), p. 7ff.

62. On the Fifth Section, see Durkheim, *La vie universitaire à Paris; Problèmes et méthodes d'histoire des religions* (Paris: Presses Universitaires de France, 1968); *Célébration du cinquantenaire de la Section des Sciences religieuses de l'Ecole Pratique des Hautes Etudes* (Paris: Ernest Leroux, 1937); and the *Annuaire* of the section. There are several portraits of leading figures in the Fourth and Fifth sections in Marcel Mauss, *Oeuvres* (Paris: Les Editions de Minuit, 1969), Vol. 3, section on "Maîtres, Compagnons, et Disciples."

Table 1. Mean Salaries at Various Institutions (in francs)

Institution	1850	1871	1880	1890	1899	1914	1939	1960
Paris Faculty of Letters	5,000	7,500	14,500	14,300	14,100	13,400	74,500	28,200[a]
Provincial Faculties of Letters	3,980	5,060	–	7,900	7,680	8,780	–	28,200
Collège de France	5,000	7,500	10,000	10,000	–	12,000	–	31,000
Ecole Normale Supérieure	2,905	4,100	–	–	–	–	26,000	10,293
Ecole Pratique des Hautes Etudes	–	–	–	2,593[b]	2,835[b]	3,954[b]	30,195[b]	10,851[c]
Académie des Sciences Morales et Politiques	1,500	1,500	1,500	1,500	1,500	1,500	5,000	–
Provincial Primary Schoolteacher (Starting salary)	–	–	700	800	900	1,100	10,500	–

Sources: Ministry of Education archives. Primary schoolteacher figures (approximations for 1881, 1891, 1913, and 1930) from Prost, L'enseignement en France, p. 372.
[a] All Faculties combined.
[b] Fourth Section only.
[c] Fourth Section, cumulants only.

to one-half as large as the Fourth Section in terms of budget and personnel.[63]

Official statements about the section always claimed it was not anti-Catholic, and that it included from the outset *croyants* as well as *in-croyants*. But in largely avoiding theological discussions, and by subjecting Christianity to historical and comparative analysis, it was not seen as quite the same as the old Faculties of Catholic Theology.[64]

When such comparative analyses of religion as those in the *Année sociologique* began to appear, the ideological implications of this scholarship were clear: erudite comparisons of Catholicism with Australian totemism did not please the *bien pensants*. The major link between the EPHE and the *Année* was Marcel Mauss. He studied Indian religions under Sylvain Lévi and Near Eastern religions under Léon Marillier after completing his agrégation. It was here that Mauss learned the painstaking procedures of textual analysis and some of the vast substantive knowledge that went into the *Année sociologique*. Mauss guided several younger Durkheimians to the EPHE, and in 1901 he replaced Marillier as maître de conférences of Religions of Non-Civilized Peoples. In the same year, Henri Hubert also became maître de conférences, initiating instruction at the EPHE in Primitive Religions of Europe. In 1913, Marcel Granet was appointed director of Far Eastern Religions. Mauss and Granet both served as presidents of the Fifth Section in the interwar years. Mauss's position was taken over by Maurice Leenhardt in 1941, and in turn by Claude Lévi-Strauss in 1951 (the title of the post was changed to Comparative Religions of Non-Literate Peoples in 1954). Gabriel Le Bras, an active force in the sociology of Catholicism, held the post of History of Canon Law in the section from 1931 to 1965.

63. The Fourth Section had twenty-nine directeurs d'études, directeurs adjoints, and maîtres de conférences in 1892, and forty by 1925; the budget of the Fifth Section remained just under half that of the Fourth from 1890 to 1925, when it supported nineteen directeurs d'études and maîtres de conférences.

64. Its emphasis was marked by the number of faculty positions devoted to non-Christian religions: seven were essentially non-Christian and five Christian when the Section was founded in 1886; by 1936, sixteen were non-Christian and four Christian; but Christianity had made some progress by 1967, when it claimed the attention (at least in the titles) of twelve of the thirty-seven positions.

Despite the quality of many EPHE faculty, prior to 1945 there was no more than a handful of serious students.[65] Persons like de Saussure and his linguistic associates, Simiand, Alexandre Koyré, Granet, or even Mauss or Lévi-Strauss, in their early years at the EPHE were not particularly appreciated. Koyré became better known after moving to the Institute for Advanced Study at Princeton; the linguists needed others, such as Claude Lévi-Strauss, to demonstrate more general applications of their work. Mauss had a certain following of students, but these came largely from his contacts with other institutions.

Two factors hindering dissemination of ideas from the EPHE were associated with student career lines and patterns of professional organization. Unlike most other institutions, there were no requirements that students had to meet to attend courses: a particular age, nationality, former degrees (even secondary), or registration fees were not demanded; virtually anyone could come in. But in turn the EPHE neither helped prepare for nor awarded any degree of immediate use for a career. In principle, one could undertake research for a state doctorate at the EPHE; but in fact few persons did, even though some financial support was available. In later years, the creation of degrees for specialized research, such as the Third Cycle Doctorate, would in themselves do little to change the EPHE from being more than an ill-equipped institute for distinguished scholars and a very few protégés. Certain cultural prejudices — largely antispecialization[66] — worked against the EPHE, but these were less significant than other factors in discouraging students. More important was the

65. Mauss recounted that in 1895 and 1896, as students of Sylvain Lévi and his disciple Finot, there were only Lacote, who attended irregularly as he was preparing the agrégation, "Joe" Stickney from Harvard, Mabel Bode who went to the University of London, and Mauss. In later years, he reported, there were also a few Hungarians. Mauss, *Oeuvres*.

66. In Anatole France's *Monsieur Bergeret à Paris,* the EPHE is mentioned as a place where a language is taught from a grammar written by a German scholar, who had learned it from a parrot in the South Seas, who had been the sole companion of an old woman, who had died a few years before, the last of a small tribe to use the language.

Arnold van Gennep published an essay in 1912, *Les demi-savants,* that parodied the ritualism of specialized scholarship, recently translated by Rodney Needham as *The Semi-Scholars* (London: Routledge & Kegan Paul, 1967). His early irreverence toward academic norms seems to have been a factor in preventing him, a former EPHE student, from ever holding a position in the French university system.

structure of careers, taken up in the next chapter. For EPHE directors would be unlikely to develop a following unless they were linked with more central institutions.[67]

This interpretation is supported by the leading role of the EPHE Sixth Section. Duruy sought to create a fifth section in economic sciences when the original four were launched in 1868. Although a note in the founding Report stated that "subsequently

---

67. A degree at an earlier stage might nevertheless have attracted more foreign students. At least this was the opinion of Alfred Binet, who wrote to Gaston Paris, president of the EPHE Fourth Section and close associate of Louis Liard, as follows:

Paris, 29 rue Madame
le 3 Octobre '95

Monsieur le Professeur,

Je me permets de vous écrire pour attirer votre attention sur une question qui, je sais, vous paraît importante, celle de certificats ou diplômes pouvant être accordés par l'Ecole des Hautes Etudes. Je reçois souvent à mon laboratoire des étrangers, notamment des Américains, qui ont fait de la psychologie dans leur pays et viennent chercher en Europe un complément d'instruction. Vous savez, sans doute, qu'en ce moment, en Amérique, le nombre de laboratoires de psychologie augmente rapidement et dépasse 30. Les étudiants américains ne sont cependant pas satisfaits des diplômes accordés là-bas, et ils viennent demander aux laboratoires de la vieille Europe un titre qui a toujours plus de prestige que les leurs. Longtemps ils se sont dirigés vers l'Allemagne, particulièrement vers le laboratoire de Wundt, à Leipzig, et s'ils s'arrêtent à Paris, ça a été tout simplement pour visiter l'opéra et les Musées. Mais depuis un an ou deux, nous recevons quelques uns d'entre eux à notre laboratoire des Hautes Etudes, ils désirent travailler chez nous. Jusqu'ici j'ai dû les éclairer sur l'état de choses actuel, leur avouer que notre Ecole ne confère aucun titre, aucun diplôme; aussi, en hommes pratiques, se sont-ils retirés au bout de peu de temps, et ils sont allés grossir le nombre des élèves de laboratoires allemands.

J'ai toujours pensé que nous étions coupables de ne pas lutter contre un état de choses qui assure une prépondérance écrasante aux idées allemandes, en psychologie. C'est pour cette raison que je fais appel à votre concours pour défendre les intérets de la science française.

Permettez-moi de terminer ma lettre par le souvenir personnel d'un service que vous avez bien voulu me rendre il y a une vingtaine d'années, en me recommmendant, par la prière de Madame Lubanska, à M. Léopold Delisle, pour que je fusse admis à travailler dans la Salle des Imprimés. Votre recommandation m'a été singulièrement utile; car ce sont mes travaux à la Bibliothèque Nationale qui ont décidé ma vocation.

Veuillez agréer, Monsieur le professeur, l'hommage de ma haute considération.

Alfred Binet

Directeur du Laboratoire
de psychologie des
Hautes-Etudes

(Letter provided by Dr. Theta Wolf from the Salle des Manuscrits, Bibliothèque Nationale.)

a fifth section could be created," for "les sciences économiques," [68] this was not done. Duruy pleaded for such a section in a major report to the Emperor,[69] as well as for teaching positions in economics and related fields at the Collège de France, Faculties of Letters, and Faculties of Law; but he was unsuccessful. There were allusions to the "missing section" of the EPHE throughout the last part of the century, but only in 1947 was life given to the provision of the founding Report. The section of "economic and social sciences" grew rapidly, and by 1951 it listed twenty-eight faculty members; then by the 1960's it had far surpassed the other sections in personnel as well as its ministerial budget.[70] Other parts of the university had supplemented their ministerial budgets, but the Sixth Section developed a considerable reputation in this respect: the Congress for Cultural Freedom, the Ford

68. Victor Duruy, "Rapport à sa majesté l'Empereur sur l'enseignement supérieur, 1865–1868," *Statistique de l'Enseignement Supérieur, 1865–1868* (Paris: Imprimerie Nationale, 1868). There has been some disagreement about the initial designation of the Fifth Section. Hauser suggests that it was first "juridical studies," but that after a negative reaction at the Paris Faculty of Law, this idea was abandoned in favor of a more general definition of the social sciences. Henri Hauser, *L'enseignement des sciences sociales* (Paris: Marescq, 1903), pp. 130–132. But in turn it was restricted to economic sciences before Duruy's 1868 "Rapport," perhaps to avoid offending further vested interests.

69. *Ibid.* Although printed, the Report seems to have been a relatively privileged document. It was located (Summer 1968) with most of its pages uncut in the rear of the stacks (closed to the public and entered only with special permission) of the library of the Institut Pédagogique National; it was not included in the regular card catalogue listings of the Institut or the Bibliothèque Nationale.

Duruy's arguments appealed to many motives. They included:
A brief history of economics, emphasizing its French roots.
Details on courses in social science in German universities.
Demands which had led to fifty-three authorized *cours libres* in political economy in France during 1867–68.
The example of the Lyon Chamber of Commerce: founding a course and hiring a professor for it.
The suggestion that if political economy had been more developed, the 1848 Revolution might have been avoided.
But the caution that time was necessary — chemistry took eighty-five years before industrial applications began.
The self-supporting position of higher education — 3.8 million francs expenditures and 3.6 million receipts in 1866.
The far greater outlays for higher education in Belgium, Germany, and Great Britain.

70. In 1968 it included 211 persons in some teaching capacity.

Foundation, and the intermediary Fondation Marc Bloch were among the sources supplementing ministerial funds, although to what extent remains a subject of some disagreement.[71] Under Lucien Febvre and then Fernand Braudel it supported numerous individual research institutes, field trips, international congresses, and scholarly publications; it also developed a considerable following of advanced students. Comparison of the Fourth and Fifth sections thus suggests that the EPHE could indeed develop a considerable following if it were sufficiently linked with the rest of the system and careers were open to its students.

The Collège de France

Similar in many ways to the EPHE was the Collège de France.[72] From the outset both predominantly supported original research by senior scholars. Both recruited their faculties from a broad pool of talent as, unlike the universities, they did not require the Doctorat d'Etat. EPHE courses generally drew only a handful of students; sometimes this was also the case at the Collège de France — for neither prepared students for particular examination sequences. But generalizations about the Collège in this respect are difficult; the type of following around chairs there varied considerably with the position of the incumbent in the more general "intellectual field," to use Pierre Bourdieu's term.[73] Certain highly specialized scholars would lecture to a few disciples as at the EPHE; indeed, they were often the same few disciples and same professor: the linguists Sylvain Lévi and Antoine Meillet held positions at both the Collège de France and the EPHE, and lectured to the same small followings at both institutions. Sanskrit and other rare languages somehow never attracted

71. The first three sections of the EPHE were largely replaced in the twentieth century by the Centre National de la Recherche Scientifique.

72. As the institutional histories of the Collège de France are only brief commemorative volumes, one must rely on its *Annuaire* and fragments of other works. See, however, the chapter by Maurice Croiset in Durkheim, *La vie universitaire à Paris,* pp. 144–160; and *Les quatre siècles du Collège de France* (Paris: Bibliothèque Nationale, Galérie Mazarine, 1931). Abel Lefranc's articles in the *Revue internationale de l'enseignement* around 1890 and his *Histoire du Collège de France* (Paris: Hachette, 1893) deal largely with its early years.

73. Pierre Bourdieu, "Champ intellectuel et projet créateur," *Les temps modernes,* No. 246 (November 1966), pp. 865–906.

the *grand public*. But this pattern, followed by the *érudit,* was only one of several. It was most frequent in esoteric subject matters which led to few possible careers.

A second alternative was the *mondain,* the accomplished speaker who captured the interest of the general, nonacademic public. Prior to the 1880's, of course, this was the dominant model inside the universities. At the Collège de France, literary critics like C. A. Sainte-Beuve, the historian Jules Michelet, Gabriel Tarde, and Henri Bergson tended toward this pattern. All wrote prolifically, but unlike the erudites, their books sold well with the general public. They also frequently wrote for general intellectual and even popular magazines and newspapers, serving as critics of plays and best-selling books, debating political issues, and acting generally as arbiters of the *goût public.* Their subjects — often history, philosophy, or literature — were institutionalized at the secondary level and had a broad potential appeal. The *mondains* remained outside the Ecole Normale and Sorbonne circuit of traditional *universitaires.* Perhaps of higher social background than the *universitaires,* and self-taught in certain areas, they often had not completed the full sequence of university degrees. In style, they were more spontaneous than cartesian.

The third type was the classic *universitaire.* If the erudite might hold *postes cumulants* at scholarly institutions, and the *mondain* become involved in general public activities, the *universitaire* might hold a chair at the Ecole Normale (Pasteur, Monod, Lavisse) or the Sorbonne (Alfred Croiset, Lavisse). He would be integrated into a cluster as discussed in the next chapter. He would sit on ministerial advisory boards and thesis and agrégation committees. He would probably be a *normalien* and have completed licence, agrégation, and Doctorat d'Etat. He was most likely lower rather than upper bourgeois in social background. He would tend to be of more cartesian than spontaneous temperament.

How could these different types be housed together? Such heterogeneity was extraordinary in French bureaucratic institutions — but the Collège de France was a remarkably unbureaucratic place. What most incumbents did share, despite other radical differences, was quality. In a generally elitist system, Collège de France professors were more consistently eminent than those at any other institution. The number of posts was restricted (twenty-eight in 1850, forty-two in 1968), and they were generously endowed: the salary was two to three times that of the EPHE (see Table 1).

Since its beginnings, the Collège had maintained an untraditional tradition of innovation. The openness to new ideas derived from the same factors fostering its diversity. Foremost was the absence of those bureaucratic mechanisms which integrated other institutions into the national system: there were no student entrance requirements as at the Grandes Ecoles; indeed, legally there were no students, only auditors. No examinations or degrees were possible as there were no regular students. There was no need to adapt to any institutional student culture as none existed. Thus, the Collège professors did not have to meet or agree on common standards; each could go his own way, lecture as he pleased, and attract followers corresponding to his particular outlook. The only collective activity of importance was selection of incumbents for chairs, decided through a secret majority vote of at least two-thirds of the professors.[74] But even here, with so few positions, it was virtually impossible to appoint friends or disciples, as was possible inside the university, and as they had no direct impact on examinations or course requirements, established professors were less affected by new appointments. Then, with prestige and salaries so high, and positions so few, only quite outstanding persons would seek vacant posts. Unlike the Faculties or the EPHE, there were no junior positions from which men would advance only after years of scholarship and deference. Although salary increases for Faculty professors and EPHE directeurs depended largely on seniority, the fact that all Collège de France professors received the same salary from the outset eliminated this source of status differentiation.

This is not to imply that biases of one sort or another could not operate, but that the institutional culture placed such emphasis on universalistic standards that tendencies toward particularism were strongly resisted. For example, more than one Col-

74. The Institut de France also became involved, and various alternative nomination procedures were utilized before the twentieth century which will not be treated here. These matters are discussed in Gabriel Monod "Une élection au Collège de France," *Comptes rendus des Séances et Travaux de l'Académie des Sciences Morales et Politiques,* 167 (1907), 336–358.

lège de France professor, when forced to vote on candidates in areas beyond his personal competence, would solicit the advice of eminent foreign specialists. Such individual and often secret inquiry by nonspecialists should be sharply distinguished from official invitation of outside testimonials, as is routine at many American and British universities.

The basic structural features of the Collège all discouraged the formation of cliques which might influence nominations. Since changes in titles of chairs did not affect the national system, as they did in the Faculties, the Collège could respond to intellectual developments more rapidly than other institutions. The Collège was also an innovative force in another way; not only could it institutionalize new lines of thought, but the faculty was sufficiently free from committee work and the burdens of theses that it could help disseminate innovations in other institutions. The prestige of the Collège was considerable enough that participation of one of its professors in a new activity helped provide academic legitimation. The importance of this sort of activity, which might be called academic pump-priming, was especially evident in the social sciences during the nineteenth century.

Two chairs in the social sciences were created in 1831: Eugène Lerminier was appointed Professor of History of Comparative Legislation, and Jean-Baptiste Say, Professor of Political Economy. Say was succeeded by Pellegrino Rossi, Michel Chevalier, and Paul Leroy-Beaulieu, all of whom continued the tradition of liberal, theoretical economics. Duruy's emphasis on economics led to a chair in the History of Economic Doctrines in 1871. Emile Levasseur occupied the chair for forty years and was succeeded by Marcel Marion; in 1933 it was changed to Economic and Political Geography and given to André Siegfried. In 1907, when Levasseur's reputation for work on history of the working class was at its height (and he was *administrateur* of the Collège), a chair was created in the History of Labor, filled by Georges Renard and then François Simiand (1932–1935). Simiand was succeeded by Emile Coornaert, and when he left the chair, its title became Démographie Sociale: La Vie des Populations and it was given to Alfred Sauvy. François Perroux was appointed to a new chair in Analysis of Economic and Social

Facts in 1955. Although the strictly economic contributions of these men, with the possible exception of Say, were not particularly great, almost every chair evolved from economics toward one of the other social sciences. In this respect, these Collège de France professors were most influential.

Théodule Ribot lectured from the chair of Experimental and Comparative Psychology after 1888, and was replaced in 1902 by Pierre Janet, who played a crucial role in advancing laboratory work in France. The social psychological tradition which Ribot hoped to develop was strengthened considerably by Gabriel Tarde, who assumed the chair of Modern Philosophy in 1900 (after failing to have its title changed to sociology.) However, his death just four years later, and other factors to be examined below, prevented him from exercising a continuing influence. Jean Izoulet held a chair of Social Philosophy created in 1897; although he remained distant from the Durkheimians, his chair was renamed Sociology and occupied by Marcel Mauss (1931–1942), and then, as Collective Psychology, by Maurice Halbwachs (1944–1945.) Claude Lévi-Strauss was named to a new chair of Social Anthropology in 1959, and Raymond Aron to a chair of Sociology of Modern Civilization in 1970.

Muslim Sociology and Sociography was a chair created in 1902 with funds from the Governor General of Algeria and the protectorates of Tunisia and Morocco; a former military man, Alfred le Chatlier, was appointed. Though his descriptive volumes on sources of potential insurrection may have assisted army intelligence, their scientific value was meager. Another unimpressive appointment was Pierre Laffitte, whose contacts in the Senate helped create the first chair in the world in the History of Science in 1892.

These poor appointments were nevertheless only minor deviations of an outstanding institution. Changes over the years at the Institut de France were an entirely different matter.

The Institut de France

Although not an educational institution, the Institut, in some periods and fields, played an important role in the development

of new ideas.[75] Created in 1795, the Institut replaced the Académies of the ancien régime abolished two years earlier. Three
"classes" were included in the new Institut. The first, physical
and mathematical sciences, covered the same area as the former
Académie des Sciences; the third, literature and fine arts, also
had its antecedents under the ancien régime; but creation of the
second, moral and political sciences, constituted recognition of a
sort that previously was politically inconceivable. Members of the
second class included Destutt de Tracy, Georges Cabanis, and
other "ideologues." Although they completed studies on public
health and welfare which the government found useful, eight years
later Napoleon abolished the class; he felt uneasy supporting potential political opponents. In 1832 the two remaining classes
were transformed into four Académies, and under the influence
of Guizot, a fifth was created: the Académie des Sciences Morales
et Politiques. No major organizational changes have taken place
in the Institut since that time.

The Académie Française, the oldest and most respected
Academy, had as its major function the maintenance of the
French language. The Académie des Inscriptions et Belles Lettres was the official organization for scholars of Antiquity, the
Middle Ages, and certain associated fields. The Académie des
Beaux Arts was concerned with the plastic arts, architecture, and
musical composition. The Académie des Sciences, under the ancien régime and Napoleon, included some of the most eminent
of French natural scientists. They provided important advice for
the government in several applied areas: gunpowder and arms,
navigation instruments, irrigation systems, and so forth.[76] Some
of the natural scientists also occasionally turned a hand to social
questions. D'Alembert, Bernoulli, and Laplace wrote a number
of papers on statistical and demographic phenomena, and Condorcet calculated probabilities of jury verdicts and election results. Lavoisier conducted a study of hospital organization.[77] This

75. The basic sources for the Institut are the *Mémoires, Travaux,* and similar reports of its various sections.
76. See Maurice Crosland, *The Society of Arceuil* (Cambridge: Harvard
University Press, 1967), especially chaps. 3 and 4.
77. Bernard Lécuyer and Anthony Oberschall, "Sociology: Early History
of Social Research," *International Encyclopedia of the Social Sciences* (New
York: Macmillan and Free Press, 1968).

perspective of the natural scientist turned governmental consultant had an important influence on the early work of the social statisticians.[78]

When the Academies wanted to encourage work on a topic, they would frequently offer a prize. In the nineteenth century such prizes might range as high as 10,000 francs, more than the annual salary of high civil servants. The Institut also performed a supervisory function: organizations and projects were created "sous le haut patronage" of Académies, which would administer funds, supervise the scientific activities, and provide a link between the new venture and governmental agencies. In this way the Société de Statistique de Paris was founded under the Académie des Sciences Morales et Politiques,[79] and Frédéric Le Play's family monographs were supported by the Académie des Sciences.[80]

The liberalism of Guizot, as founder of the Académie des Sciences Morales et Politiques (ASMP), was characteristic of its membership for much of the nineteenth century. His close contact with the higher civil service and political leadership has also marked the ASMP throughout its life.[81] The ASMP generally sought to avoid political controversy by focusing on distant historical periods and on contemporary questions considered legitimate by political leaders of the day. Difficulties could nevertheless arise with changes in political leadership. Thus, after the June days of 1848, the provisional government commissioned the ASMP to set forth the political, social, and economic principles of a "well-ordered Republic." Victor Cousin, Adolphe Thiers, and others contributed to the effort. But even though the results were not widely distributed, after the 1852 coup d'état, the Sec-

78. See Chapter 4.
79. See Chapter 4.
80. See Chapter 3.
81. For this reason, more than one critic of the French establishment has focused his attack on the ASMP. Proudhon, for example, wrote that "C'est au palais de l'Institut, à l'Académie des Sciences Morales et Politiques, tribunal suprême des moeurs françaises, que se tiennent ces conférences. Ceux qui prennent part à la délibération sont les plus haut placés dans l'administration et l'enseignement . . . tous défenseurs de la religion, de la morale, du mariage et de la famille, contre le socialisme anti-malthusien, et, hors ce qui regarde la procréation des enfants, partisans du laissez faire, laissez passer . . ." *De la justice dans la révolution et dans l'Eglise* (1858), cited in Louis Chevalier, *Démographie générale* (Paris: Dalloz, 1951), p. 61.

ond Empire leaders imposed membership restrictions and had a political monitor attend all sessions.

In the mid-nineteenth century the effective control of crime and of the growing working classes were recurrent subjects at the ASMP. Under its auspices Louis Villermé conducted outstanding working class investigations in the 1840's, combining official statistics and personal observation with interviews of factory managers (although not direct interviews with workers.)[82] His report became a model in subsequent years for parliamentary commissions on factory conditions.[83] Alexis de Tocqueville's reports were examples of this same tradition of policy-oriented field research.

In later years, several statistical studies were conducted either by ASMP members or nonmembers competing for prizes. Members with statistical concerns near the turn of the century included Emile Lavasseur, Paul Leroy-Beaulieu, and Emile Cheysson.

Social philosophy included such representatives as Théodule Ribot, Gabriel Tarde, and Henri Bergson. Even these grand theorists could perform mundane activities for the ASMP. Tarde, for example, supervised the Prix Carnot, established by the wife of the national politician to support some two hundred working-class widows each year. Another prize was awarded in 1901 to the two best reports on "Methods Applicable to the Study of Social Facts." René Worms and A. Bauer thus won 1,000 and 1,500 francs respectively.

The emerging social sciences found modest financial support through such prizes. In the 1860's, for example, the ASMP offered one annual prize of 3,000 francs through its state budget, and nine others ranging from 1,500 to 5,000 francs founded by private donations in the areas of pauperism, "la morale," political economy, primary school education, moral and political science, ancient philosophy, and marriage.[84] Competitions would generally be publicly announced, candidates would submit book-length

82. Bernard-Pierre Lécuyer has reported on Villermé in a number of unpublished studies.
83. Cf. Hilde Rigaudias-Weiss, *Les enquêtes ouvrières en France entre 1830 et 1848* (Paris: Alcan, 1936), and Bertrand Gille, *Les sources statistiques de l'histoire de France* (Paris: Minard, 1964).
84. *Statistique de l'enseignement supérieur* (Paris: Imprimerie Nationale, 1868), p. 739.

manuscripts on the subject, these would be judged by a committee of a few *académiciens,* who would recommend granting the prize to one manuscript, dividing it, or not awarding it at all.

More important for institutionalization, however, was the ASMP's linkage to other institutions. One outstanding example was that of Gaston Richard, a lycée professor who won a prize near the turn of the century. Louis Liard, ASMP member and Directeur de l'Enseignement Supérieur, was impressed enough with Richard to help him be named Durkheim's successor in the Bordeaux chair of Social Science.[85]

Occupying an Institut *fauteuil* was an honor highly respected by the general public even while ridiculed by the avant garde. Although not directly influential in diffusing ideas, it was indirectly important in several ways. Especially in the early nineteenth century, the appropriate Academy was a major source of electoral support for Collège de France chairs.[86] Membership also provided additional income, and before other sources developed, remained desirable for this reason alone.[87] For a writer whose books appealed to the general public, membership in the Académie Française could increase his reputation and royalties. For a natural scientist, even in the mid-twentieth century, the Académie des Sciences maintained one of the most convenient rapid publication outlets in France. For policy-oriented social scientists, ASMP membership could facilitate contacts with governmental agencies. Then, too, in some Academies, in some periods, even intellectual stimulation was to be found. But as the number of positions was not increased with the growing intellectual population, and as older men were given priority and life membership, by the twentieth century most members were quite old. Even if eminent in earlier years, their Institute presentations were seldom as significant as those in other institutions. For university professors, membership was a resource that could influence votes of other Faculty members tempted by the Institute. The Ministry of Education, especially when its Director of Higher Education was a member, could sometimes be effectively influenced from

85. See Chapter 7.
86. See Monod, "Une élection."
87. See Table 1 for salary figures of ASMP members.

the Institute. For these various reasons, *grands patrons* tended to become members of the Institute, and it thus became more closely linked with the national educational system. This more general process of institutional linkage through informal contacts among patrons is a major focus of the next chapter.

Table 2. Nonsocial Science Chairs in Paris and Provincial Faculties of Letters and Collège de France, 1865–1966

Title of Chair	1865	1878	1898	1928	1952	1966
1. Modern and Contemporary History	1 *1*	1 *1*	2 *1* (5)	3 (12)	4 *2* (13)	6 *1* (26)
2. French History			1 (4)	1 *2* (6)	3 *1* (4)	3 *1* (4)
3. Medieval History			1 (4)	1 (6)	2 (9)	3 (13)
4. Ancient History, Historical Geography of Antiquity	1	1 (3)	1 (6)	*2* (10)	1 (5)	(11)
5. Greek History				1 (1)	1 (1)	3 *1* (2)
6. Roman History, Epigraphie et Antiquités Latines				(1)	1 *1*	2 *1* (1)
7. Religious History			*1*	1 *1* (1)	1 *1* (1)	1 *1* (1)
8. Archaeology, Oriental Archaeology		1	1 *1*	1 *2* (3)	1 *1* (2)	2 *1* (12)
9. History of Art		*1*		2 *1* (4)	1 (5)	3 *1* (8)
10. History of Music					1	1 (1)
11. Egyptology, Antiquités Egyptiennes et Ethiopiennes	*1*	*1*	*1*	*1*	*1* (1)	4 *1* (2)

Table 2. (*Continued*)

Title of Chair	1865	1878	1898	1928	1952	1966
12. Byzantine Studies				1	1 (1)	2 *1* (1)
13. Islamic Studies, Langue arabe	*2*	*2*	*1*	1 (4)	1 2 (3)	5 *1* (2)
14. South East Asian Civilization	*1*	*1*	1 *1* (1)	2 (1)	1 3 (1)	2 5
15. Slavic Language and Literature	*1*	*1*	*1* (1)	2 *1* (1)	*1*	4 *1* (6)
16. Linguistics				1 *1*	2 *1* (3)	2 (7)
17. Semitic Languages; Langues persane, Syriaques, Zende, Sandscrite; Paléographie	*2*	*2*	*3*			1 *1*
18. Ancient Greek Language, Literature, Philology	1 *1*	2 *2* (5)	2 *2* (12)	3 *2* (12)	4 *1* (10)	7 *1* (16)
19. Latin Language, Literature, Philology	2 *3*	2 *3* (5)	2 *3* (13)	1 *3* (14)	6 *2* (14)	9 *1* (21)
20. French Language, Literature	2 *2* (15)	2 *2* (14)	3 *2* (17)	6 *2* (17)	6 *2* (28)	20 *1* (58)
21. Non-French Romance Language, Literature		*1*	1 *1* (2)	4 *1* (7)	3 2 (14)	8 *1* (16)
22. Germanic Language, Literature		*1*	2 (1)	2 *2* (9)	1 *1* (18)	8 *1* (22)
23. English Language, Literature			(2)	3 (13)	3 (16)	10 (18)
24. American Language, Literature				1 (1)	1 *1* (1)	2 *1* (1)

Table 2. (*Continued*)

Title of Chair	1865	1878	1898	1928	1952	1966
25. Slavic Language, Literature					(3)	
26. Comparative Literature	*1*	*1*	1 (1)	1 (3)	1 (2)	3 (9)
27. Scandinavian Language, Literature				1	1	
28. Dutch Language, Literature						1
29. Chinese Language, Literature	*1*	*1*	*1*	*1* (1)	*1*	1
30. Japanese Language, Literature				1		1
31. Classical Language, Literature	*1* (15)	2 (9)	(3)	(7)	(6)	(5)
32. Foreign Language, Literature	1 (15)	*1* (14)	1 (10)			
33. History	(15)	(12)	(11)			
34. Histoire et Technologie des Systèmes Philosophiques					*1*	
35. Civilisation Indo-Européenne					*1*	
36. Assyriologie					*1*	*1*
Total, Paris Faculty of Letters	8	10	16	37	47	114
Total, Collège de France	*18*	*22*	*22*	*25*	*24*	*24*
Total, Provincial Faculties of Letters	(60)	(62)	(93)	(134)	(161)	(263)

Source: Minerva, Jahrbuch der Gelehrten Welt, issues from 1865 to 1966.
Note: Figure in upper left is for Paris Faculty of Letters.
Figure in italics in upper right is for Collège de France.
Figure in parentheses in lower left is for provincial faculties of letters.

Table 3. Social Science and Related Chairs in Paris and Provincial Faculties of Letters and Collège de France, 1865–1966

Title of Chair	1865	1878	1898	1928	1952	1966
1. Philosophie	1 (15)	1 (14)	1 (13)	1 *1* (11)	2 *1* (19)	(22)
2. Logique, Histoire de la Philosophie, Philosophie Médiéval, Moderne, Générale, Comparée, Aesthétique	1 *1*	1 2	2 4 (1)	2 *1* (2)	4 *1* (5)	12 *2* (6)
3. Morale, Philosophie Morale	*1*	*1*			1	1
4. Psychologie				1 (1)	1 (2)	2 (2)
5. Psychologie Expérimentale				1		1
6. Psychologie Pathologique					1	1
7. Psychologie Sociale						1 (2)
8. Psychologie de l'Enfant						1
9. Géographie	1	1 (3)	1 (7)	1 (7)	1 (14)	1 (28)
10. Géographie Régionale, and all specific regions			1 *1*	1 (2)	3 *1* (3)	4 *1* (2)
11. Géographie Humaine, Economique, Politique, Appliquée		*1*	*1*	1 *1* (1)	*1*	4 *1* (2)
12. Géographie Générale						1
13. Histoire et Géographie		(3)		(2)		
14. Climatologie and geographic specialties tending toward the natural sciences					(1)	2 (1)
15. Sociologie				(1)	1 (1)	2 (4)

63

Table 3. (*Continued*)

Title of Chair	1865	1878	1898	1928	1952	1966
16. Science Sociale			(1)	(1)	(1)	
17. Science de l'Education, Pédagogie			1	(1)		1
18. Morale et Science de l'Education, Morale et Pédagogie				1 (1)		
19. Psychologie de l'Enfant et Pédagogie					(1)	
20. Psychologie et Pédagogie						(1)
21. Sciences Auxiliaires de l'Histoire				(1)	(1)	(3)
22. Histoire Economique						(3)
23. Histoire de l'Economie Sociale				1		
24. Ethnologie					1	1 (2)
25. Ethnologie Sociale et Religieuse						1
26. Ethnologie de l'Afrique Noire						1
27. Démographie						1
28. Economie Politique	*1*	*1*	*1*			
29. Psychologie Expérimentale et Comparée				*1*		
30. Faits Economiques et Sociaux				*1*		*1*
31. Enseignement de la Coöpération				*1*		
32. Histoire du Travail				*1*	*1*	
33. Sociologie et Sociographie Musulmannes				*1*	*1*	*1*

64

Table 3. (*Continued*)

Title of Chair	1865	1878	1898	1928	1952	1966
34. Prévoyance et Assistance Sociales				*1*		
35. Anthropologie Sociale						1
36. Démographie Sociale						1
Total, Paris Faculty of Letters	3	3	6	10	15	38
Total, Collège de France	*3*	*5*	*7*	*9*	*6*	*8*
Total, Provincial Faculties of Letters	(15)	(20)	(22)	(31)	(48)	(78)

Source: Minerva, Jahrbuch der Gelehrten Welt, issues from 1865 to 1966.
Note: Figure in upper left is for Paris Faculty of Letters.
Figure in italics in upper right is for Collège de France.
Figure in parentheses in lower left is for provincial faculties of letters.

Table 4. Chairs in Letters at the Ecole Normale Supérieure, 1865–1898

Title of Chair	1865	1878	1898
Medieval History (3)[a]	–	–	1
Ancient History (4)	–	–	1
Ancient Greek Language, Literature (18)	2	2	2
Latin Language, Literature (19)	2	2	2
French Language, Literature (20)	2	2	2
Comparative Grammar (26)	1	1	2
History (33)	2	2	–
Philosophy (1)	2	2	1
Logic, History of Philosophy (2)	–	–	1
Geography (9)	1	1	1
Total	12	12	13

Source: Minerva, Jahrbuch der Gelehrten Welt, issues from 1865 to 1966.
[a] The number in parentheses after each chair corresponds to the listings in Tables 2 and 3.

Chapter 2

Patrons and Clusters: The Informal Structure of the French University System

Au moment où je clos cette lettre, j'apprends officieusement que cette chaire de — serait à nouveau vacante . . . L. surchargé l'abandonnerait. Je ne voudrais pas avoir l'air trop gourmand, mais c'est un morceau dont j'aurais vraiment bien envie. D'autre part, je voudrais n'agir qu'avec beaucoup de circonspection et ne pas donner l'impression de me mettre au travers de L. Je sais que déjà en la matière vous m'avez donné de precieux conseils. Pouvez-vous à nouveau vous informer et m'informer? Merci encore et bien vôtre — Letter to a friend in Paris from a professor in the provinces.

Critical as well as enthusiastic commentators on French higher education have confronted more than one paradox. Brilliance and mediocrity have coexisted more closely than in other national systems. The shining lights of Parisian institutions like the Collège de France or the Sorbonne contrasted markedly with most provincial Faculties. But even at the Sorbonne, while some fields maintained impressive standards, occasionally others had difficulty doing just an average job. Still, in most fields since the late nineteenth century, the most eminent foreign universities would consider a Sorbonne professor a prize — if they could ever attract him.

Such quality was maintained even though a righteous tone was often sounded when "corrupt" practices of selecting professors were discussed. The results, however, suggest that strictly intellectual standards remained prerequisites to other qualifications more continuously than critics generally cared to admit.

If critics might grudgingly concede quality, however, innova-

66

tiveness was seldom listed, even by admirers, as a leading attribute of the system. Nevertheless, certain changes were introduced with almost revolutionary speed. The goal of the present chapter is to isolate certain characteristics of the French university system behind its peculiar mixture of both brilliance and mediocrity, and of conservatism and innovation. To this end this chapter focuses on informal patterns of organization which emerged inside the formal structures.

The Basic Unit of Academic Organization: the Cluster

Most accounts touching on French higher education have focused on individual professorial chairs.[1] The tenacious preference for *situations acquises* was persistent enough that many observers have taken it as a dominant characteristic of French administration.[2] If portrayals emphasizing the egocentric rigidity of the individual professor contain some truth, however, they err in implying that chaired professors were insensitive to those around them. From the standpoint of intellectual organization and innovation, the most important unit was not the individual incumbent of a chair, but an informal grouping that might be termed a "cluster."[3] The cluster was an association of perhaps a dozen persons who shared a minimal core of beliefs about their work and who were prepared to collaborate to advance research and instruction in a given area. They also generally hoped thereby to advance their careers. The term cluster is used in preference to "school," for though certain clusters were sufficiently large and intellectually cohesive to warrant the term school, many were not.

The cluster was generally organized around one or two incumbents of central chairs — at the Sorbonne or, less often, the

---

1. See Robert Gilpin, *France in the Age of the Scientific State* (Princeton: Princeton University Press, 1968), chap. 4, and the many works summarized there, as well as Joseph Ben-David, *Fundamental Research and the Universities* (Paris: Organization for Economic Cooperation and Development, 1968), pp. 89ff.
2. Michel Crozier, *The Bureaucratic Phenomenon* (Chicago: University of Chicago Press, 1964), especially chap. 9.
3. No single term is accepted by participants in the system. Alternatives to the rather neutral "cluster" might be clan, circle, clique, cabal, empire, family, regiment, or militia.

Collège de France[4] — who shall be referred to as the patron(s). Most other members were in less central positions — provincial university chairs, lycées, nonuniversity teaching institutions, or, especially in more recent years, various research institutes. The cluster was integrated through several channels, of which the most visible, and most common means of identification, was often a journal. Books might appear in a series directed by the patron for one of the leading publishing houses. When large-scale research, and research grants, grew more frequent, having a patron on leading review boards became crucial for obtaining essential resources. But probably the most important mechanism uniting the cluster was the patron's influence on the careers of lower status members.

The processes through which patrons would influence appointments were many and complex; they seem to have varied rather systematically, however, with certain of the cluster's structural characteristics. Clusters that were large, socially cohesive, intellectually united, and which enjoyed a wide network of contacts were able to exercise far more influence in placing their members than clusters without these characteristics. The Durkheimian cluster met these four criteria admirably. The polar opposite was the academic isolate who might have no following at all — Gabriel Tarde approximated this ideal type.

In most disciplines, at least until World War II, the classic university *cursus* would begin with a teaching position in a lycée — but the varying quality of the lycées and their distances from Paris made some more desirable than others. Appointments to lycées depended largely on the itinerant Inspecteurs Généraux, many of whom jealously guarded their independence from the Parisian patrons. But a large and cohesive cluster, such as that of the Durkheimians, could include an Inspecteur who would look after younger cluster members. The Inspecteurs also frequently played important roles in conjunction with patrons on agrégation examination committees. When a cluster was intellectually uni-

4. Although the internal logic of the cluster model, and fragmentary evidence, suggest its generality, our central focus remains the Paris Faculty of Letters. Its sometimes unsystematic conceptual schemes and close ties with the lycées no doubt make some of the following remarks more true for it than for other institutions.

fied, its orientation could thus be disseminated through the examination system.

Appointments at the next level, in provincial Faculties or such Parisian institutions as the EPHE and the Ecole Libre des Sciences Politiques, would depend largely on a vote of professors in that institution. If the cluster had appropriate contacts, it could help influence the outcome. So crass a procedure as seeking to influence votes would offend both the norms of universalism and of autonomy of the institution. But many other mechanisms were available, frequently involving timing of the announcement of a vacant position and of presentation of a particular set of candidates. These points will be discussed shortly. Such influence was possible, however, only if the cluster was linked to the particular institution through cooperative members. Clearly this was not always the case. Certain provincial Faculties may have been so closely integrated into the national system that section (department) meetings were held on trains to Paris. But others, such as Strasbourg and Aix-en-Provence in certain fields, had powerful local traditions that led them to resist the temptations of the capital. Decisions were thus often made according to local criteria which did not articulate with those elsewhere.

For appointments at the highest levels as well, the pattern of patronal sponsorship would generally break down. After announcement of an opening, candidates would be given an opportunity to present themselves, and perhaps three to five persons would submit their candidacies. Candidates would generally be persons in leading positions in provincial universities, or in leading research institutes or private teaching institutions. They would often be leaders of competing emerging clusters. Although the small number of central posts and the centralized structure of the system seriously discouraged interinstitutional competition,[5] these same factors generated enormous competition among clusters, and their potential patrons.[6]

5. Cf. Ben-David, *Fundamental Research*.
6. At this point it seems useful to illustrate these general remarks with one of the most extended discussions of a social scientific candidacy recorded in the proceedings of the Council of the Paris Faculty of Letters. The various appeals and attempted strategies provide a small but illuminating sample of the institutional culture. The meeting took place on November 23, 1907. It was an

One major dimension was competition between members of an established cluster and outsiders. A younger man in an existing cluster might be appointed to a central chair, and the life of the cluster could continue with minimal change. The natural

---

important event in institutionalizing social science. (The events surrounding it are discussed further in Chapter 6.)

Désignation d'un chargé de cours d'histoire de l'Economie sociale pendant la durée du congé accordé à M. Espinas. Le Doyen communique à ses collègues les lettres de candidature des MM. Bouglé, professeur à l'Université de Toulouse, Hauser, professeur à l'Université de Dijon, Marion, professeur à l'Université de Bordeaux. Invité, M. Espinas a exposé les titres des candidats. Après avoir déclaré que dans la circonstance l'intérêt de l'enseignement doit passer devant tous les autres, qu'il est impossible de séparer les doctrines économiques des faits économiques, car les idées naissent souvent des faits ou sont modifiées par eux, que l'histoire de l'Economie sociale ne comprend pas seulement les rapports de ces questions avec les systèmes philosophiques, M. Espinas propose au Conseil, en vertu même des principes qu'il vient d'énoncer, de désigner M. Hauser qui poursuit depuis plusieurs années des études pénétrantes sur les théories économiques des 16e et 17e siècles dans leur rapport avec les faits économiques contemporains, et qui est qualifié d'ores et déjà par ses études antérieures et qui remontent à 1896 pour donner l'enseignement devenu vacant. Sans doute M. Hauser n'est pas un philosophe, et sa philosophie semble assez courte et même imprécise. Mais M. Bouglé n'est pas historien et son zèle pour la sociologie l'a tenu assez éloigné jusqu'ici de l'Economie et de son histoire. C'est un logicien, un sociologue et un politique servi par un rare talent d'orateur. Il a touché en quelque sorte *du dehors* l'histoire de l'Economie en rappelant les idées de Wagner sur la méthode de cette science. M. Espinas estime qu'il y a en présence, d'un côté un historien économiste, qui, il est vrai, n'est pas philosophe, et de l'autre un philosophe, un polémiste et un politique, un publiciste brillant et grave qui n'est pas économiste et qui n'est pas historien, que s'il faut une préparation à l'enseignement de l'histoire de l'Economie, M. Hauser a une bonne partie de cette préparation, et que ses travaux antérieurs le désignent plus pour la situation vacante que M. Bouglé qui manque de toute préparation économique et historique, mais dont le talent est incontestable. Après cet exposé, M. Durkheim fait connaître l'opinion de M. Brochard qui par lettre explique que s'il fallait choisir entre plusieurs historiens il voterait pour M. Hauser, mais que c'est un philosophe sociologue qui doit être chargé de l'enseignement qu'il s'agit de pourvoir. C'est à cette idée qu'on s'est conformé en choisissant M. Espinas qui a prouvé par son exemple qu'on avait eu raison. D'autre part la Cte de Chambrun en fondant cette chaire a eu certainement l'intention de la rattacher aux études sociologiques. En outre les études sociologiques intéressent jusqu'à la passion un grand nombre d'étudiants. M. Durkheim est obligé de diviser ses efforts entre la sociologie et la pédagogie, il n'a plus pour le seconder M. Henry Michel dont l'enseignement a été supprimé. Enfin dans le programme d'agrégation figure parmi les textes à expliquer l'oeuvre d'un écrivain politique ou d'un économiste; si le cours d'économie sociale cessait d'être professé par un philosophe, ou un sociologue, il y aurait dans la préparation à l'agrégation une lacune qu'il faudrait combler un jour ou l'autre. Pour toutes ces raisons, la candidature de M. Bouglé semble à M. Brochard devoir être recommandée au choix de la Faculté. Le nombre et la variété des sujets qu'il a traités dans ses ouvrages attestent sa force de travail et l'étendue de ses connaissances. M. Bouglé est jeune, plein de zèle, doué d'un véritable talent de parole qui a assuré un brillant succès à son enseignement à Montpellier

scientists of the Society of Arceuil, for example, presented by Crosland in terms generally consistent with the conception of the cluster used here,[7] maintained a certain continuity over the first half of the nineteenth century. The Henri Berr cluster of historians was continued by Marc Bloch and Lucien Febvre, and then Fernand Braudel and the group of the *Annales,* for more than half a century.

One device which an aging patron could use in an effort to maintain continuity was the "suppléance." There was also an economic incentive, for by inviting a younger man to provide substitute lectures the patron would retain part of his salary, while the younger man would receive only a portion of remuneration from the chair, the amount varying with his status and other sources of income. In the nineteenth century the device seems to have been used frequently as a means of providing anticipatory socialization for the candidate, the other members of the cluster, and one's colleagues in the particular teaching institution.[8]

---

et à Toulouse. M. Durkheim de son côté fait remarquer qu'il s'agit d'un cours sur l'histoire des doctrines. Or si l'étude des doctrines suppose la connaissance des réalités économiques, elle implique surtout l'aptitude à analyser les idées, et la connaissance des doctrines philosophiques qui sont à la racine de toutes les grandes théorie économiques. Après un échange d'observations entre M. Bloch qui demande l'avis de ses collègues sur les deux historiens en présence, MM. Hauser et Marion, et M. Denis qui déclare que la question ne se pose pas, puisque de l'avis de la plupart des historiens l'enseignement vacant est d'un caractère philosophique, il est procédé au scrutin qui donne les résultats suivants:

Nombre de votants: 31 — M. Bouglé 25 voix, M. Hauser 4 voix, M. Marion

1 voix, M. Milhaud 1 voix.

En conséquence de ce vote, la Faculté présente en lère ligne M. Bouglé, pour être chargé du cours de l'histoire de l'Economie sociale pendant la durée du congé accordé à M. Espinas.

7. Crosland's focus on "patronage" is an important step in transcending the formal view of university organization. Although Crosland never explicitly formulates the idea of a cluster, and does not focus distinctly on the university, the graphic portrayal of the procedures by which senior men "placed" their young associates in important positions makes his book one of the richest case studies of a cluster available in print. Maurice Crosland, *The Society of Arcueil: A View of French Science at the Time of Napoleon I* (Cambridge: Harvard University Press, 1967).

8. For example, seven professors at the Collège de France were listed as having a substitute take over half or all of their lectures for the 1885–86 academic year. *R.I.E.,* 10 (July–December 1885), 484. And the chair in General Physics and Mathematics at the Collège de France was held by only five men

Still, in many instances the patron was not successful in assuring continuity. If he was not skillful enough in establishing sufficient indebtedness on the part of his colleagues, or if *le dauphin* did not possess the requisite merits for the position, the cluster would risk destruction. On the other hand, this was also the moment when radical change could be instituted, as an entirely new cluster might come to the fore for the first time.

The key to the system clearly lay in the occupancy of Sorbonne chairs, but selection of their incumbents inevitably remained the least predictable. Nomination depended essentially on the system of relationships among leading incumbents, each often the patron of his particular cluster. Their normal pattern of relationships resembled what is designated "senatorial courtesy" in American politics. Each was considered the legitimate and total master of his particular constituency, and, whenever possible, constituency decisions (for examinations, promotions, appointments, and so forth) would be referred to him by his colleagues and his judgment accepted without question. Monopoly remained the unquestioned organizational principle. For "zero-sum" situations, however, where the gain of one patron could be only at the expense of others, a system of exchange of favors served to regulate the system. Over time, favors performed among patrons would tend to balance out. Those most adept at arranging favors would tend to benefit most, while those in relative isolation would benefit least from the exchange system.

Exchanges of favors could be channeled through common memberships on examination committees, advisory boards to the Ministry, governmental commissions, or one of the several Academies of the Institut de France. Of course, not every professor would come as an equal to meetings with his colleagues. Formal equality with regard to votes would be weighted by the range and number of resources which could be brought to bear for a particular decision.[9] Aspects of the individual — his cul-

---

from 1769 to 1950! Biot, incumbent from 1801 to 1862, lectured for only fifteen of these years and used *suppléants* for the other forty-six. Jean Laval, *Leçon inaugurale* (Paris: Collège de France, 1950), p. 10. See also Charles Benoist, *Souvenirs* (Paris: Plon, 1932), I.

9. This discussion draws on the exchange theory and interchange systems of resources outlined in Terry N. Clark, ed., *Community Structure and Decision-making: Comparative Analyses* (San Francisco: Chandler, 1968), chap. 3.

turally appropriate personality, proper social and educational background, and, certainly not to be neglected, his creativity as a scholar — could all play a role. So could association with institutions disposing of resources of various sorts: important publishing houses or journals, the Institut de France, Collège de France, Sciences Po, ENS, EPHE, CNRS, the Ministry, Parliament, or political parties. International contacts with centers of culture, science, or money would also weigh in the scale. Resources such as these could implicitly or explicitly be introduced in conversations with colleagues before a meeting with an important vote — although the time period for reciprocity could extend over many years.[10]

Of course, a prerequisite to use of such resources was knowledge of the desires of colleagues — income or status through supplementary courses, having a disciple named to vacant post, and so forth. Such knowledge would increase with communication. But as the time investment for such matters could become enormous, role specialization would often develop: a few individuals would become, to use a slightly awkward expression, patrons' patrons. Men such as Ernest Lavisse, Alfred Croiset, Gustave Lanson, Lucien Lévy-Bruhl, Fernand Braudel, and Jean Stoetzel

---

10. Although the example concerned a corresponding membership in the Institute, Proust's portrayal of the rituals of exchange demands brief quotation:

> Rongé depuis des années par cette ambition d'entrer à l'Institut, [le prince] n'avait malheureusement jamais pu voir monter au-dessus de cinq le nombre des Académiciens qui semblaient prêts à voter pour lui. Il savait que M. de Norpois disposait à lui seul d'au moins une dizaine de voix . . . Mais il avait eu beau multiplier les amabilités, faire avoir au marquis des décorations russes, le citer dans des articles de politique etrangère, il avait eu devant lui un ingrat, un homme pour qui toutes ces prévenances avaient l'air de ne pas compter, qui n'avait pas fait avancer sa candidature d'un pas, ne lui avait même pas promis sa voix!
> [Then one night at the Opera the prince invited Norpois and his mistress to a dinner with the King and Queen of England. Norpois immediately spoke of the ASMP:] je déjeune précisément, de demain en quinze, pour aller ensuite avec lui à une séance importante, chez Leroy-Beaulieu sans lequel on ne peut faire une élection; j'avais déjà laissé tomber devant lui votre nom qu'il connaît, naturellement, à merveille. Il avait émis certaines objections. Mais il se trouve qu'il a besoin de l'appui de mon groupe pour l'élection prochaine, et j'ai l'intention de revenir à la charge; je lui dirai très franchement les liens tout à fait cordiaux qui nous unissent, je ne lui cacherai pas que, si vous vous présentiez, je demanderais à tous mes amis de voter pour vous (le prince eut un profond soupir de soulagement) et il sait que j'ai des amis. — Marcel Proust, *A la recherche du temps perdu* (Paris: Gallimard-Pléiade, 1961), II, 257–263.

seem to have played such roles at one point in their careers. And even persons who were not professors at leading institutions might assume such roles on occasion, for example, the Ecole Normale librarian Lucien Herr, and to a lesser degree the astute Jeanne Weill (alias Dick May).[11] Clearly the relative balance of resources — scholarly creativity, contacts, money, political acumen — varied considerably from one patron's patron to the next, as did, correspondingly, the particular style with which he managed his leadership role. What they had in common was a capacity to structure the supply and demand of resources so that exchanges could approximate market characteristics.

The converse of the patrons' patron role was that of the "academic isolate." Although more frequent in provincial universities and lesser Parisian institutions, there have been many isolates at the Collège de France. Personal idiosyncracies of all sorts and a disdainful attitude toward other scholars were always perfectly appropriate for a patron, and militant defense of such "individualism" should in no way be confused with isolation from one's following. On the other hand, the more creative the man, the more automatically his ideas would spread, and the more students, younger faculty, and senior colleagues would respect his views. Hence, to be listened to by his colleagues, he needed to invest far less time and accumulate fewer outside contacts and material resources than did less gifted men. Generational variation for a cluster in this respect also occurred: the first patron might neglect academic politics; but less original successors might have to rely more on nonintellectual resources to maintain their position. Although Durkheim, unlike Tarde, was no academic isolate, his successors increasingly devoted time to cluster organization rather than original thought. A crucial variable for continuity was openness to innovation within the cluster; otherwise one could be entirely displaced, as were the Durkheimians.

One source of instability in replacing incumbents at the highest levels was the limited resources at the disposal of candidates. Largely excluded from the system of favors among patrons, they had neither the time nor opportunity to develop sufficient "debts" to be called in a vote for a chair. Just as important as one's gen-

11. See Chapter 6 on Lucien Herr, and Chapter 5 on Jeanne Weill.

eral qualifications was the state of the competition; hence the importance of selecting the appropriate moment for presentation of one's candidacy. Although failures at first attempts in examinations and in efforts to enter a leading institution were recognized as frequently necessary — in contrast to the United States, for example, where despite enormous faculty mobility it is considered improper actively to seek a particular appointment[12] — failures were nonetheless to be avoided if possible. Thus it was essential to estimate the likely competing candidates in advance.[13] One way of regulating the matter, of course, was through the relationships among patrons. In many fields and periods, patrons apparently arranged positions in the provinces for their disciples by working through the cluster system. Three simultaneous procedures were essential for such operations. First, one would persuade the local Faculty to delay in declaring a chair vacant ("geler le poste") until the proper candidate had completed his thesis and the field was reasonably clear of rivals.[14] Second, possible rival candidates in other clusters would be dealt with through their patron. Finally, those in the same cluster would be persuaded to wait their proper turn. The Braudel-Labrousse and Renouvin clusters even seem to have been able to utilize the same arrangement for allocating positions in the Paris Faculty of Letters.

Nevertheless, in most cases it was still necessary for at least two persons to apply for a post. Hence the institution of the "phantom candidate": a person who would perform the rituals of presenting his candidacy and making visits, but with the knowledge that he was almost certain to be defeated. Célestin Bouglé, for example, served as the phantom candidate when Durkheim presented himself for Ferdinand Buisson's chair.[15] Because one

12. In the United States a professor is "called" or "named"; in France he "presents his candidacy."

13. Something of the flavor of the contest is provided by the quotation at the beginning of the chapter.

14. See Crosland, *The Society of Arcueil,* pp. 161–168 for an impressive case of delaying tactics.

15. At the meeting of the Conseil on 16 June 1906, with not one person absent (a rare occurrence), the matter was handled with dispatch: "Le Doyen donne lecture des lettres de candidature de M. Durkheim, *chargé de cours* de Science de l'Education à la Faculté, de M. Bouglé, professeur à la Faculté des Lettres de l'Université de Toulouse, et de M. Malapert, professeur de philosophie

would not choose voluntarily to be a mere phantom candidate, the stronger candidate (or the patron) might have to persuade a younger or less capable man to play the role. The inducement might remain vague, but the stronger candidate would be expected somehow to look after the phantom in his subsequent career.[16]

Serious and phantom candidates would traditionally pay a visit to every voting member of the Faculty. The origin of this institution may be seen as an attempt by potential patrons, lacking other resources, to enter the patronal exchange system. Be-

---

au lycée Louis-Le-Grand. Il donne ensuite la parole à MM. Boutroux et Séailles qui exposent brièvement les titres des concurrents; ils mettent hors de pair et en première ligne M. Durkheim dont les travaux et la suppléance de M. Buisson pendant quatre années sont présents à tous les esprits. Après M. Durkheim ils placent M. Bouglé, esprit distingué, professeur éloquent; M. Malapert, qui ne manque ni de finesse ni de pénétration, leur semble avoir une moins grande envergure.

Après ces observations, il est procédé au scrutin qui donne les resultats suivants:

> M. Durkheim: 29 voix, à l'unanimité, 1ère ligne.
> M. Bouglé: 20 voix   2ème ligne."

Source: Minutes of the Conseil de la Faculté des Lettres, Paris, Sorbonne Archives.

16. A variation was that of the aspiring phantom candidate: the role assumed by the candidate expecting to lose, but who nevertheless hoped to benefit at a later point from having gone through the procedures. Consider the following letter from a notorious academic failure:

A Monsieur LAME, Membre de l'Académie des sciences

Samedi soir 16 août 1845

Mon cher Lamé,

Je me suis présenté chez vous ce matin pour vous expliquer spécialement ma candidature actuelle à la Direction des études de l'Ecole polytechnique, récemment vacante par la démission de notre ancien camarade Duhamel.

Ne croyez pas que je me fasse aucune illusion sur le succès d'une telle demande. D'après l'ensemble de la situation, je suis très persuadé que vous allez cette fois obtenir sans difficulté un poste dont je sais combien vous êtes digne. Mais, la règle actuelle obligeant le Conseil à présenter deux candidats, j'ai cru devoir me mettre loyalement sur les rangs . . . Cette candidature est d'abord destinée à signaler ouvertement mes prétensions ultérieures à un tel office . . . C'est, sous cet aspect, un mode énergique, quoique indirect, d'avertir que j'attends toujours avec confiance, sous les diverses formes qui peuvent successivement devenir convenables, la légitime réparation qu'une sorte de surprise légale a empêché le nouveau Conseil dirigeant de m'accorder jusqu'ici . . .

Tout à vous,
Ate Comte

Correspondance inédite d'Auguste Comte (Paris: Société Positiviste, 1904), IV, 246–247.

cause all professors in the Faculty would vote, but only a few could appreciate the work of the candidates, less directly intellectual qualities could play a role. Hence the visit. The aspiring candidate would attempt to learn of the major interests and attitudes of Faculty members, and seek to respond favorably to them. The most common resource seems to have been flattery. Petty as most observers, patrons included, might consider simple flattery, the candidate unable to uncover easily fulfilled desires of his electors could attempt to offer flattery in sufficient quantity and variation to tip the balance.[17]

Flattery may also involve more than deference. It can imply symbolic presentation of a carte blanche which the visited person may, during the visit or later, take up and utilize as the first favor in a new exchange. But just how widespread or important a role was played by such carte blanche distribution remains unclear. Because of the considerable ego involvement of the candidate and the absence of clear norms defining the role of the "visitor," all parties relied on classical forms of *politesse* to keep the situation manageable. The consequent indirectness of any requests or suggestions, and inability of those involved to verify an "agreement" in case of later misunderstanding, further complicated portrayal of the visit to outsiders. It is important, however, not to underestimate the ritualistic elements of the visit; the proportion leading to specific exchanges of resources was doubtless very small.

Beyond flattery, obvious criteria for decisions were political and social views, an agrégé style, general culture, and social background and personality of the candidate — but these were matters over which he had limited control in a visit. The professor visited, however, could sound out the candidate on such matters. This opportunity to scrutinize the candidate may help explain the homogeneity of political and social views within many Faculties.

For an isolate or younger scholar seeking to join a cluster,

17. Julien Luchaire recounts the custom of his father (Sorbonne professor of history, Member of the French Institute, etc.) to receive visits in his study at home: "Un matin qu'il avait reçu la visite d'un candidat à l'Académie, il me dit avec un soupir: 'Tu ne peux pas t'imaginer jusqu'où peuvent s'abaisser de grands esprits, quand ils ont envie d'un fauteuil académique.' Je venais de voir sortir de son cabinet l'illustre philosophe Boutroux . . . ," Julien Luchaire, *Confession d'un français moyen* (Florence: Olschki, 1965), I, 57. See also p. 62.

the same protocol of visits could be used. In addition, as the potential cluster member generally would be intellectually closer to the patron than patrons were to one another, it was more essential to demonstrate the quality and proper orientation of his work. To this end, reprints and books with deferential inscriptions could be addressed to the patron, or at a later stage, manuscripts could be submitted for a patron's journal or monograph series. Indirect efforts — such as impressing junior men whom the patron consulted for evaluations—could be equally important.[18] Laboratory experiments demanding special knowledge or equipment could be performed, local archives could be searched for an essential document, geological samples could be sent to Paris. Writing enthusiastic book reviews or review articles on work by cluster members could add more points. And less directly intellectual favors should not be ignored: a provincial professor could delay in declaring a post in his Faculty vacant or help a cluster

---

18. Having no patron, Alfred Binet continually sought to bring pressure to bear when posts at the Collège de France or the Sorbonne became vacant. Here is a letter he sent to Paul Passy, a colleague at the EPHE, which Passy sent on to Louis Havet:

4 juillet 1901

Mon cher ami,

Tu sais peut-être que Ribot vient de démissionner et que je me présente contre Pierre Janet pour le remplacer. Ce sera une rude campagne, dans laquelle je suis heureusement soutenu de la manière le plus vigoureuse, et si je succombe, ce ne sera pas ma faute. J'ai pensé que parmi les professeurs du Collège de France, dont je brigue les voix, tu as deux amis, Chavaune et surtout Havet. Je te demande de faire auprès d'eux une démarche en ma faveur. Il est évident qu'ils ne voteront pas pour moi uniquement parce que tu es mon ami; mais je désire qu'ils ne s'engagent pas à fond, de suite, avec Janet, sans avoir écouté le pour et le contre et sans avoir eux-mêmes consciencieusement examiné mes titres. Il y a plus de 20 ans que je fais de la psychologie, tu le sais; je me suis formé tout seul, sans aucun maître; et je suis arrivé à une situation scientifique actuelle par la seule force de mes poignets; *personne,* tu m'entends bien, personne ne m'a jamais aidé. J'ai fait de la psychologie expérimentale, c'est le titre de la chaire de Ribot. Je suis même le seul en France qui en ai fait; ni Ribot ni Janet n'en ont fait; le premier est un critique et le second fait de la psychologie pathologique avec l'hypnotisme, l'hystérie, etc. Mais j'arrete plaidoyer, ce n'est pas le moment. Tout ce que je te demande en ce moment c'est de bien vouloir préparer les voies auprès de tes deux amis. Ecris-moi un mot à ce sujet.

Cordialement
Alfred Binet

Janet was elected to the chair. When Binet subsequently presented his candidacy for Janet's former position as chargé de cours at the Sorbonne, he again failed. (Letter provided by Dr. Theta Wolf from Salle des Manuscrits, Bibliothèque Nationale.)

member be named to it; he could send his best students to the patron; he could perform various administrative tasks for the cluster.[19]

Similar if less advanced activities could be completed by students or young agrégés seeking to join a cluster. Performing a few such tasks was also a way of learning about a cluster in order to decide whether or not to continue with it.[20] In evaluating alternatives, he could consult with junior cluster members and other available advisers — certain staff members of the Ecole Normale played crucial roles of this sort (for example, Lucien Herr as librarian, and Gustave Lanson and Célestin Bouglé as directors).[21] In conversations with such persons a young man could assess the contribution which he could make to a cluster, and the number and types of posts in the system likely to become available at appropriate times for his own career. After the turn of the century, when new posts were created more readily, career lines

19. The editor of *Lucien Leuwen* tells us that, apropos of Leuwen's cousin, Ernest Dévelroy, Stendhal included the following note on the manuscript: "Modèle: M. Lherminier, professeur à moustaches au Collège de France.

"Caractère d'Ernest Dévelroy. Il assiste chaque jour au dîner du savant qui le protège et ôte les arêtes au poisson que son savant, presque aveugle, aime avec passion. Il fait ce métier trois ans. Son savant lui procure quelques voix à chaque élection, mais sous main l'empêche d'être élu. — Il ne m'ôterait plus les arêtes, et je ne me fie pas à mon domestique, qui d'ailleurs se lave mal les mains. Ernest suit son savant aux eaux, où le savant meurt après une maladie de sept mois. Ernest est comme M. Lemoine pour M. Guerin." Stendhal, *Romans et nouvelles,* I ([Henri Martineau, ed.] Paris: Gallimard, 1952), 1490–1491.

20. For an outstanding young man to choose among competing clusters was often a decision filled with anguish. Hubert Bourgin describes the torments of not allying himself with a cluster at the outset of his career. After achieving national fame in philosophy at the baccalauréat, he was repelled by the subject at the Ecole Normale Supérieure. And by a hairsbreadth, he "escaped being seized by the historical schools." Some years later he collaborated with the Durkheimians, although, while still at the Ecole Normale, he tells us that "I did not yet know the sociological school, and this was perhaps my greatest luck: it had a great force of apprehension and of adhesion, and it held on solidly to those that it had seized; in addition, it chose them well. But its members of least value would no doubt have astonished, wounded, worried me by their superior conduct, by their intransigence, by their rigidity. Brought to collaborate some years later by a friend who surpassed almost all of them, I owe to this delay in acquaintance, a period during which my personality could develop, to have always conserved my independence toward the master and his disciples, and to have always freely worked toward an objective which, in my eyes, never was that of a school." Hubert Bourgin, *Cinquante ans d'expérience démocratique 1874–1924* (Paris: Nouvelle Librairie Nationale, 1925), p. 45.

21. See Chapters 6 and 7.

could remain relatively fluid, but especially in earlier years it was imperative to calculate the availability of chairs very closely, and the order in which cluster members were likely to be appointed. Obviously a field blocked by advanced cluster members would be less desirable, ceteris paribus, than one with several men in chairs nearing retirement or another in rapid expansion.[22] Personality and social background factors could enter in selecting a cluster, and in certain periods, political affiliations took on almost caste-like importance. Assessments of the future prosperity of various political groups thus had to be made as well.

Successions in Cluster Leadership

Clusters could be affected considerably by shifts in the Latin Quarter climate, some of which may be classified along a continuum of cartesianism and spontaneity. After the 1880's, the ideal typical cultural configuration for a cluster was cartesianism. But as the Latin Quarter climate shifted away from cartesianism, a cartesian cluster would have difficulty attracting qualified members. Cluster leaders might shift their orientations, but such shifts were usually small. Critics could then invoke spontaneous arguments, and might weaken the cluster or drive off less convinced members. There might be efforts to create a cluster around a spontaneous professor, but the instabilities of spontaneity were such that these efforts were largely unsuccessful.[23]

Cyclical variation between cartesianism and spontaneity was also associated with succession crises inside individual clusters. If an obvious successor to the patron could assume leadership, the change might take place with only a small manifestation of spontaneity. But if there were no *dauphin,* or if for some reason he could not assume leadership and the alternatives contrasted sharply in style and orientation, the succession crisis could generate an outburst of spontaneity. When a succession crisis co-

22. Joseph Ben-David's studies have illuminated the importance of such expansion. See for example, "Scientific Productivity and Academic Organization in Nineteenth-Century Medicine," *American Sociological Review,* 25 (1960), 828–843.

23. One such example was the Bergson enthusiasts who would meet with Sorel and Péguy at the Cahiers de la Quinzaine. See Chapter 6.

incided with a Latin Quarter period of spontaneity, the result could be a particularly strong anticartesian reaction.

One set of cycles was thus associated with the careers of individual patrons. But when a man was also important in linking other patrons together, his succession would generate reverberations throughout the system; compounded with political turmoil, the crisis could become even more extended. Thus, succession crises would vary in intensity as a function of the number of persons involved, the number and level of the units undergoing succession, and the amount of change in intellectual outlook. The larger the number of such changes, ceteris paribus, the greater the outburst. Dramatic changes of this sort seem to have taken place soon after the 1870 war, in the last five years before World Wars I and II, after the Liberation, and in conjunction with the May 1968 events.

The impact of such crises on members of changing clusters could be considerable, but the effect would vary according to the individual's position. Although numerous gradations in originality within a cluster might be distinguishable, the hierarchical organization of the system would tend to stratify individuals into (at least supposedly) brilliant *grands patrons* on the one hand, and more pedestrian followers on the other. Patrons would be expected to present general programmatic theories, while followers would tend toward more narrow scholarly activities, often testing and extending hypotheses implicit in the patron's theory.[24] Hence the paucity of middle-level theorizing in traditional clusters. But as the general theory might be vaguely formulated or wrong on some points, and as the patron might not be competent (especially in a rapidly changing field) to advise his followers on testing it, followers might well be led to blind alleys and inconsequen-

---

24. When Charles Gerhardt took the liberty of publishing a theoretical article in 1840, Liebig, with whom he had studied in Germany, warned him against continuing such work: "Vous vous croyez toujours sur le sol neutre de l'Allemagne, et vous êtes sur un sol qui contient des matières combustibles de toutes sortes. Si vous partagez l'avis d'un tel, vous en avez aussitôt dix contre vous. Il n'y a qu'un moyen sur de gagner les sympathies de tous, c'est de fournir des faits nouveaux et interéssants utiles à chacun. Rappelez-vous ce que je vous dis; vous brisez votre avenir et vous irritez tout le monde, comme Laurent et Persoz, si vous continuez à faire des théories." Cited in Maurice Daumas, "L'école des chimistes français vers 1840," *Chymia,* I (1948), 55–65.

tial results. When an aging patron would also resist extension or revision of his theory, research prospects for followers could become sterile. The aging chemist J. B. Dumas seems to have been an extreme case in this respect.

The same rigidity could, of course, be experienced in the American system by graduate students, or in the German system by students and assistants; but after a few years in such a situation, the younger American or German scholar could still advance on his career independently of his former professor. In France, with dependence on a single patron for as much as a lifetime, prospects for younger scholars were much less attractive. Most students, without the local intellectual alternatives present in most American departments, would feel blocked. Older followers, without the alternative professors and mobility available in the German system, or the support of the disciplinary organization in the United States, could easily become overwhelmed. With theoretical inspiration, career advancement, and intellectual and social control largely concentrated in the individual patron, he would understandably become both adored and feared by his followers. Similarities between the patron and the authoritarian father figure are obvious enough; but the extension of this analysis along psychoanalytic lines will be left to others.

In times of turmoil, with clusters disintegrating but not yet replaced, the sense of crisis and anomie of the followers would be especially acute. Hence the profound ambivalence of simultaneous resistance and embrace of radical change. Hence also the sense of near-permanent crisis that certain social sciences experienced after the late 1950's when the traditional cluster patterns were eroding, but no strong and viable alternatives had emerged.[25]

In anticipation of the patron's retirement or death, one or more followers would make themselves visible to cluster members and others important in determining succession. A major research contribution was a prerequisite; hence the abundance of grand theoretical statements by contenders for cluster leadership. The Doctorat d'Etat was the normal vehicle for presentation of such a work to the academic public, from which followed the

25. See Chapter 7.

great ceremony attached to the thesis defense. But as there were inevitably fewer positions for patrons than there were aspirants, the system tended to generate an excess of grand, programmatic works. When informed by originality, they have become classical monuments of scholarship — Durkheim's *Division du travail social,* Bergson's *Essai sur les données immédiates de la conscience,* for example. But inevitably some contenders would be sadly incompetent, as attested by the ponderous but too often unimaginative tomes found in French secondhand bookstores. Creation of a "monument" sometimes left its author incompetent to continue less spectacular but more cumulative work. After the fierce competition for cluster leadership, the narrowly-defeated would not easily assume the role of followers; they might well sulk in a provincial Faculty for the rest of their careers.[26]

The situation for advanced students and younger researchers in time of turmoil was perhaps even more unsatisfactory, as many had not developed a cognitive map of the intellectual terrain under a dominant patron. With vague, incompletely accepted, and constantly changing criteria for research and for career advancement, the young could easily condemn the whole bickering gerontocracy and find other reference groups. This might be some foreign group, work in another field, classics from an earlier period, or the forum centered around general intellectual journals. Of course, if pressures became too great, these wandering scholarly activities could give way to intense political activity, extended vacations, or other occupations.

Origins of the Cluster Pattern

Certain congruencies between this pattern of university authority and the paternalism of the traditional French family are apparent. Analogous patterns are also found in the governmental administration, the military, the Church, and certain national industries. Doubtless paternalistic patterns in other institutions could provide models for those inside the university. But although legitimation for patronal authority may be found in French cul-

26. Consider such international sociologists as René Worms, Gaston Richard, G. L. Duprat, and Emile Lasbax. (Discussed in Chapters 5 and 7.)

ture,[27] this same culture also offered a good deal of support for more egalitarian patterns. If the more paternalistic cultural elements may have supported the cluster, the specific organizational structure of the university system was also crucial.

The centralization of formal authority made it essential for persons on the peripheries, especially the ambitious, to establish communication channels with the center if they were to have some control over their individual destinies. But since the sheer number of actors in the system made direct communication with leading decision-makers impossible, and since few formal channels were realistically available, intermediaries were a virtual necessity. Here lay the fundamental structural constraint toward creation of clusters. Analogous groupings in industry performing similar functions were the special interest groups. The political parties performed some analogous functions, but, forced to aggregate and articulate demands from so many varied social groupings, they were more oriented, in principle, toward broad ideological goals than specific favors.

International Comparisons: Germany and the United States

The importance of centralization as a prerequisite to the cluster is made clearer by comparison with the German system. German culture furnished ready support for authoritarian organizational patterns, but the cluster as it existed in France was far less salient in Germany. The major social unit in the German university appears to have been rather the individual chair and its associated structures — the seminar and the research institute or laboratory — supporting what could be called the "apprenticeship grouping." [28] In contrast to France, this apprenticeship grouping was principally composed of advanced students and assistants — not of other chairholders. They formed a more integrated social unit and interacted much more frequently than the ecologically dispersed members of French clusters. The Ger-

27. See the review of culturalist approaches in Viviane Isambert-Jamati, "L'autorité dans l'éducation française," *European Journal of Sociology,* VI, no. 2 (1965), 149–166.

28. Among other sources on Germany, see Fritz K. Ringer, *The Decline of the German Mandarins: The German Academic Community, 1890–1933* (Cambridge: Harvard University Press, 1969).

man pattern was essentially one of apprenticeship: the professor was the unquestioned intellectual and administrative leader, even though his grouping may have included as many members as the French cluster. Like the French professor, he was traditionally the sole representative of the discipline at his university. But in sharp contrast to France, his authority, like that of the feudal German prince, was limited to his realm: it seldom extended beyond his own university. When a former student or assistant acceded to a chair at another university, even a definitely less eminent one, he generally developed a similar following. In the decentralized German system he did not need to rely upon his former professor: his budget for institute, library, and staff derived largely from his own university. He set the content of courses and seminars in his field and established subjects and standards for examinations and theses. He might edit a small journal, or, more frequently, a monograph series subsidized through his university budget. Such apprenticeship groupings developed only infrequently at provincial French universities, and seldom did they have a vitality comparable to those in Germany. This was understandable as the agrégation was not administered by any single professor, there was no Dr. phil., and the Doctorat d'Etat was too advanced for apprentices.

Of course, the classical German system included its "schools," but these were generally quite different from French clusters.[29] The German schools were collections of individuals united more by an intellectual outlook than the necessities of academic politics, although nonintellectual criteria certainly could become involved.[30] The prestige hierarchy of German universities, while obviously present,[31] was far less steep than in France; without administrative centralization, it was an insufficient structural incentive to create clusters. The German schools seem to have been structured more around disciplinary associations and eminent in-

29. On the German schools, see Paul Honigsheim, *On Max Weber* (New York: Free Press, 1968) and Franz Schnabel, *Deutsche Geschichte im Neunzehnten Jahrhundert* (Freiburg: Herder, 1934, 1954), III, especially 128–142.

30. See Max Scheler, "Probleme einer soziologie des Wissens," in Scheler, ed., *Versuche zu einer Soziologie des Wissens* (Munich and Leipzig: Dunker and Humboldt, 1924), p. 66.

31. See the ingenious ranking developed by Awraham Zloczower in "Career Opportunities and the Growth of Scientific Discovery in 19th Century Germany," M.A. thesis, Hebrew University, Jerusalem, n.d.

dividuals than central councils or a ministry. There were separate ministries for each *Land,* and most included only one or two universities. The major exception was of course Prussia, and the most frequently discussed schools centered around Berlin. But this fits directly into the present analysis, for Prussia was the sector of the German system least distant in structure from the French. A university system with centralization and hierarchy similar to France should develop groupings similar to the French clusters. Conversely, the greater the competition among institutions, given minimal integration into a single system, the more rapid the diffusion of ideas and the institutionalization of new fields.

The disjunction between secondary and higher educational levels also distinguished the German system from the French. Whereas the traditional career of the young Frenchman would take him through several provincial lycées while completing his Doctorate, his Germany analogue would remain an assistant in a university institute while completing thesis and *Habilitationsschrift*. Although the German might shift from one apprenticeship grouping to another, he usually would not accept a Gymnasium teaching position. The obligation of the Frenchman to enter secondary school teaching reflected not only greater administrative integration of the two levels, but also the longer period necessary (more pronounced in letters than science) to complete a French Doctorat d'Etat. The necessity of the young Frenchman to spend an extended period in lycée teaching, research institute work, and lower-level university positions maintained his dependency on the patron, and recommendations to the Ministry for holding these temporary positions were correspondingly more important for a young man than in Germany.[32]

Rather than the German apprenticeship grouping or the French cluster, the dominant social units in the American system are the academic department and the national professional organization. The distinguishing characteristic of the department is

32. As the percentage of German university staff in subordinate positions increased near the end of the nineteenth century, younger staff members occasionally were forced into situations more like those of their French counterparts. See Helmuth Plessner et al., *Untersuchungen zur Lage der deutschen Hochschullehrer* (Göttingen: Vandenhoeck & Ruprecht, 1956) and Ben-David, *Fundamental Research*.

the presence of several professors in the same discipline with roughly equal authority.[33] The department is similar to the individual chair in Germany in that it has some budget for library, laboratories, and staff, it offers courses, and it establishes standards for examinations and theses. But in contrast to Germany, there is generally some range of outlook within the same department, so that students dissatisfied with one professor need not change universities. Despite stratification within the department, the chairman's authority is more limited than that of the French patron. Not only does the chairmanship rotate among departmental faculty at many American universities, but the constraints which administrators or colleagues may impose on a faculty member are limited by the competitiveness of other universities in the national system. Mobility existed in the French system, but it was largely vertical: there was only one Paris at the top. With no institution so dominant as the University of Paris, and with many more involved, a great deal more horizontal mobility takes place at all levels in the American system.[34] Equally important, this mobility is not supervised or regulated by any central minis-

33. Of course, this has not always been the case. One visitor to Europe who helped create the American department perceived exactly the opposite situation in the 1850's. In contrast to the scholastic and "impractical" character of American higher education (the Morrill Act was only passed in 1862), he observed that in the Grandes Ecoles of France and the Fach-Schulen of Germany, "The thorough and yet comprehensive character of the instruction . . . [is] in contrast with what has thus far been provided in our own country. The utmost which has been done in our institutions, has been to establish *a* professorship of agriculture, or *a* professorship of engineering; but in the best continental institutions such sciences would be considered as demanding the attention of several well trained men . . . and in some countries each would be taught in a separate school with several professors, and all the necessary accompaniments of buildings and apparatus. For any one man to be willing to 'profess' a knowledge of two such sciences as 'mining' and 'metallurgy' would in Germany be considered to show an indication of emptiness of mind or emptiness of purse." Daniel C. Gilman, "Scientific Schools in Europe," *American Journal of Education,* I (1856), 319.

On the origins of the American academic department, see Joseph Ben-David, "The Universities and the Growth of Science in Germany and the United States," *Minerva,* VII (Autumn-Winter 1968–69), 1–35.

34. Apparently such mobility has increased in the last few decades, but Veysey, in his outstanding volume, considers the ever-present possibility of such mobility crucial in restraining would-be authoritarian administrators near the turn of the century. Laurence R. Veysey, *The Emergence of the American University* (Chicago: The University of Chicago Press, 1965), chap. 5 and passim. Howard D. Marshall, *The Mobility of College Faculties* (New York: Pageant Press, 1964) reviews more recent mobility patterns.

try, council, or patron; it is undertaken largely at the initiative of the individual faculty member and the inviting department. Such competitive bargaining had its counterpart in Germany, but was virtually unknown in France.

The extensive mobility in the American system is linked to the importance of the national professional organizations. Organized around disciplines and similar specialties, they maintain intellectual standards — through congresses, special meetings, journals and monograph series, and various awards and prizes — that most individual universities cannot. Leading publications in the United States do not represent a cluster or an individual professor, but the more universalistic standards of the profession. The professional organizations also help integrate competing departments into a national system, but are themselves generally too large to be controlled by any single department; they can thus assure institutional and intellectual continuity for a discipline even when major departments temporarily suffer mediocrity or faddism.

Temporary mediocrity or faddism in Paris, however, would generate a national disaster. Precisely because of the absence of strong professional organizations in France, intellectual continuity among clusters, at the same period or over time, was much more limited. For students, outside witnesses, and even many participants, observing the almost revolutionary introduction of new paridigms and the redefining of entire subfields or disciplines following a *coup d'université* often led to a uneasy feeling that no knowledge was legitimately established. When textbooks were radically revised, the history of the field rewritten, and references to work abroad entirely changed — repeatedly, every few decades — alienation from the entire discipline and the university system was the not infrequent result.[35] Such discontinuity was of course more damaging in the humanities and social sciences than in the natural sciences, which had more firmly established results at an earlier date.

35. Without referring to more recent years, one may cite the considerable changes between 1870 and 1920 associated in history with Lavisse and Berr, in philosophy with Boutroux and Bergson, and in literary criticism with Brunetière and Lanson. The criticisms of such changes by a quasi-permanent student are illuminating: Pierre Leguay, *La Sorbonne* (Paris: Grasset, 1910).

Dogmatism in the American system is most often found at institutions where the faculty undertake little or no research; without the generalized exchange medium of published research linking them to the national system, they are forced to rely on more particularistic local contacts. Even at these lesser institutions, however, the authority of the thesis-supervisor seldom extends beyond his own university, except for placing disciples in their first job.

The authoritarianism in less outstanding American institutions has also been reinforced by reliance on institutional budgets, rather than outside grants and contracts. Annual institutional budgeting has been most frequent in the state universities, which also superficially resemble the French national system in their civil service rules and dependence on an elected legislature. But the absence (at least traditionally) of the highest quality faculty and students from the state institutions, their location in culturally retarded areas, and frequent interference by legislators distinguished them from the French system. On the other hand, the enormous growth of federal support since World War II has made the American national system more integrated and responsive to the national government and thus more similar to the French. But here again, important differences persist: most support is awarded through specific, limited contracts from "mission-oriented" agencies rather than on a continuing basis from a single basic science-oriented ministry. The diversity of possible sources, the turnover in granting committees, and simply the larger number of participants in the system make the crystallization of authority far more difficult. American academic despots are small fry compared to their French counterparts.

Sources of Structural Change

What particular elements are most crucial for maintenance of the traditional patterns, and what specific structural modifications would most likely affect the functioning of the system? [36] These questions have been posed many times, especially since the

36. The present tense is used in the next few pages as the general characteristics of the system at this writing still seem to apply even if some specifics no longer hold.

events of May 1968. But recent discussions, as in earlier years, have vacillated between narrow, legalistic interpretations on the one hand, and emotionally charged ideological demands for "restructuring" on the other. Between these two, where one might hope for a social scientific analysis encompassing legal as well as informal patterns, precious little has appeared.[37] Until the elements maintaining the system are isolated, attempts at change are likely to yield insignificant or unintended results. Thus such frequently discussed measures as abolishing the agrégation or Doctorat d'Etat, strengthening the Doctorat du Troisième Cycle, or changing representation in councils are unlikely, in themselves, to influence seriously the operation of the system as analyzed here.

Four elements may be distinguished, however, which are central to maintaining the system. To some degree interdependent, together they form characteristic points of support for a moving equilibrium.

1. Centralization of control. The basic authority for setting budgets, making appointments, and establishing examination sequences — not to mention less academic matters, such as library, laboratory, classroom, and dormitory operation and expansion — resides largely with the Ministry in Paris. Permitting formal authority to remain with the Ministry in no way implies that all decisions would in fact have to be taken at the center: any of these decisions could in large part be transferred to different groups (specially constituted committees, individual advisers, and so forth) in Paris, or to bodies constituted by members of the individual universities.

2. Monopolistic character of the system. A corollary of centralization is the absence of competition among the major subunits: the various provincial universities and the many Parisian institutions. Lack of competition implies in turn a strictly vertical mobility pattern for most students, junior, and senior faculty. When vertical upward mobility for individuals is no longer possible — whether because of age, the quality of their work, block-

37. Probably the most insightful recent analyses are Raymond Aron, *La révolution introuvable* (Paris: Fayard, 1968) — although many of the points were developed earlier in *Le Figaro, Preuves, Minerva,* the *Archives Européennes de Sociologie,* and even *Les sciences sociales en France* (Paris: Centre d'Etudes de Politique Etrangère, 1938) — and Alain Touraine, *Le Mouvement de mai ou le communisme utopique* (Paris: Editions du Seuil, 1968).

age of higher positions, or any other reasons — they are virtually condemned to remain in place. If competition among units at approximately the same quality level existed, horizontal mobility could develop, and the antagonisms of many-year-long associations would be eased. The simple knowledge that horizontal mobility was possible should decrease tensions among those remaining in any given institution.

3. Few central posts. The smaller the number of central posts in a field, the smaller the number of potential patrons, and the smaller the number of clusters. If the number of central posts were increased sufficiently to develop numerous centers of intellectual activity and academic power, the conditions would at least be present for competition among their incumbents. The enormous expansion since World War II, and especially since 1960, of posts with the CNRS, EPHE, and quasi-autonomous research institutes in Paris represents a considerable step in this direction. The provincial universities might also be made more inhabitable if they could become sufficiently strong in certain areas to reduce the need for constant contact with Paris — a task probably easier in the natural sciences than the humanities. However, specialization and strengthening of the provincial universities have been discussed since well before Louis Liard, who could not force the plan past regional opposition in the National Assembly near the turn of the century. The possibility of strong and specialized institutions in the Paris region seems much more politically and culturally feasible — the examples of Nanterre and possibly Vincennes and the other recent campuses seem to be cases in point, despite recent difficulties.

But most of these new institutions, especially those involved almost exclusively in research (often part of the CNRS or EPHE), have lacked the prestige of the traditional university posts and have generally not attracted the most eminent persons, except as *cumulants* holding positions in a more central institution (mainly the Sorbonne or the Collège de France). More important, perhaps, is that such newly created posts have often remained subordinated to and integrated into the structure of the older system. Such integration has depended in turn on the fourth characteristic.

4. Inflated status-sets for the patrons. When new institutions

are added to the system, they can potentially become centers of rivalry and competition for the older ones if they develop autonomously. But in many cases, new institutions — sections of the CNRS or the EPHE, new laboratories, research institutes, journals, governmental advisory boards, or, especially important, fund-granting committees — have been placed under the general supervision of the traditional patrons. The short-run consequence may be to increase his authority considerably through the increase of resources, but as the size and number of these new institutions increase, it becomes more and more difficult to remain in touch with any one of them. The patron then must either become a mere administrator and renounce most ambitions for intellectual creativity, and even intellectual domination of his growing empire, or he must restrict his attention to a small number of statuses within his total status-set.

Changes in any of these four system characteristics would curtail the domination by clusters. As one moves from the first to the fourth characteristic, the role of the central government decreases, and that of individual academics increases. Whether modifications at any of these levels will take place in the near future, however, remains to be seen.

Part II

The Institutionalization of the Social Sciences

Introduction

The next four chapters deal with specific groupings of social scientists and the patterns by which they became institutionalized. In the most general sense, institutionalization refers to the adoption of specific cultural elements or cultural objects by actors in a social system. For many new intellectual fields, including the social sciences in France, it involved (1) differentiation from existing fields and institutional structures, (2) creation of new institutions (professional organizations and journals, centers of instruction), and, ideally, (3) entering the university system. In general the prophetic style of the originators was succeeded by a patronal style appropriate to the university.[1] Each of these processes was achieved with varying degrees of success by the social scientists under consideration.

Chapter 3 treats certain precursors to the three groupings[2] that are considered in detail. Each of these precursors — the official positivists, the Le Playists, and the Broca grouping of anthropologists — developed a distinctive but comprehensive approach to the study of man. Their leaders were often prophetic in style. Each started from a natural scientific background from which it was necessary to break away, intellectually and institutionally. Such differentiation was facilitated by creation of new institutions. Virtually none of the precursors, however, succeeded in entering the university.

Comte, although he supported himself by tutoring mathematics, wrote and offered public lectures on positive philosophy. He gradually developed disciples who came to represent official

1. For further discussion see my "Institutionalization of Innovations in Higher Education: Four Models," *Administrative Science Quarterly*, XIII, no. 1 (June 1968), 1–25.
2. In the following pages, the term cluster has been reserved for persons around a patron holding a chair in such an institution as the Collège de France or the Sorbonne. The more general term grouping is used for clusters as well as collections of persons associated with a journal or scholarly society outside the university system.

positivism. They were institutionalized in official committees, in their distinctive journals, *La philosophie positive* and later the *Revue occidentale,* and in instruction offered at the famous rue Monsieur-le-Prince residence of Auguste Comte. Le Play gave up his professorship in metallurgy after the Académie des Sciences agreed to support his social research. He thus directed many younger collaborators in fieldwork and in preparing monographic reports. The Le Playists were formally united in the Société d'Economie Sociale and published a journal, *La réforme sociale,* as well as a series of books. In the 1880's they began to offer formal courses on Le Playist doctrines. Broca followed a career as professor at the Paris Faculty of Medicine, but encouraged a grouping of anthropologists outside the Faculty. Like other young groupings, they founded a Société, a *Revue,* and an Ecole, through which they developed and disseminated their ideas.

The social statisticians followed another path to institutionalization, originating in the needs of various governmental ministries for regular and detailed information. Certain civil servants increasingly specialized in statistics, and eventually separate statistical bureaus were formed in several ministries. However the statisticians' social and intellectual identities became defined largely through professional organizations and their respective journals, which developed outside the ministries (Adolphe Quételet's Congrès International de Statistique, the Société de Statistique de Paris, the Institut International de Statistique). After the 1850's, scattered courses touching on statistics were offered in several extrauniversity institutions, but the field had difficulty achieving the intellectual authority necessary for university entry. In part this was due to the emphasis on the administrative components of the role of statistician. The high social status of the statistical bureau director tended to attract talented persons to the position, and led them in turn to interact with one another and to avoid the unsystematic precursors of social science. Such social isolation, however, retarded the intellectual differentiation of statistics at the same time that it discouraged social scientists from moving toward quantification. Isolation also impeded entry into the university. It was not until 1892 that Fernand Faure, a lawyer with general interests in statistical matters, was given a chair in statistics at the Paris Faculty of Law. He offered only elementary courses for law students, however, and the field did not become institutionalized in a separate examination or degree sequence at the Faculty of Law. Perhaps a more ambitious and capable individual could have disseminated a quantitative orientation into the emerging social sciences. But it is interesting to contrast Faure's failure in spreading his ideas with the success of others.

In the early 1890's social and moral questions attracted considerable popular attention in France. Men of letters, journalists, natural scientists, lawyers, and others lectured and wrote on social issues of the day. At the same time there was an increasing demand for more disciplined social thought. The time was thus ripe for two entrepreneurs to channel this enthusiasm into institutional structures. René Worms created several professional structures — the Institut International de Sociologie, *Revue internationale de sociologie,* Société de Sociologie de Paris; and Jeanne Weill such teaching institutions as the Collège Libre des Sciences Sociales and the Ecoles des Hautes Etudes Sociales — which assembled aspiring social scientists irrespective of orientation. In contrast to the dogmatic precursors, René Worms and Jeanne Weill encouraged contacts among persons of divergent views in hopes of an eventual creative synthesis. These activities also attracted students and faculty from the university. With an intellectual climate and political leadership sympathetic to the social sciences, leading university administrators offered support for such developments. But most persons involved in the institutions of René Worms and Jeanne Weill could not meet university standards, and were not appointed to university posts.

However, when a scientifically-oriented young philosopher came to the attention of Louis Liard, Director of Higher Education, he was encouraged to move toward the social sciences. Emile Durkheim was given a fellowship to study in Germany, and then in 1887 was appointed chargé de cours of Social Science and Pedagogy in Bordeaux. His reputation grew rapidly through his scholarly contributions, his more popular writings on crime, social solidarity, and other topics, his lectures, and his public statements as a Dreyfusard. For an *universitaire* in the politicized Third Republic, Durkheim represented an ideal blend of scholarship and ideology, so when Ferdinand Buisson left his Sorbonne chair in pedagogy in 1902, Durkheim was chosen as his successor.

Durkheim soon became a leading patron, gathering a cluster of followers around the illustrious *Année sociologique*. In contrast to Georg Simmel, Tarde, and others, Durkheim used a very broad and loose definition of sociology. Such breadth made it possible for talented persons of diverse interests both to aspire to existing university chairs (in philosophy, history, law, area studies, and linguistics) and, in collaboration with the *Année,* to develop a sociological orientation in their particular specialty. Some of the most able young *normaliens* were thus attracted to Durkheim, and they became a large, cohesive, and powerful cluster. To outsiders they often seemed dogmatic, intolerant, and deadly serious. Despite political attacks from without, however, and resentment of non-Durkheimians from within the university, by 1914 enough cluster members had been appointed to permanent university positions that the cluster seemed destined to continue for many years.

These successes notwithstanding, sociology did not attain complete institutionalization: it had no distinct examination or degree sequence, and no lycée posts. Without these foundations for a traditional academic field, the Durkheimians did not dispose of the traditional incentives for recruiting followers. With time, this weakness became disastrous. But in 1914, the Durkheimians were the most completely institutionalized grouping of social scientists in France, and their success in this regard certainly eclipsed all others.

Chapter 3

Prophetic Precursors: Positivists, Le Playists, and Anthropologists

Pour retrouver le secret des gouvernements qui procurent aux hommes le bonheur fondé sur la paix, j'ai appliqué, à l'observation des sociétés humaines, des règles analogues à celles qui avaient dressé mon esprit à l'étude des minéraux et des plantes. J'ai construit un mécanisme scientifique. — Frédéric Le Play, *Les ouvriers européens,* second edition (Tours: Mame, 1879), I, vii–viii.

J'ai plus appris par les voyages et la conversation que par la lecture. Ma méthode est celle du reporter. — André Siegfried, quoted in *André Siegfried 1875–1959* (Paris: Imprimerie Foulon, 1961).

Saint-Simon, Comte, and Latter Day Positivists

The central current of cartesian social thought was strengthened considerably by Comte Henri de Saint-Simon.[1] He provided an important link between the Enlightenment philosophers of the eighteenth century and the young *polytechniciens* of the nineteenth. Born a nobleman, and, by turns, an adventurer, soldier in the American Revolution, canal builder, speculator in confiscated Church properties, stagecoach operator, and textile manufacturer, at forty-one he decided to devote himself exclusively to projects bettering mankind. He steeped himself in the best ideas available by inviting leading thinkers — especially Polytechnique professors — to sumptuous dinners at his home. Without absorbing the full content of the new sciences, Saint-Simon captured the essence of a scientific spirit which he elaborated, in the

---

1. Particularly useful on Saint-Simon are the works by Frank E. Manuel, *The New World of Henri St. Simon* (Cambridge: Harvard University Press, 1956), and *The Prophets of Paris* (Cambridge: Harvard University Press, 1962), chaps. 3 and 4.

style of a prophet, for the rest of his life. His first publication was an inflated version of the Voltairian cult of Newton: he proposed a subscription to finance a "Great Council of Newton." Each subscriber could nominate three mathematicians, physicists, chemists, physiologists, *littérateurs,* painters, and musicians. This Council of twenty-one, presided over by the mathematician with the most votes, would become the representative of God on earth. The ecclesiastical hierarchy of the Catholic Church would thus be replaced by numerous local Councils of Newton, which everywhere would supervise research, thinking, and worship. This was but the first of many proposals for social reconstruction that Saint-Simon generously offered mankind.

To maintain contact with new scientific developments, and to help put his disordered thoughts onto paper, Saint-Simon hired bright young men as secretaries. After employing one Augustin Thierry for several years, he found a nineteen-year-old supporting himself by tutoring mathematics named Auguste Comte. Comte had recently been expelled from the Ecole Polytechnique for inciting students against the administration. During the next eight years the production of Saint-Simon was difficult to distinguish from that of his young secretary; the relative contribution of each subsequently generated no little debate.[2]

The death of the master, as so often happens, led to division among his followers. The disciples, organized around Olinde Rodrigues and then Prosper Enfantin and Michel Chevalier, exaggerated the religious implications of Saint-Simon's writings and declared themselves no longer doctors of science but apostles of religion. Their colorful rituals and preaching of free love attracted a few spirited followers and terrified the bourgeoisie: in 1832 they were brought to court and sentenced to a year in prison for outrages against public morals. The prison term served its purpose and broke the back of the organized movement; many of its key figures went into business. In banking, railroad construction, and canal digging, former Saint-Simonians distinguished

2. In later years, Comte referred with scorn to that "depraved juggler" by whom he had been employed in his youth. See Henri Gouhier, *La jeunesse d'Auguste Comte et la formation du positivisme,* 3 vols. (Paris: J. Vrin, 1933 to 1941) for one interpretation of the relationship, and Manuel for a more balanced picture.

themselves — these were, after all, activities praised by the master — but they did little to develop his ideas.

It was in the work of Saint-Simon's dissident disciple that "positive philosophy" or "positivism" found its most influential statement. In a series of private lectures delivered in his rooms, Comte summarized the *Cours de philosophie positive* (6 volumes, 1830–1842), probably the most important single presentation of positivist thought (albeit seldom actually read).[3] His law of three stages was essentially a sober restatement of Saint-Simonian prophesies. In the positive stage, life would be regulated in harmony with the laws of man and nature established by the positive sciences. Comte's hierarchy included not only those sciences specified by Saint-Simon for the Council of Newton, but also, at the very top, a new discipline: the "queen of the sciences," which he baptized "sociology." The new science of society would develop by applying to mankind the same methods of exact observation and analysis used in the "lower," "more simple" sciences.

If Comte was dreadfully unsuccessful in impressing high officials, it was not from lack of trying. He wrote long personal letters to the general of the Jesuits, the czar of Russia, and the Egyptian Viceroy Mehemet Ali, soliciting their moral and financial support. He wrote to Guizot as Minister of Education suggesting that a chair of history of mathematical and physical sciences be created at the Collège de France, which he would agree to occupy.[4] His bold requests ignored, he supported himself for years as tutor of mathematics and entrance examiner for the Ecole Polytechnique. But mathematics was a sorrowful subject for the prophet who had unraveled the laws of history, created sociology, and proclaimed himself High Priest of Humanity. The 1826 and 1829 lectures had not attracted a large audience, but it was a distinguished one: Alexander Von Humboldt, the mathematicians Binet and Fourier, the physicians Broussais and Esquirol, and the economist Dunoyer were among the listeners.[5] Subsequent lectures were less successful and poorly attended. He ac-

---

3. Talcott Parsons's *The Structure of Social Action* (New York: McGraw-Hill, 1937) remains the most conceptually, if not stylistically, clear analysis available of variations of nineteenth-century positivism.
4. See also his letter quoted in Chapter 2.
5. W. M. Simon, *European Positivism in the Nineteenth Century* (Ithaca: Cornell University Press, 1963), p. 74.

cused the intellectual Establishment of a "conspiracy of silence" concerning his achievements. In the 1840's and 50's, he nevertheless attracted a small band of followers who participated with the High Priest in elaborating the Positivist Religion. Concerned that his work continue after his death, Comte sought to appoint a successor, but, not surprisingly, found all candidates lacking and was thus not able to reach a decision. Emile Littré appeared a likely choice at one stage, but in 1852 he broke with Comte over personal and intellectual issues. Littré nevertheless continued to propagate the faith: in 1867 he created a journal for philosophy and science with the Russian émigré crystallographer Grégoire Wyrouboff, *La philosophie positive*. Littré did not seek to compete with the official positivists, but he attracted a number of collaborators for *La philosophie positive*. They even met as the Société de Sociologie in 1872. The Société included twenty-five founding members, among them a future president of the Senate, Antonin Dubost, and the social and medical statistician Dr. Louis-Adolphe Bertillon; John Stuart Mill and Eugène de Roberty were corresponding members. The president was Littré, and vice-president, Wyrouboff; Dubost served as secretary. But despite auspicious beginnings, the Société de Sociologie left only its list of officers, a few statutes, and four short articles (read at the February 8, 1872 meeting) defining sociology and its boundaries. Bimonthly meetings were intended, according to the statutes, but were not held — apparently due to Littré's fear of rivaling the "official" positivists.[6] Perhaps the major sociologist collaborating with Littré was the Russian émigré Eugène de Roberty, whose elaboration of the "bio-social hypothesis" and sociologistic theory of knowledge and morals helped transmit the Comtean heritage to Worms, Durkeim, and others at the end of the century.

Littré was appointed to a chair of history at the Ecole Polytechnique in 1871, but was deposed almost immediately following the political turmoil. Although *La philosophie positive* was discontinued in 1883, a concluding article argued, quite rightly, that it had fulfilled its mission of diffusing positivist ideas throughout the intellectual public. Littré served as senator after 1875,

6. See *La philosophie positive*, VIII, no. 5 (March–April 1872), 298–336, and Simon Deploige, *Le conflit de la morale et de la sociologie* (Paris: Alcan, 1912), pp. 252ff.

and led his fellow senators to encourage positivism, as demonstrated in their subsequent actions concerning Pierre Laffitte.

Laffitte was a leading positivist and a more serious candidate than Littré for the Comtean heritage. He was president of the commission of executors of Comte's will, and after an unseemly period of intrigue following Comte's death in 1857, he emerged victorious. But he did not become High Priest of Humanity, only "president of the religious committee," which he soon renamed simply "positivist Committee." Although maintaining control of Comte's property and house at rue Monsieur-le-Prince, he only grudgingly performed religious ceremonies under pressure from other positivists. Unlike Littré, however, who rejected the later religious writings of the master, Laffitte accepted all of his works. But Laffitte was not of prophetic temperament and continued to teach mathematics while administering the positivist legacy. His lack of religious fervor infuriated certain disciples, and in 1877 they attempted to depose Laffitte in favor of Richard Congreve, leader of the "Positivist Church" of England. Laffitte compromised by founding the *Revue occidentale* to spread the faith, but many remained dissatisfied.

If negligent in maintaining the priesthood, Laffitte was a spirited lecturer with a more general audience. Beginning in 1869 he lectured at the Salle Gerson, and in 1880 obtained ministerial permission for a *cours libre* at the Collège de France. In the following years, his lively discussions of positivist ideas filled the largest lecture hall in the Collège to capacity. By 1890 he had won enough followers so that Senators Léon Bourgeois (also Minister of Education), his successor Charles Dupuy, and the scientist-politician Marcelin Berthelot led a large majority to vote for a chair of history of science for Laffitte at the Collège de France.[7]

The further triumph of positivist ideas was symbolized in 1903 at the unveiling of a statue of Auguste Comte, conspicuously placed in the Place de la Sorbonne. The next year Laffitte

---

7. Laffitte taught the history of science by mixing it with liberal doses of positivist philosophy. A motion was presented to the Senate in 1896 to create a chair of positivist ethics at the Collège de France and thus permit Laffitte to sermonize legitimately on his favorite topic. But this was considered too great a step from traditional scholarship, and the project failed. See "Une proposition au Sénat," *Revue occidentale,* Second Series, XII (May 1896), 388–405.

died, however, and to succeed him the Collège faculty voted for the eminent historian of science Paul Tannery. Although his nomination was confirmed by the Académie des Sciences, the Ministry created a scandal by appointing the second-line candidate, Littré's former associate Wyrouboff.[8] Tannery's Catholicism seems to have been too much for the anti-clerical Ministry. The case was interesting, however, for two reasons. It demonstrated the importance of a candidate's religion. It also showed the considerable outburst resulting from violation of the norm that the Ministry accept the faculty's recommendation.

Near the turn of the century positivist instruction was also offered by the Deputy from Seine-et-Marne, Ernest Delbet, at the Collège Libre des Sciences Sociales, and by half a dozen other disciples at 10 rue Monsieur-le-Prince.[9]

Although direct disciples of Auguste Comte may have been few, his impact on philosophers and social scientists was clearly considerable. Laffitte's audiences were tiny compared to the many persons who were directly or indirectly influenced by Comte. But to trace the less direct influences of positivism is an onerous task;[10] the focus here is limited to institutionalization of the official positivists, with the other threads of Comte's legacy left to subsequent sections.

The Le Playist Traditions of Social Reform and Social Science

Over the nineteenth century, probably the major line of French social thought after positivism was that of Le Play.[11] Frédéric Le Play (1806–1882) lived with a conservative uncle in Paris before attending the Ecole Polytechnique and Ecole des Mines. The technocratic enthusiasm of students at these two

8. On the incident, see George Sarton, "Paul, Jules, and Marie Tannery (with a note on Grégoire Wyrouboff)," *Isis*, XXXVIII (1947), 33–50.

9. Dick May, "L'enseignement positiviste à Paris," *Revue internationale de l'enseignement*, XXXIV (July–December 1897), 28–45.

10. D. B. Charlton, *Positivist Thought in France* (Oxford: Oxford University Press, 1959), and Simon, *European Positivism*, perform this task only very fragmentarily.

11. A useful summary and guide to further materials is Jesse Pitts, "Frédéric Le Play," *International Encyclopedia of the Social Sciences* (New York: Macmillan and Free Press, 1968). Catherine Bodard at Columbia has completed much unpublished work on the Le Playists.

schools disturbed him and conflicted sharply with conversations in his uncle's salon. He debated social questions with fellow students, and in 1829, while Comte offered one of his first private courses, he took a field trip in France and Germany with a Saint-Simonian friend. They collected information on working-class families that might support their conflicting views. Le Play took extensive notes which he later organized around a detailed budget for each family. This was the origin of his famous family monographs, published in 1855 as *Les ouvriers européens.* Le Play became professor of metallurgy at the Ecole des Mines, but resigned when the Académie des Sciences offered to support his monographic work. In 1856 he founded the Société d'Economie Sociale to conduct studies of families throughout the world. His assumption was that studying the family, as the basic cell of every society, would result in a better understanding of social stability. Thus began the series of *Les ouvriers des deux mondes,* which eventually included over two hundred monographs of families throughout the world.

The monographs' mixture of conservative Catholicism, praise of patriarchal authority, and modern scientific methods appealed to several statesmen, and came to the attention of Napoleon III. The Emperor requested that Le Play prepare a popular volume summarizing his conclusions; the result, in 1864, was *La réforme sociale.* One of a few leading intellectuals to support the Empire, Le Play became popular in political circles: he carried on an extensive correspondence with Napoleon III,[12] and was appointed to numerous governmental positions. These activities led him to abandon field work, although he continued to supervise the monograph series. For Le Play the fall of the Empire, understandably, was a disaster; excluded from leading governmental circles, he undertook several new activities to diffuse his ideas.

Basic works by Le Play and the Société d'Etudes Sociales were published by the Catholic house Mame, which in 1874 formed a nonprofit Bibliothèque with the Unions de la Paix Sociale: for

12. This correspondence is preserved in the archives of the Institut de France. It includes, among other things, careful instructions from Napoleon III on the organization of World's Fairs. For example, he urged Le Play to be careful that the electricity to the various exhibits was turned on when he was conducting Queen Victoria through the Fair, and just as careful that it was turned off immediately after they passed.

a nominal fee, members could participate in Union congresses and obtain the publication series. Unions were organized by conservative industrialists, landowners, and clergymen throughout France; they were a great financial and ideological success. Once assured of a public and of financial support, Le Play sought to maintain viable intellectual leadership. He thus created the Ecole des Voyages to provide fellowships for students to do field work; two of his close associates of prophetic temperament, the Abbé Henri de Tourville and then Edmond Demolins, began to offer private courses on Le Play's methods and doctrines; a journal, *La réforme sociale,* was formed to publish the group's results. By the time Le Play died in 1882, these new institutions were expanding rapidly: in that year there were 12 students; four years later there were 120.

As the leading teacher of social scientific methods, de Tourville had carefully studied Le Play's many works (although he never personally engaged in field work). He developed what he called "la Nomenclature des faits sociaux" — essentially an elaborate classificatory framework — as a guide to future field work and monograph preparation.[13] Although popular with many younger disciples, the Nomenclature, in the hands of de Tourville and Demolins, was too creative a vehicle for traditional Le Playists. They protested such revisionism and in 1886 forced Demolins to resign the editorship of *La réforme sociale.* Confident of his ideas and his young associates, de Tourville provided funds for a new journal of which Demolins became editor: *La Science sociale suivant la méthode de Le Play.* The title indicated their stronger concern for science than reform while affirming their Le Playist ties (although in a few years it became simply *La science sociale*).

The new group prospered. De Tourville, for reasons of health and temperament, withdrew from Paris to his family manor of Calmont in Normandy. He remained the intellectual leader of the group (and financial patron), but published only occasional articles in *La science sociale.* His influence was exercised principally through conversations with younger associates at the manor and through his extensive correspondence. The Abbé, by all re-

13. Terry N. Clark, "Henri de Tourville," *International Encyclopedia of the Social Sciences* (New York: Macmillan and Free Press, 1968).

ports erudite, brilliant, and slightly mystical, was complemented nicely by Demolins: this articulate and urbane editor would present the group's ideas at annual courses at the Société de Géographie[14] and at meetings throughout France, attracting students, providing them with a basic set of ideas, and leading the most capable in pilgrimages to the manor of Calmont.

De Tourville was not merely didactic; he learned with his followers as new discoveries were made. Perhaps the most important example was a study by a leading disciple, Paul de Rousiers. De Rousiers was the first Le Playist to complete a serious investigation of the United States, *American Life* (1892), and a central element of Le Play's theory was contradicted by its findings: the American family was generally stable and the economy prosperous, but as in France the paternal estate was equally divided among all children. Since Le Play had argued that family stability could only result from integral transmission of the paternal estate, de Tourville resolved the conflict by deemphasizing the economic relationships and stressing socialization by families into distinctive value patterns. Thus developed his theory of the particularistic family. These families were comprised of autonomous households established by each self-reliant child. Such families, he argued from his colleague's monographs, were most dominant in the Anglo-Saxon countries and Scandinavia — which he traced to the geographic peculiarity of the Norwegian fjord: these narrow strips of land permitted only small, nuclear families; hence self-reliance of each child was essential for survival there. The seafaring Norwegians diffused their family structure, but not to the plains of Central Europe where patriarchal families could operate large farms, nor to wooded Western Europe where isolated, but unambitious nuclear families could eke out an existence. Over the centuries, families from these regions transmitted their basic values without fundamental changes.[15]

14. In 1886 the courses reputedly drew about 120 students. *La science sociale* (January 1886), pp. 90–92.

15. The theory was first published in articles in *La science sociale* between 1897 and 1903, and then as *Histoire de la formation particulariste* (Paris: Firmin-Didot, 1905), (English translation, 1907).

The most active social scientist continuing the Tourvillian tradition in the 1960's, Philippe Perier, has sought further support for the basic thesis of the rise of the particularistic family. See his "Recherches d'un 'Comité des Fjords'," *Revue internationale de sociologie*, Series 2, II (December 1964), 67–95.

The implications of this new theory were several. It stressed geographic factors as the ultimate source of social organization — a tendency exaggerated by Demolins in particular — which led to considerable criticism by such outsiders as the Durkheimians. It also suggested that a society could be reformed by socializing children to new values, rather than by changing inheritance patterns. Demolins again carried this conclusion to its extreme: he gave up his scholarly activities and created a model private school, the Ecole de Roches, to inculcate an elite with particularistic values. (It served as one of John Dewey's models in founding the University of Chicago Laboratory School.) The theory was also congruent with a laissez faire ideology which found the sources of French decadence in too much rather than too little state intervention; it glorified private enterprise. These ideas appealed to many leading businessmen, and several *Science sociale* collaborators followed Le Play's example of serving as ideologue for industrialists. Robert Pinot thus became general secretary of the steel manufacturers' interest group, the Comité des Forges, and Paul de Rousiers served as president of the armaments lobby. Pinot and de Rousiers also both taught at the leading business school in Paris, the Institut des Hautes Etudes Commerciales. Many capable followers left the grouping after a few years for business, the professions, or the diplomatic corps. But Pinot and de Rousiers served as ideological spokesmen for industrialists at the same time that they wrote in *Science sociale*. This lent a distinctive character to the journal and grouping.

De Tourville died in 1903, leaving almost no financial support to his associates. Without his intellectual and financial leadership, the grouping gradually fragmented. The Société Internationale de Science Sociale was organized in 1904, mainly to raise money for *Science sociale* activities; it was only moderately successful.[16]

A Second Series of *Science sociale* was initiated. As monographic studies had often appeared serially, the format was changed to permit their separate publication; these sold better and thus provided additional revenue. Demolins had been the only salaried member of the grouping and was succeeded by Paul

16. In 1935 it merged with the orthodox Le Playist Société d'Economie Sociale to form the Société d'Economie et de Science Sociale.

Descamps, who continued to edit the journal. Official instruction was maintained by Descamps and on a voluntary basis by Pierre Roux and Paul Bureau. As this was the period when social science became extremely popular, speakers were in great demand by other institutions: Joseph Durieu taught at the Collège Libre des Sciences Sociales from 1907 to 1914; Paul Bureau offered instruction at the Catholic Faculté Libre de Droit in Paris; Paul de Rousiers held a chair at the Ecole Libre des Sciences Politiques from 1908 to 1932.

Although publication of *Science sociale* continued after de Tourville's death, the vitality of the 1880's and 90's gradually diminished. Research trips were still supported, but the reports declined into elementary descriptions. Such intellectual leaders as Demolins, de Rousiers, and Pinot turned increasingly to other activities. When the 1914 war came, it almost eliminated the remains of the grouping.

In several respects the history of the *Réforme sociale* grouping was similar to that of the *Science sociale*. Both remained creative and self-critical as long as a leading figure was alive. But soon after his death, the organizational structures weakened, no individual could assume leadership, and application became stressed over generation of new ideas.

Following Le Play's death and the ousting of de Tourville and his associates, the *Réforme sociale* grouping sought to apply the master's insights to social problems, but seldom were operating assumptions questioned or the framework extended. Conferences of the Unions de la Paix Sociale were held to discuss what affluent Catholics defined as pressing issues of the day, such as industrial working conditions, public health, and care for widows and orphans. The major concerns in such discussions were "social peace" and "family stability"; social disruptions were avoided at all costs. Two of the most capable members of the grouping, Emile Cheysson and Pierre du Maroussem, illustrate its general tendencies.

Cheysson, *polytechnicien,* was an engineering consultant for public works; he thus collaborated with Le Play in organizing the 1867 World's Fair. Le Play's social ideas attracted him to the *Réforme sociale*. He directed the graphic statistics section of the Ministry of Public Works until the section was abolished in 1885.

As recompense, the Minister of Education, Raynal, created a chair of industrial economies for him at the Ecole des Mines.[17] He also occupied the chair of Political Economy at the Ecole Libre des Sciences Politiques after 1887, and had its name changed to "social economy" in 1901. His courses included a mixture of economic statistics and working-class monographs; he treated such practical questions as how to deal with strikes, working-class family crises, and wage disputes. These were immediate problems to students at the two institutions where he taught, as many would occupy high positions in industry.

The distinctive social and political character of the professor and his students was nicely illustrated in an incident recounted in his autobiography. It occurred at a public lecture he presented on capital in 1895. The hall at the Hôtel des Sociétés Savantes was crowded with an impolite audience of "souteneurs, filles de mauvaise vie, repris de justice, et rôdeurs de barrières" who continually interrupted with hooting and *grossièretés*. But a devoted corps of his Sciences Po students came to "form a rampart" for their professor, and their active participation in the audience saved the occasion from becoming a disaster.[18] Latin Quarter lectures could be spirited affairs.

Cheysson's bibliography includes 546 items, but most were concerned with specific problems rather than systematic social theory. However, Cheysson was particularly proud of one article presenting summary statistics of expenditures by country and region for the 100 family monographs in *The European Workers* and *The Workers of Two Worlds*.[19] The article also demonstrated how Cheysson transcended a frequently troubling dichotomy, that of case studies versus statistical methods. He held that statistical information could help select representative units, but that monographs provided essential insights into numbers in the tables. He also encouraged monographs on social units other than the family: factories, communities, regions, and so forth.

Cheysson's writings on monographs, however, were largely

17. The appointment was resisted by the faculty as he did not have a degree from the school, but from the rival Ecole des Ponts et Chaussées. See Emile Cheysson, *Oeuvres choisies* (Paris: Arthur Rousseau, 1911), I, 61ff.

18. Cheysson, *Oeuvres choisies,* I, 64–65.

19. "Les budgets comparés des cents monographies de famille," *Bulletin de l'Institut International de Statistique* (Rome: Botta, 1890).

prescriptive; the more active monographic researcher was Pierre du Maroussem. A collaborator on family monographs in *The Workers of Two Worlds,* du Maroussem conducted extensively documented, generally volume-long monographs of department stores, wholesale food markets, workers' associations, clothing industries, and other working groups. He worked alone as well as with others, especially at the research team of the Ministry of Commerce, the Office du Travail: some of the most elaborate studies of the working class at the end of the century were conducted by this bureau, where du Maroussem was director of "moyenne et petite industrie." He also conducted monographs with students. From 1890 to 1902 he presented a *cours libre* at the Paris Faculty of Law; after 1895 he lectured at the Collège Libre des Sciences Sociales; he was appointed to the Ecole Libre des Sciences Politiques in 1912. His volume *Les enquêtes* (1900) summarized the French monographic tradition and helped spread the method.

He later boasted not only of the proliferation of monographs, but also of the "influence on a philosophical level" of Le Play's followers.[20] His examples form an interesting collection: Taine's *Origins of Modern France*; the philosophical studies of Théophile Funck-Brentano; the school of historians "who exalt the memories of old France"; the new "roman ennobli" of Paul Bourget, René Bazin, and Henri Bordeaux; *La Dépopulation de la France* by Jacques Bertillon; the Ecole des Roches in Normandy; the Musée Social.

Du Maroussem may have exaggerated slightly in crediting Le Play with these creations; nevertheless, they did represent a similar orientation, and in many cases overlapping memberships. A few remarks on the most enduring of them are in order.

Private Social Institutions: Sciences Po
and the Musée Social

The 1870–71 events generated a crisis for Le Play and other Frenchmen; several were consequently led to create new institu-

20. Pierre du Maroussem, "Soixante années d'enquêtes et de doctrine," *La réforme sociale,* LXXIII (January–June 1917), 37–73.

tional structures. Hippolyte Taine, a leading critic of the educational system, called for a political institute to train statesmen and diplomats scientifically — and thus perhaps limit future political catastrophes. Emile Boutmy, Protestant, Anglophile, and economic liberal, took up the cause.[21] In 1871 he created a private corporation with about two hundred stockholders. Numerous statesmen and writers — Taine, A. Adam, and Jean Casimir-Perier — helped enlist public support. The most important patrons were bankers and industrialists, including Edouard André, Jacques and Jules Siegfried, and Adolphe d'Eichtal, who together contributed over 200,000 francs.[22]

In January 1872, the Ecole Libre des Sciences Politiques opened its doors, and ninety-five persons enrolled, the majority students at the Faculty of Law, but also businessmen, lawyers, staff members from the Ministry of Foreign Affairs, and two Protestant ministers. The ministers reflected the important role that Protestants continued to play in the institution. From the outset the Sciences Po asked only one or two courses of its faculty, and recruited professors holding chairs at the Faculty of Law and the Collège de France, as well as officials in ministries and the diplomatic corps, eminent bankers and industrialists, and occasionally freelance writers and journalists. It began with a faculty of six; by 1896 there were forty professors and ten maîtres de conférences for a student body that fluctuated between three and four hundred. An ideology of policy-oriented, noblesse oblige instruction, coupled with economic liberalism (of the Manchester variety), appealed to that part of the nobility and upper bourgeoisie known as the *grand monde;* many students as well as faculty were drawn from its ranks. This ideology was part of an active institutional culture: in distinct contrast to most university Faculties, the Sciences Po provided language courses, vacation trips, course sequence requirements, and even organized

21. Emile Levasseur, "Boutmy et l'école," *Annales des sciences politiques,* XXI (1906), 141–179.

22. See Pierre Rain, *L'Ecole Libre des Sciences Politiques* (Paris: Fondation Nationale des Sciences Politiques, 1963). More often useful are the publications of the school: *Annales des sciences politiques* (more recently the *Revue française de science politique*) and the *Bulletin de l'Association des anciens élèves de la rue St. Guillaume.*

athletics for its students.[23] Still, their work load was sufficiently light that many simultaneously took courses and prepared degrees elsewhere: the Faculty of Law was a favorite choice, but students would also watch newspapers and billboards for new courses of interest. Sciences Po students thus helped fill many audiences at the budding institutions devoted to social science.

Among the Le Playists, as noted above, Paul de Rousiers of the *Science sociale* grouping held a chair at Sciences Po, as did Emile Cheysson, Théophile Funck-Brentano, and Pierre du Maroussem of the *Réforme sociale* tendency. The sociological historian of England, Elie Halévy, was at the Ecole for years, as was the statistical historian of the working class, Emile Lavasseur. Gabriel Tarde offered a course on political sociology at the turn of the century. But probably the social scientist most associated with Sciences Po was the son and nephew of two of its founders, a professor for decades and its president after 1945: André Siegfried. Siegfried and the Sciences Po are best understood in the context of his family.

Jules Siegfried (1836–1922), the father of André Siegfried, was born of a Protestant Alsatian family and entered his father's cotton business at fourteen.[24] In 1861 he traveled to America, the source of most raw cotton for France, and in Washington his conversational tact led to acquaintance with leading political figures; their comments about the Civil War helped him make a sizable fortune in cotton speculation. With the 1870 loss of Alsace to Germany, he settled in Le Havre, continuing his commercial activities and was elected mayor. Then in 1885 he was elected as a deputy to Parliament and moved to the capital where he soon became a leading figure in political, financial, and philanthropic circles. His upright character and concern for the common man were viewed as eccentric, while his belief in "individual initiative" and progress through industry marked him as Anglo-Saxon. He was impressed with an exposition on "Social Peace" at the 1889 Paris World's Fair (organized by Cheysson), and when he

---

23. See Claude Desportes, *L'atmosphère des Sciences Po* (Paris: Editions Spès, 1935).
24. See André Siegfried, *Mes souvenirs de la IIIe république: mon père et son temps* (Paris: Presses Universitaires de France, 1952).

became Minister of Commerce four years later, he proposed a permanent "Social Museum" to demonstrate working-class living arrangements, and, in charts and tables, the success of various paternalistic devices.[25] The Ribot cabinet, including Siegfried, fell soon thereafter and the project was shelved; but a private offer to revive it came from the Comte de Chambrun. A wealthy dilettante, in his later years the Comte supported numerous projects for (gradual) improvement of the working class; those of Le Playist inspiration he found particularly worthy. Thus, in 1895, he donated a splendid maison de ville on the Left Bank which became the Musée Social. In addition to items like those at the World's Fairs, it included a valuable library on the working class, held lecture series, and sponsored research projects on the condition of workers in France and abroad. Le Playist sympathizers were especially active at the Musée: Emile Cheysson served as a life member of the Musée's Comité de Direction; Paul de Rousiers and Pierre du Maroussem both undertook monographic studies with Musée Social financing and presented numerous lectures there; Robert Pinot was its first director.[26]

The Musée Social resembled the social charity organizations then in London and the Russell Sage Foundation in New York. Neither the Sciences Po nor the Musée Social would have stood out in Britain or the United States, where private philanthropists long supported such institutions; in France they were exceptional. Religion seems to have been an important component, judging from the many Protestant and Jewish names on ceremonial plaques. Certainly, André Siegfried stressed his father's Protestantism; and there were many resemblances to Protestantism in the self-reliance and personal initiative of Le Playist ideology.

The contrast between Protestant-inspired idealism and Catholic conservatism was brought home to André Siegfried in 1902,

25. See Henri Deroy, "Du Musée Social au CEDIAS," *CEDIAS* (Paris: Musée Social-OCOB, 1964); André Siegfried, "Discours: Cinquantenaire du Musée Social," *Les Cahiers du Musée Social,* no. 3 (1945), pp. 157–174; and the *Annales du Musée Social,* especially 1896–1914.

26. Also *secrétaire-adjoint* at Sciences Po, Robert Pinot was considered by some as overenthusiastic in his Le Playism: "par mainmise à l'américaine de l'individu sur l'association," he and his associates, it is said, wasted no time in spreading the doctrine. See Dick May, *L'enseignement social à Paris* (Paris: Arthur Rousseau, 1896), p. 38. (Dick May–Jeanne Weill is discussed in Chapter 5.)

1906, and 1910, when he was defeated in elections by more conservative candidates.[27] He had met leading figures of the Third Republic at his parents' home, and at age twenty-five became acquainted with the Musée Social by attending its opening banquet with his father. He spent a year at Sciences Po and earned degrees in law and letters, but was also educated by personal travel, mainly in the United States, New Zealand, and Canada. He wrote two books on his travels (*La Démocratie en Nouvelle Zélande,* 1904; *Le Canada: les deux races,* 1906) in a style quite similar to that of the monographic studies of Paul de Rousiers. When his electoral defeats convinced him to abandon "l'ivresse de l'action" for "la volupté de comprendre," he combed the published sources, regional archives, and held numerous interviews in the region where he had campaigned, and in 1913 published the monumental *Tableau politique de la France de l'Ouest.* It combined the best Le Playist traditions with the emerging university field of "human geography." Comparing subregions of differing land tenure patterns, religious composition, and class relationships, he demonstrated associated configurations of electoral behavior in ingenious graphs and charts.

In the 1920's Siegfried was sent to England and the United States by the Musée Social and published volumes on these countries. He taught at the Sciences Po (irregularly) from 1900, held a chair at the Collège de France after 1933, served as president of the Musée Social after 1941, and of Sciences Po after 1945, remaining active as teacher, traveler, administrator, and political commentator until his death in 1959. He thus witnessed the cold reception which greeted the *Tableau politique de la France de l'Ouest* in 1913 change to active interest in France, Germany, and the United States in the interwar years, and finally to recognition as basic inspiration for an entire tradition of work on political behavior.[28] Just as his father had been central in locating

27. Jean Pommier, "Notice sur la vie et les travaux de André Siegfried," *Séances et Travaux de l'Académie des Sciences Morales et Politiques* (19 June 1961), pp. 1–23; *André Siegfried 1875–1959* (Paris: Imprimerie Foulon, 1961).

28. This tradition is outlined in Rudolph Heberle, *Social Movements* (New York: Appleton-Century-Crofts, 1951), and F. Goguel and G. Dupeux, "La sociologie électorale," in Georges Gurvitch, ed., *Traité de sociologie* (Paris: Presses Universitaires de France, 1963), II, 46–75.

private funds for Sciences Po and the Musée Social, André Siegfried was instrumental in reorganizing these institutions after World War II with public support. At that time, symbolizing the academic respectability it had earned, the Sciences Po became part of the University of Paris.

Anthropology and the Science of Man: The Broca Cluster

If the positivists derived inspiration from Enlightenment philosophy, and the Le Playists from field work among the (principally European) working classes, a third current of thought emerged from studies of non-European societies. Accounts of preliterate peoples sold well in the eighteenth century, but the traveler's urge to please with tales of the exotic, and especially the erotic, was often stronger than his ability to maintain objectivity. Many accounts aimed no higher than salon conversation, but a few were scientifically concerned with differences among peoples of the world. The initial focus was often physical differences, partially, it seems, because the eighteenth-century traveler with intellectual concerns was often a ship's doctor or military surgeon. Between battles or epidemics he would collect observations on the weight, height, and facial features of indigenous populations, and bring home souvenirs such as skeletons, clothing, tools, and pottery. Constantin Volney was one of the most serious of these traveling physicians.

In 1799 the Société des Observateurs de l'Homme was created for these international scavengers to compare notes, but it also included a religious element: actual or would-be missionaries were concerned with alleviating the condition of the poor savages.[29] The charitable motivation was evident three years later when the Société des Observateurs merged with the Société Philanthropique. In these years of colony formation, however, the mere existence of a society concerned with natives' welfare was a political act; not surprisingly the Société was soon terminated by political upheavals. Then, in 1839, the ideologue Destutt de Tracy introduced a motion to the Chamber to emancipate slaves in the colonies. Antislavery movements were springing up throughout the world, and Thomas Hodgkin, previously active

29. Cf. George W. Stocking, Jr., *Race, Culture, and Evolution* (New York: Free Press, 1968), chap. 2.

with abolitionist groups in London, sought to further such efforts in Paris with his compatriot William Edwards.

Surprisingly enough, they were successful: the result was the Société Ethnologique de Paris, authorized on 21 August 1839. It was not a simple lobby, however, but included many dedicated scholars: they undertook scientific voyages and published research reports in its *Bulletins* and *Mémoires*. The political implications of these activities, however, especially discussions on slavery, were simplified and publicized by the popular press. Opponents or proponents of slavery sought support for their respective positions in evidence on monogenetic or polygenetic origins of the human race. As national politics became more agitated, so did the Société; with the revolution of 1848 it broke up altogether. But before long, subterranean activities dealing with race and evolution surfaced inside the established scientific bodies, especially the Société de Biologie and the Paris Faculty of Medicine. Discussion of such matters was strongly resisted by their leading members, however, and in 1858 a group of seven dissidents met to discuss forming a new set of institutions.[30] The intellectual and administrative leader was Paul Broca, lecturer and then professor at the Paris Faculty of Medicine. His specialty was the physical location of cerebral functions, but he sought to found with his associates a Société d'Anthropologie to consider "all matters dealing with the human race." The Imperial government viewed the proposal as a likely cover for revolutionary propaganda, or at the very least, an unchristian enterprise; it was strongly discouraged. After considerable petitioning, the Ministry of Education nevertheless authorized the Société to hold meetings, subject to three conditions: that no more than twenty persons attend, that there be absolutely no discussion of politics or religion, and that an Imperial police officer attend every session to assure compliance with regulations. The contrast with the official subsidy accorded Frédéric Le Play three years earlier is sufficient comment on the politico-religious implications of social science at the period.

Broca and his associates scrupulously observed these regula-

30. Paul Broca, *Mémoires d'Anthropologie* (Paris: Reinwald, 1874), II, 488–509; L. Manouvrier, "La Société d'Anthropologie de Paris," *Revue internationale de l'éducation*, LX (1910), 234–251.

tions, however, and the police officer eventually stopped attending. Broca's writings at this time argue for pure research divorced from ideology; they provide a case study of adaptability of scientific values confronting adverse forces — like Max Weber, and in contrast to Durkheim, Broca sought a solution in value neutrality.

Not only a diplomatic scientist, Broca was a gifted organizer: he was the active patron of an emerging cluster. He formed a Laboratoire d'Anthropologie in conjunction with the Faculty of Medicine, and obtained access to a small building next to the Faculty for his activities. Disciples — mostly advanced medical students — gradually formed around him. He was restricted to a narrow curriculum in the Faculty, however, and to expand formal training for his disciples he proposed an Ecole d'Anthropologie. This was too much for the Imperial Ministry; it refused. Things changed substantially with creation of the Third Republic: a *Revue d'anthropologie* was founded in 1872 with Broca as editor. Then he solicited contributions from wealthy benefactors, and with the same spirit of private innovation behind the Sciences Po, the Ecole d'Anthropologie de Paris was founded in 1876. Initially it included six chairs, whose titles reflected the dominant concern with physical anthropology: Broca, Anatomical Anthropology; Topinard, Biological Anthropology; Gabriel de Mortillet, Prehistorical Anthropology — but with more social concerns there were Abel Hovelacque, Linguistic Anthropology; F. Dally, Ethnology; and L.-A. Bertillon, Demography and Medical Geography.[31] Although the stamp of medicine was visible, over the years professors sought to develop their specialties beyond medicine. L.-A. Bertillon's courses, for example, dealt initially with "statistics of races," but came to include "intellectual and moral qualities of social groups."

A more impressive example was provided by incumbents of the sociology chair. As the number of chairs at the school increased — there were eight professors and seven others of lower rank by 1906 — a chair of sociology was created for Charles Letourneau in 1885, apparently the first such chair in the world.

31. See *L'Ecole d'Anthropologie de Paris* (Paris: Félix Alcan, 1907). Announcements of courses were often included in the *Revue internationale de l'éducation* and *Revue internationale de sociologie*.

Although trained in medicine, Letourneau was independently wealthy and thus pursued his scholarly interests without practicing. He joined the Société d'Anthropologie in 1865, apparently from an interest in the scientific study of religion.[32] He translated works on this subject by Ernst Haeckel and Ludwig Buchner, and collaborated with the journal *La pensée nouvelle*. Simultaneously, however, he followed more medical pursuits with volumes on *La Biologie* and *La Physiologie des passions*. In the decade after the appearance of Charles Darwin's *Origin of the Species* (1859), the long-term French interest in human evolution was stimulated to more intense activity. Letourneau studied the theoretical literature and reexamined empirical work on non-European societies, searching for evidence to specify evolutionary stages of particular institutions: religion, the economy, the state, and so forth. After presenting several papers on these subjects to the Société d'Anthropologie, he was given a chair of sociology (which initially was subtitled "history of civilizations"). During each of the seventeen years that he held the chair, Letourneau presented a course on evolution of a particular social institution, and published twelve volumes dealing, for example, with *L'Evolution de la morale,* or *L'Evolution du mariage et de la propriété. La Sociologie d'après l'ethnographie* summarized his approach. For each of these institutions, he would review ethnographic materials from animal societies through preliterate groups, ancient Egypt, Japan and China, ancient Greece and Rome, and contemporary European societies.

The Ecole was popular with Latin Quarter students, and even the arrogant young Durkheimians occasionally attended the lectures. The same year (1902) that Letourneau died, however, Durkheim came from Bordeaux to the Sorbonne, and Gabriel Tarde had been at the Collège de France for two years. Such official competition made the chair at the Ecole d'Anthropologie less attractive, but promising young men were invited as guest lecturers in 1903 and 1904: Maurice Vernès of the EPHE, and Paul Fauconnet (who succeeded Durkheim at the Sorbonne). But whether they refused the chair or were never offered it remains unclear; in 1905 it was given to Georges Papillaut.

32. Société d'Anthropologie de Paris, 741st Session, 6 March 1902, *Bulletins et mémoires de la Société d'Anthropologie de Paris,* 1902, 168–175.

119

Although Letourneau was surpassed by many *universitaires,* he at least commanded respect. Dr. Papillaut, however, was the object of continual jokes. His major claim to the chair seems to have been eight loyal years of work on skulls in the Laboratoire d'Anthropologie. He offered courses on what he called "anthropological methods," emphasizing an "anthropological questionnaire" of a sort then widely used: it was a checklist for colonial administrators and travelers (that an ethnology professor should leave the capital was almost unthinkable) to guide the collection of information about a society. There is little indication, however, that Papillaut's questionnaire stimulated any significant research.[33]

The decline in quality of the instruction from the chair of sociology symbolized the general decline of the Ecole after the turn of the century. With new private institutions developing, the Ecole lost the near monopoly on anthropological and sociological instruction of its early years. Then with creation of the Institut d'Ethnographie by Paul Rivet, Marcel Mauss, and L. Lévy-Bruhl in 1925, the Ecole was dealt a near-fatal blow; after that time, it was frequented by only a very marginal group of physicians (even though it was still in operation in the late 1960's).[34]

Conclusion

Thus throughout the nineteenth century scattered groupings of individuals developed ideas with implications for the social sciences. They often gathered a small but committed core of disciples, and they began to create new supporting institutions: generally professional societies and journals, and then private teaching institutions. But they had virtually no success inside the university, and most of their fragile institutions faltered after a few years. Nevertheless these early prophets of social science provided a set of programs, a scattering of studies, and a handful

33. George Montadon, "Le squelette du Professeur Papillaut," *Bulletins et Mémoires de la Société d'Anthropologie de Paris,* Eighth Series, VI (1935), 17–22, presents a careful analysis of the skeletal remains of the professor, suggesting that he had exaggerated his height on official forms.

34. H. M. Vallois, "La Société d'Anthropologie de Paris 1859–1959," *Bulletins et Mémoires de la Société d'Anthropologie de Paris,* Eleventh Series, I (July–September 1960), 295–309, and personal communications from H. M. Vallois (former Secretary of the Société d'Anthropologie de Paris, Professor at the Sorbonne, and Director of the Musée de l'Homme).

of individuals who would seek to carry the flame in later years. Certain social and intellectual linkages established among the disparate groupings will be taken up in Chapter 5. First, however, another line of development will be considered, one associated with the social statisticians.

Chapter 4

The Social Statisticians

Another great lacuna is the absence of all instruction relative to method in economic science, and more especially, relative to mathematical political economy. It is really humiliating to think that in France, a country which occupies a prominent rank in the mathematical sciences, and which, in Cournot, inaugurated mathematical political economy, there is not a single course on this subject, probably not even a single professor who would be capable of giving it. And by a singular irony, it happens that this branch has been brilliantly represented at Lausanne for twenty years by a Frenchman, but who is known throughout the world as a Swiss: M. Walras. — Charles Gide, "France," in *Annual Reports of the Department of the Interior, Report of the Commissioner of Education,* Vol. 2, House of Representatives, 55th Congress, 2nd session (Washington: Government Printing House, 1901), p. 1469.

Empirical Social Research and Statistics

If positivists, Le Playists, and anthropologists helped formulate perspectives on the study of man, another tradition was more adaptable to changing theoretical or ideological superstructures: the tradition of empirical social research. It had roots in Germany and Britain as well as in France. *Statistik* was initiated by Hermann Conring in seventeenth-century Germany, and political arithmetic by John Graunt and Sir William Petty in Britain. Under the ancien régime the *enquêtes* of the French civil service also contributed to a distinctive type of empirical investigation. Its goal was to provide information about aspects of society essential to directing the affairs of state. Hence the origin of the term statistics, which initially did not imply that such information need be quantitative.

The importance of regular and systematic information for setting policies on military conscription, tax rates, tariffs, and other matters led to periodic requests for information from civil servants. Not until about 1800, however, did most European countries institutionalize such efforts in national statistical bureaus. Censuses of basic information about the population and the economy were subsequently conducted on a regular basis; they were supplemented with more detailed and specialized studies at less frequent intervals.

Especially in Britain an important complement to governmental efforts was the private social survey. During the early nineteenth century, a number of successful industrialists became concerned about the condition of the poor. Whatever their motives, they clearly perceived that recent urbanization stimulated by their enterprises had created a working class both socially unattached and potentially revolutionary. Frequently religious nonconformists, the industrialists used their religious contacts to establish charity organizations. A continuing concern then became documenting the actual extent of poverty, disease, and crime, and evaluating the impacts of charity efforts to alleviate these difficulties. Information for these purposes was garnered from open-ended questionnaires administered to doctors, ministers, and other informants, and later directly to the poor. France and Germany saw similar efforts, but the number and scale of such surveys were much greater in England and, by the early twentieth century, in the United States. Such endeavors depended on substantial private donations, which maintained the Manchester and London Statistical Societies, later the studies of Charles Booth and Seebohm Rowntree, and in the United States, the Russell Sage surveys. Their lesser importance on the Continent seems related to the low level of private charity there.

Common to the various branches of empirical social research was a concern with reliable reporting of factual information. But despite exemplary clarity and organization, by their disregard for underlying assumptions and neglect of systematic explanations, these reports stand quite apart from contemporary empirical social science. To say that no guiding framework existed is certainly incorrect. But instead of theoretical statements, these largely consisted of dominant beliefs of the political leadership of the period. Basic conceptions of the probable origin of social ills, and appropriate solutions, followed largely from unstated assumptions; readers of the reports, as right-thinking men, were presumed to share these with the authors. For example, Frédéric Le Play would declare, articulating the views of many others, that eternal truths of social organization had been discovered centuries before, and achieved their clearest statement in the Decalogue and doctrines of the Roman Catholic Church. Socialist and working-class groups increasingly criticized such studies. Near the end of the century exponents of more radical reform, learning the propaganda value of a documented exposé, conducted many such studies themselves.

While established beliefs of the bourgeoisie were increasingly questioned, a more refined substitute to guide empirical research became seriously considered: systematic social theory. This crucial step held revolutionary consequences for the social sciences. No longer was social theory part of a doctrine to support the status quo or a program for reform, it was elaborated by men seeking to create truly scientific disciplines. A cursory examination of natural science showed close linkage between theoretical advance and data collection; philosophers of science proclaimed the necessity of analogous efforts for social science. Simultaneously, specialists in data collection grew more aware of the precariousness of ad hoc interpretation. Statistical bureaus in particular became so diversified that their directors assembled no longer solely for methodological issues; specialized conferences for population expansion, agricultural organization, and similar topics became frequent. Accumulation of data on specialized issues and conflicting interpretations of these data increased considerably. More refined analyses gradually emerged which sought to articulate with specific social theories. Simultaneously, exponents of social theories sought more systematic support for their ideas. Durkheim's *Suicide* was one outstanding example of a theory tested with such empirical data. Jacques Bertillon's work on population growth represented the trend from ad hoc interpretation toward more theoretical analysis. Walras, Vilfredo Pareto, and L. T. Hobhouse were among the others who undertook analogous activities.

The naïveté of much early empirical work and the theoretical preferences of most historians of social science, to mention only two factors, have resulted in less attention to past empirical efforts than to social theory.[1]

For the present study it was decided to include one grouping of researchers from this empirical tradition. Likely candidates were field studies supported by the ASMP, working-class investigations by parliamentary commissions, or the tradition of *enquêtes* culminating with the Office du Travail — but it seemed best to focus mainly on the social statisticians. Their early institutionalization in governmental ministries, their formation of active professional organizations and journals, the seriousness of their work compared with most other empirical traditions, and their late and unimpressive entry into the university make them especially interesting to compare with the independent sociologists and Durkheimians.

Institutionalization in Ministries

The institutionalization patterns of the statisticians were quite different from the Le Playists, the international sociologists, or the Durkheimians: the statisticians enjoyed research institutes, in the form of statistical bureaus, before professional or teaching organizations were created and before statistics penetrated the university.[2]

Although efforts toward a French national census can be traced back as far as 1328, only in the late eighteenth century — and then only irregularly — was a modicum of methodological sophistication developed in collecting statistical data. The first general statistical bureau was created by François de Neufchateau

1. This has been changing significantly in recent years. Paul F. Lazarsfeld and Stein Rokkan have inspired such historical work, and important efforts are under way by Anthony Oberschall, Bernard Lécuyer, and others. See the works cited in the rest of the chapter.

2. On the histories of statistical bureaus, see Statistique Générale de la France, *Historique et travaux de la Statistique Générale de la France à la fin du XVIIIe siècle au debut du XXe* (Paris: Imprimerie Nationale, 1913); Pascal-Gaston Marietti, *La Statistique Générale en France* (Paris: Presses Universitaires de France, 1948); Fernand Faure, "The Development and Progress of Statistics in France," in John Koren, ed., *The History of Statistics* (New York: American Statistical Association, 1918), pp. 215–330; Jacques Bertillon, *Cours élémentaire de statistique administrative* (Paris: Société d'Editions Scientifiques, 1895), pp. 13–42; Bertrand Gille, *Les sources statistiques de l'histoire de France* (Geneva: Droz, 1964).

in 1796, but it never conducted a full-scale census. In 1801, a large-scale, albeit hasty, census was carried out under Lucien Bonaparte. In principle Napoleon favored statistics — his remark "statistics are the budget of things, and without a budget there is no salvation!" was often quoted — but despite ambitious reorganization of the government and educational systems, he did comparatively little to institutionalize statistical activities.

The Restoration (1814–1830), however, realized important advances. In 1818 a special agency for statistics on army recruitment was established, and another for customs in 1819. A judicial statistical bureau was organized in 1825 under the Ministry of Justice, later directed by Gabriel Tarde (1894–1904). The Paris statistical bureau grew after 1817 and included as directors Louis-Adolphe Bertillon and his son Jacques Bertillon. In 1833 a statistical agency for mining was created, directed by Frédéric Le Play until 1847. After 1840, savings bank statistics were collected. The Paris Chamber of Commerce conducted major studies of Parisian industry in 1848, 1860, and 1872. After 1852, penal institutions were covered by the statistical section of the Ministry of the Interior.

These many agencies, however, were generally only small subdivisions of particular ministries. The bureau director and a few assistants might be specialized in statistical matters, but most personnel was assuredly not. The Ministry would send questionnaires to local officials much as it sent out administrative directives. Local and regional officials were thus responsible for interviewing or data collection, and even a good deal of analysis, often sending only summary tables to Paris. Weekly or monthly data collections facilitated standardization of procedures, but for irregular *enquêtes* or a five-year census, the lack of uniform procedures introduced considerable confusion.

Most ministerial officials lacked skill in statistical matters, but ignorance was not the only source of error: officials at each level frequently had a personal interest in altering figures before passing them on to a superior. Thus, when information eventually did reach a statistician, it was likely to be unreliable; this led professional statisticians (largely the bureau directors) to plead for a specialized and centralized agency solely concerned with data collection.[3] They were only partially successful, however.

Centralization was the ideal behind the general statistical bureau of 1796, but it disappeared in 1814–15, reappearing only in 1834 when Thiers felt compelled not to let the English, with their Board of Trade created two years before, outshine the French. Moreau de Jonnès was the first director of the resurrected bureau, charged with collecting data on population, foreign trade, and, occasionally, agriculture and industry. Individual ministries continued considerable data collection, however, and the statistical section of the Ministry of the Interior grew especially large. Then in 1891 the Office du Travail was formed under the Ministry of Agriculture and Commerce to collect materials on working conditions. The Office expanded rapidly and increased coordination with other ministries until it merged in 1907 with statistical bureaus of the Ministry of the Interior into the Statistique Générale de la France, the central statistical agency after that time.

Definition of the Status of Statistician

Full-Time Self-Supporting Activity

During the nineteenth century, a large number of full-time posts were thus created for directors of statistical bureaus, filled on the whole by distinguished individuals. Highly committed to their work, the bureau directors undertook far more statistical activity than demanded by their ministries. They continually urged collecting more extensive data, and in addition to their official reports, they performed elaborate secondary analyses on specific questions, published in statistical and popular journals.

Consequently, while most would-be social scientists were still struggling to create full-time self-supporting activities — to move from their developing professional organizations into bureaucracies — the statisticians followed the opposite trend: originating in bureaucracies, they only subsequently created professional organizations, journals, and teaching institutions. Prior to development of these professional activities (largely in the last quarter of the nineteenth century), a sharp distinction separated the

3. Cf. Bertillon, *Cours.*

usually capable bureau directors from *franc tireurs* whose quality varied as much as their seriousness.[4] These occupational differences corresponded to distinct conceptions about the nature and goals of statistics.

Professional Ideologies

In the early nineteenth century, the statistical vision was manifestly utopian; the style of its spokesmen, prophetic. Louis Chevalier comments on the fervor of the period:

> A spirit of youth in statistical research? That might be saying too much. It was far more a passionate effort to realize — with new and more powerful means, thanks to much more considerable documentation — the ambitions of the great eighteenth century to introduce measurement into the description and prediction of human, physical, and moral phenomena.
>
> Such were the ambitions of a Moheau, whose *Recherches et considérations sur la population de la France* presented in advance the entire program of our qualitative demography, continually taken up and yet never achieved . . . Such was the ambition of a Buffon, writing an *Essai d'arithmétique morale*. Of a Condorcet especially, continuing and perfecting previous efforts of political arithmetic — and affirming that "the truths of the social and political sciences may be interpreted with the same certainty as those forming the system of the physical sciences . . ."

At least this was the program that the statisticians of the first half of the nineteenth century, strengthened with their new riches, wanted to take up and carry out. It was the program of the eighteenth century, assumed by persons who con-

---

4. In this respect the contrast with England was pronounced. There were almost no French analogues of the large-scale private social surveys in Britain. Quantitative analyses by British amateurs also evidenced more sophistication than those of their French counterparts, although, like most of the French, they seldom moved beyond ad hoc interpretation of individual tables. The British social survey tradition is treated in unpublished papers prepared at Columbia University by Steven Cole and David Elesh, in Walter F. Willcox, "Cooperation Between Academic and Official Statisticians," *Publications of the American Statistical Association*, XIV (1914), 281–293, and Philip Abrams, *The Origins of British Sociology* (Chicago: University of Chicago Press, 1968), especially pp. 13–31.

sidered themselves the successors of the men of the eighteenth century, the heirs of the grand designs, and who actually were so in their techniques and in their concerns. Whence this intransigence and this manifold curiosity in statistical forays. Whence this audacity in utilizing figures and in interpreting them.[5]

Although echoes of these comprehensive claims occasionally reverberate in the second half of the century, by 1900 they had grown considerably more modest, for several reasons. As greater quantities of data were collected, it became increasingly evident that the statisticians' achievements lagged far behind their initial aspirations. Second, certain unqualified amateurs presented exaggerated claims and unsound interpretations, thus discrediting the activities of all statisticians.[6] Third, practitioners in the emerging social sciences were not loath to point out that the statisticians' imperialistic claims did not square with reality. But the proper relationship of statistics to these adjoining fields continued to be debated for some time.

Delimiting Intellectual Boundaries and Specifying the Content of the Status

Although consensus was never reached, in the nineteenth century statistics was widely viewed as a general science which sought to formulate quantitative social laws. Dufeau, for example, wrote in 1840 that "statistics is the science which deduces laws for the succession of social facts from analogous numerical terms."[7] In 1847, Moreau de Jonnès stated: "Statistics is the science of social facts expressed in numerical terms. It has as its object the inves-

5. Louis Chevalier, *Classes laborieuses et classes dangeureuses* (Paris: Plon, 1958), pp. 21–23. Cf. also Maurice Crosland, *The Society of Arcueil* (Cambridge: Harvard University Press, 1967), pp. 89ff. on Laplace and his associates as "pre-positivists" linking Condorcet and the *ideologues* to natural science and Saint-Simon.

6. One founder of the Société de Statistique de Paris argued that an important rationale for the organization was to distinguish serious statistical work from that of "serviteurs incapables, courtisans perfides, faux savants, prestidigitateurs habiles à grouper les chiffres." A. de Malarce, "Les origines de la Société de Statistique de Paris," *Journal de la Société de Statistique de Paris*, XXXV (1894), 68–77.

7. Cited in Emile Levasseur, *La population française* (Paris: Arthur Rousseau, 1889), I, 2.

tigation of society considered in terms of its elements, its economy, its situation, and its movement." [8]

Initially, designation of phenomena for investigation posed no problem: they were largely defined by the administrative jurisdictions of the ministries. Before long, however, it became evident that these materials could not be examined in an intellectual vacuum, but that certain social scientific theories pertained to their interpretation. Near mid-century a few social scientists — mainly economists and geographers — began to make serious use of governmental statistical materials, and simultaneously to criticize the imperialism of the statisticians.

One consequence was the field baptized by Achille Guillard as *"démographie,"* the "mathematical knowledge of populations, their general movements, their physical, civil, intellectual and moral composition." [9] The substantive emphasis of demography on population distinguished it from the broad methodological concerns of statistics. [10]

By the end of the century, even bureau directors were less prone to define statistics as a *substantive discipline;* they and others had come to see it as a *method* applicable to a variety of subject matters. Maurice Block in 1880 distinguished statistics "as a science" from statistics "as a method." [11] Emile Levasseur went still further in 1889. Asking if statistics was a scientific discipline, he replied "we see in it a method of research, an instrument, and not an end." [12] Although the older conception claimed its adherents, by the turn of the century they had become rare. [13]

8. *Ibid.*

9. Achille Guillard, *Eléments de statistique humaine* (Paris: Guillaumin, 1855), p. xx. This work was originally prepared for a contest of the ASMP, but when the judges insisted that sections critical of earlier population theory be deleted, Guillard refused and had it published privately.

10. Sauvy's remarks about demography hold for statistical studies in general: "Despite Guillard's coining of the term 'démographie' in 1855, the subdivision of science toward the middle of the century was disastrous for demographic study. Being much too general, demographic studies were disregarded by the specialized faculties of the universities." Alfred Sauvy, "Development and Perspectives of Demographic Research in France" in Philip M. Hauser and Otis Duncan, eds., *The Study of Population* (Chicago: The University of Chicago Press, 1959), p. 180.

11. Cited in Levasseur, *La population française,* I, 2.

12. *Ibid.,* pp. 15–17, 66.

13. Cf. A. de Foville, "La statistique, les statisticiens et leur institut international," *Revue politique et parlementaire,* XLVI (October–November–Decem-

One structural factor retarding differentiation of substantive work from methods, and of substantive fields from each other, seems to have been the (relatively) high prestige of the statistical bureau director, and the absence of comparably prestigious and well-paid university posts. For most of the nineteenth century, careers involving quantitative analysis of social phenomena consisted mainly of teaching in the unprestigious and low-paying private institutions, or of becoming director of a statistical bureau, hence part of the respected civil service. The most capable persons chose the second alternative.[14] Their high standards led the bureau directors to associate with one another more than with others who may have been knowledgeable in particular substantive areas. The social cohesion of the bureau directors thus reinforced the intellectual cohesion of what appear a posteriori as rather incongruous elements.[15]

While some persons in the social sciences worked with statistical materials as early as the 1850's, the use of statistics (in the sense of quantitative empirical data) was by no means uniformly accepted.[16] Quantitative social scientists thus would frequently continue traditional theory simultaneously with empirical, quantitative research — a schism perhaps even more marked in Germany, with Ferdinand Toennies and Max Weber, for example.[17] Prior to 1914, the important work of Bertillon, Levasseur, and

ber 1905), 224–244; Walter F. Willcox, "Definitions of Statistics," *Revue de l'Institut International de Statistique,* III (January 1936), 388–399.

14. For example: Frédéric Le Play, Maurice Yvernès, Gabriel Tarde, L.-A. and Jacques Bertillon, Moreau de Jonnès, Lucien March. The same pattern prevailed abroad, where bureau directors included Adolphe Quételet, Georg von Mayr, and Ernst Engel.

15. Cf. Faure, "The Development," p. 217, on the artificial association of what he calls the theory and practice of statistics.

16. "Although statistics may be said to have passed through an age of enthusiasm in 1830–1850, when statistical journals and societies were being established, this enthusiasm did not really infect economics, though it may have infected some statisticians who had come to look upon economics as a branch of statistics or of (an essentially Comtean) sociology . . . Adoption of [quantitative methods] was slow but relatively steady, and the process remained so even after the 1850's when quantification began to progress more rapidly." Joseph J. Spengler, "On the Progress of Quantification in Economics," *Quantification,* ed. Harry Woolf (Indianapolis: Bobbs-Merrill, 1961), pp. 128–146, quotation at p. 140. Cf. also Paul F. Lazarsfeld, "Notes on the History of Quantification in Sociology: Trends, Sources, and Problems," *Ibid.,* pp. 147–203.

17. Cf. Anthony Oberschall, *Empirical Social Research in Germany 1848–1914* (Paris: Mouton, 1965), pp. 37–63.

others on population movements, Durkheim's suicide studies, Simiand's and Bourgin's investigations of wage and price levels, Halbwachs's work on ecology and family budgets, and René Maunier's studies of the location of industry combined theoretical generality with systematic quantitative evidence.[18] Nevertheless, even in France, social scientists' quantitative studies were often segregated from the rest of their work, and referred to as "statistical studies" rather than in terms of their substantive content.[19] Correspondingly, many quantitative social scientists associated with members of their discipline (or cluster) as well as with other "statisticians": Simiand, Bourgin, and Halbwachs, for example, collaborated with the *Année sociologique,* but also belonged to the Société de Statistique de Paris.

To recapitulate: in the early nineteenth century, analysis of quantitative data was considered largely the prerogative of "statisticians," mainly directors of statistical bureaus. The statisticians' substantive concerns included virtually all aspects of social life. But over the century, the status of statistician was pruned of many activities as they were incorporated into role-sets of substantively-oriented social scientists. In an intermediary stage, quantitatively-oriented social scientists were often considered to occupy two separate statuses, for example, economist and statistician. Three basic activities may therefore be distinguished that have increasingly differentiated since the nineteenth century: (1) the design and supervision of periodic large-scale data collection and data processing operations; (2) the development of various procedures, generally mathematical, relating to analysis and interpretation of empirical data; and (3) the investigation of substantive questions using quantitative data. Certain mid-twentieth-century statisticians hold that all three are still integral to the status of the statistician;[20] but clearly the relative importance of

18. See Appendix II.
19. For further discussion of this point, see Terry N. Clark, "Discontinuities in Social Research: The Case of the *Cours élémentaire de statistique administrative,*" *Journal of the History of the Behavioral Sciences,* III (January 1967), 3–16.
20. Cf. William H. Kruskal, "Statistics: The Field," and M. G. Kendall, "Statistics: The History of Statistical Method," both in *International Encyclopedia of the Social Sciences* (New York: Macmillan and Free Press, 1968); Vittorio Castellano, "Science, méthode, et statistique," *Revue internationale de sociologie,* Series 2, II (December 1966), 1–47. I am grateful to William Kruskal

the second sort of activity has increased considerably in the twentieth century. An important role in changing these definitions was played by the professional societies and journals.

Professional Activities

Before 1850, the bulk of the statisticians' activities centered on their bureaucratic functions, although an ephemeral Société de Statistique de France had existed shortly after the Revolution, and in 1829 César Moreau founded a Société Française de Statistique Universelle[21] including Quételet, King Louis-Philippe, the economist Jean-Baptiste Say, and numerous ambassadors and French governmental officials. Apparently more concerned with ritualistic formalities than substantive work, the organization accomplished little. In 1830, S. Bottin founded the Société Libre de Statistique. Like the early anthropological organizations, however, these societies lasted only a few years, succumbing to political tumult.[22]

The Congrès International de Statistique

The first important organization for professionalizing French statisticians was not French, but an international group created by Adolphe Quételet following the 1851 World Exhibition in London — the Congrès International de Statistique.[23] It organized nine congresses in various European capitals between 1853 and 1876. Meetings were held under official governmental auspices, and most European governments sent delegates, generally directors of major statistical bureaus.

The major goals of the Congrès were promotion of official

---

for his observations on this point and for making available an early draft of a paper involving E. Martin, Frederick Mosteller, and Conrad Taeuber, "The Profession of Social Statistician."

21. Fernand Faure, in "Procès-verbal de la séance du 17 Octobre 1906," *Journal de la Société de Statistique de Paris,* XLVII (1906), 366–367.

22. Cf. Fernand Faure, "Les précurseurs," *Notes sur Paris* (Nancy: Berger-Levrault, 1909), pp. vii–lii; Walter F. Willcox, "Note on the Chronology of Statistical Societies," *Journal of the American Statistical Association,* XXIX (1934), 418–420.

23. On the Congrès, see Harald Westergaard, *Contributions to the History of Statistics* (London: P. S. King, 1932), pp. 172–235, as well as the *Comptes rendus,* published separately for each congress.

statistical research and cross-national standardization of categories and procedures of analysis. Greater centralization and professionalization of statistical work were also advocated, including the replacement of unspecialized governmental personnel by professional statisticians.

Most meetings thus emphasized organizational more than scientific matters. With such organizational concerns, bureau directors found the attendance of amateurs particularly troublesome. They were drawn like moths by the distinguished foreign statisticians at the international congresses: the 1863 Berlin congress included 127 foreigners and 477 participants; at Florence in 1867, 85 foreigners were drowned by a total of 817 participants. Large audiences were admirably suited to reading papers and to public relations, but they all but precluded focused discussion of organizational matters. Hoping to retain the advantages of size, yet achieve the coherence of a working group, Ernst Engel, director of the Prussian statistical bureau, proposed a Permanent Commission consisting solely of directors of statistical bureaus. The proposal was accepted and the Permanent Commission met four times between 1873 and 1878. Nevertheless, the difficulties of size and the antagonisms of the Franco-Prussian War led to termination of regular meetings after the 1876 congress.[24]

The Congrès still accomplished a great deal in its twenty-three years. Cross-national standardization of categories for data collection and presentation was advanced. Second, at a time when international journals were only beginning, the congresses established communication channels among leading statisticians in many countries. Increased communication heightened professional identification, which in turn helped maintain higher standards. Finally, by exposing national achievements to an international audience, the congresses enabled bureau directors, in the name of national prestige, to gain more extensive support from their respective governments.

The Société de Statistique de Paris

In 1860 the Société de Statistique de Paris was formed under the patronage of the Ministère de l'Agriculture et du Commerce,

24. Levasseur, La population française, I, 76.

the Conseil Municipal de Paris, and the ASMP.[25] It initially included 157 members,[26] with Villermé as honorary president, Michel Chevalier as president, and Legoyt (director of the Statistique Générale de la France) as permanent secretary. After 1873, presidents served only one year, and included most eminent French statisticians at the time.

The Société's stated purpose was "to popularize statistical research through its work and its publications." [27] Although it did organize public lectures and occasional public sessions, most activities were on a relatively professional level. Organizational questions and policy recommendations were occasionally discussed at the monthly meetings, but substantive matters supplied the major focus. Much as in a seminar, two or three papers would be read or summarized, and then discussed by the other members.

By assembling the directors of major statistical bureaus and, in later periods, professors of demography, economics, statistics, and sociology, the Société helped create and reinforce professional standards among persons involved in quantitative research.

The Journal de la Société de Statistique de Paris

The monthly *Journal* of the Société included two or three articles read at the Société's meeting, summaries of the discussion, and a few short book reviews. Although very thorough, logical, and carefully organized, *J.S.S.P.* articles were seldom more than empirical generalizations about population, the economy, or political organizations; causal relationships were rarely

25. On the Société, see Lucien March, "La Société de Statistique de Paris" in *Notes sur Paris,* pp. lii–lxvi; articles by de Malarce, B. A. Rouillet, and Levasseur in the *Bulletin de l'Institut International de Statistique,* I (1896); Société de Statistique de Paris, *Annuaire de 1947* (Nancy: Berger-Levrault, 1947); *Le Vingt-Cinquième anniversaire de la Société de Statistique de Paris* (Nancy: Berger-Levrault, 1886); and the *Journal de la Société de Statistique de Paris,* particularly the 1894 and 1909 issues.

26. Of these founding members, 86 were Parisians and 71 resided in the French provinces or abroad. Parisian members included doctors, lawyers, engineers, governmental administrators, and a few industrialists; most provincial members were governmental administrators.

In 1885 there were 514 members and in 1910 approximately the same number if one distinguishes *membres titulaires* from *correspondants* and *associés.* Meetings from the 1880's to 1914 record between 70 and 138 persons in attendance. See the issues in these years of the *Journal de la Société de Statistique de Paris.*

27. March, "La Société," p. lii.

examined systematically; there was practically no attempt to link findings by use of theory.[28]

The Annales de Démographie Internationale

In 1877, Dr. Arthur Chervin, member of the Société de Statistique de Paris, organized the *Annales de Démographie internationale* in conjunction with the Congrès International de Démographie, the only international organization of demographers active between the collapse of the Congrès International de Statistique (1876) and the creation of the Institut International de Statistique (1896). Its advisory board included most eminent European demographers. Jacques Bertillon aided Chervin and became editor himself in 1882. But a year later, Bertillon assumed the directorship of the Paris statistical bureau. He was obliged to abandon the *Annales,* which were then discontinued.

The seven weighty tomes of the *Annales* contain the work of many of its advisers, including several important articles by Louis-Adolphe Bertillon and his son Jacques. Two papers on suicide (1879) and divorce (1882) by Jacques Bertillon were the starting points for Durkheim's work on these subjects.[29] These articles first formulated the "Bertillon Law": in European societies suicide varies concomitantly with divorce. Although Bertillon's interpretations were crude, he was methodologically astute in combining variations of divorce and suicide with sex, age, family status, nationality, and other factors in three and four variable tables. Rejecting Bertillon's theoretical interpretations, Durkheim still drew heavily on his methodology and his substantive results.[30]

The Institut International de Statistique

In 1885 the Statistical Society of London invited representatives from most European countries for its fiftieth anniversary celebration. It was natural that the first international meeting of

28. The membership of Société de Statistique de Paris and the content of its journal are discussed further in Appendixes I and II.

29. Cf. Terry N. Clark, "Jacques Bertillon," *International Encyclopedia of the Social Sciences* (New York: Macmillan and Free Press, 1968).

30. Through Walter Willcox, Bertillon exercised considerable influence on American students of deviance. See William L. O'Neill, "Divorce and the Professionalization of the Social Scientist," *Journal of the History of the Behavioral Sciences,* II (October 1966), 291–302.

statisticians since 1876 would seek to organize a new international statistical association. To combat unwieldy size, membership was limited to 150. To allay the fears of German bureau directors that international ties would limit their freedom, it was ruled that members would attend meetings in a purely individual capacity; no decisions would be officially binding.

The Institut International de Statistique was thus successfully created and, in subsequent years, brought together, among others, Francis Galton, Ernst Engel, Gustav Schmoller, Adolph Wagner, Léon Say, Léon Walras, Emile Levasseur, and Jacques Bertillon.[31] The *Bulletin* of the Institut, published every year or two, included many important papers, such as work by Gabriel Tarde on deviance, Emile Cheysson's analysis of one hundred family monographs, a reanalysis of Belgian family budgets by Ernst Engel, and one of the first papers on sampling methods by A. N. Kiaer.

In addition to these substantive activities, the Institut continued the organizational efforts of the earlier Congrès; Jacques Bertillon was particularly active at this task, and drew up many standardizing frameworks, including the "Bertillon Classification" for the causes of death.

The Conseil Supérieur de Statistique

Sessions of the Congrès International de Statistique and the Institut International de Statistique repeatedly recommended that every country establish a central commission for planning, supervision, and coordination of national statistical activities. Belgium took the initiative under Quételet in 1841, with Prussia, Austria, Italy, Spain, and Hungary following suit between 1860 and 1874. The Société de Statistique de Paris made efforts to establish such a commission in France, and in 1875 almost succeeded. Vested interests and fears of outside domination by several ministries proved too strong until a second campaign in 1884, directed prin-

---

31. On the Institut, see F. X. de Neuman-Spallart, "La fondation de l'Institut International de Statistique—Aperçu historique," *Bulletin de l'Institut International de Statistique,* I (1886), 1–35; and subsequent volumes of the *Bulletin;* Westergaard, *Contributions,* pp. 242ff.; de Foville, "La statistique"; J. W. Nixon, *A History of the International Statistical Institute* (The Hague: International Statistical Institute, 1960).

cipally by Emile Cheysson, convinced Parliament of the merits of such an institution.[32]

To emphasize its strictly advisory capacity, the body was designated not the *Commission* (as in several other countries), but the *Conseil* Supérieur de Statistique.[33] One-sixth of its members were senators, deputies, and administrative political officials; one-sixth representatives of scholarly societies; and two-thirds representatives from each of thirteen ministries and the city of Paris. Among the most active members were Emile Levasseur, Jacques Bertillon, and Emile Cheysson.

The Conseil, which in principle met twice a year, recommended the information that ministries and other bureaus should collect, the methods of collection and types of questionnaires, and materials for publication in the *Annuaire statistique de la France*. It also advised the ministries and Parliament on the teaching of statistics, and on relationships among various statistical agencies. It served essentially as an official lobby for the statisticians in expanding their activities. Among its accepted recommendations were studies on occupations, occupational recruitment, working hours, and hospitals. Less successful, however, were its attempts to have ministries hire professional statisticians.

Teaching Institutions

Informal Training

Prior to about 1880, anyone in France who wished to learn statistics had to read alone or work as an apprentice. Under such circumstances, the prominence of the Bertillon family for three generations was at least partially explained by its quasi-monopoly on statistical education: unwritten knowledge was passed on from father to son as were trades in earlier eras.[34]

32. Cf. Emile Cheysson, "Le Conseil Supérieur de la Statistique," *Journal de la Société de Statistique de Paris*, XXIII (1882).

33. On the Conseil, see Cheysson, "Le Conseil"; Marietti, *La Statistique*, pp. 173–189; *Bulletin du Conseil Supérieur de Statistique*; Clark, "Discontinuities in Social Research."

34. On the Bertillon family, see the notes and bibliography in *La vie et les oeuvres du Docteur L.-A. Bertillon* (Paris: Masson, 1883); the biography of her uncle by Suzanne Bertillon, the daughter of Jacques Bertillon, *Vie d'Alphonse Bertillon* (Paris: Gallimard, 1941); a more recent biography, Henry

Achille Guillard was a consulting engineer interested in the scientific study of society, and through a public lecture he gave on the subject, Louis-Adolphe Bertillon, a young physician, made his acquaintance just before 1848. The two were involved in the Revolution and spent some time in prison together where they discussed statistics. A few years later, Louis-Adolphe Bertillon married Guillard's daughter, by whom he had three sons: Jacques, Georges, and Alphonse. Achille Guillard lived with the Bertillon family for some time, and all three boys were raised in an atmosphere imbued with quantification. Jacques especially manifested an early interest in statistics, and his zeal even led him to construct indicators of seasickness from the number of times each family member leaned over the rail during a crossing of the Channel! Like his father, Jacques studied medicine, although he probably would have specialized in statistics had it been possible. He attended statistical meetings and congresses with his father and grandfather, and when his father died in 1883, Jacques succeeded him as director of the statistical bureau of the City of Paris.

Alphonse Bertillon was an unruly student, and his misconduct led to expulsion from numerous schools. He was sent to England in his late teens by his exasperated father to make the best of himself. He found a job with the English police detecting criminals. Although remiss in schoolwork, Alphonse had still absorbed a few rudiments of statistics and physical anthropology. Recording large numbers of measurements on criminals, and remembering his father's discussions of probability and measures of central tendency, he developed a new procedure for identifying criminals: he took several very precise measurements of criminals' noses, ears, and so forth, and knowing the low probability of recurrence for any single combination, he identified disguised criminals who had escaped other detection procedures. As the use of finger-

T. F. Rhodes, *Alphonse Bertillon* (New York: Abelard-Schuman, 1956), which draws heavily on the work of Suzanne Bertillon; Mlle. C. Moricourt, *Bibliographie analytique des oeuvres de la famille Bertillon (y compris Guillard), médecins et démographes, de Jean-Claude-Achille Guillard (1799–1876), à Georges Bertillon (1859–1918)* (Paris: Institut National des Arts et Métiers, 1962, typescript thesis); and Clark, "Jacques Bertillon."

A second daughter of Jacques Bertillon, Mlle. Jacqueline Bertillon, was also kind enough to discuss her family at some length, as was Professor Jean Bourdon, who worked closely with Jacques Bertillon, and Professor Louis Chevalier, who has stressed the importance of the Bertillon family.

prints was not perfected at the time, the procedure was close to revolutionary; Bertillon became internationally famous. He later became skilled at other procedures, such as handwriting analysis, and helped systematize the use of fingerprints. During the Dreyfus Affair he was called upon to examine the handwriting of numerous documents. When he declared (incorrectly) that they were written by Dreyfus, he was widely attacked in the pro-Dreyfus press. Jacques Bertillon, strongly *Dreyfusard,* was furious with his brother and refused all contact with him for years afterward. At this same time Jacques Bertillon applied for a chair at the Collège de France, but was not appointed; the family association with anti-Dreyfusards may have been a factor in the defeat of his candidacy.

Georges Bertillon studied medicine like his father and older brother and, although not especially creative, he published several papers on anthropometrics. Others interested in statistical questions, however, and less favored than the Bertillons, pressed for establishment of formal courses.[35]

Formal, Extra-University Training

Statistical instruction in France was initiated at the Conservatoire National des Arts et Métiers. Created in 1794 by the revolutionary government, the Conservatoire was envisaged as a depository for conservation (hence its name) of tools, machinery, various inventions, plans, books, and other objects related to the industrial arts.[36] A technical staff demonstrated these materials, but serious instruction began only after 1817 with course offerings in applied mechanics, applied chemistry, and industrial economics.[37] The Conservatoire did not draw students from the Latin

35. As Dick May put it when the first course in demography was offered at the Collège Libre des Sciences Sociales: "M. le Docteur Jacques Bertillon . . . par une initiative généreuse, a ouvert au Collège le trésor d'expériences démographiques accumulé dans ses biens de famille." *L'enseignement social à Paris* (Paris: Arthur Rousseau, 1896), p. 73.

36. On the Conservatoire, see L. Wolowski, "Conservatoire des Arts et Métiers," in Ch. Coquelin and Guillaumin, *Dictionnaire de l'économie politique* (Paris: Guillaumin, 1864), I, 461–463; Henri Hauser, *L'enseignement des sciences sociales* (Paris: Chevalier-Marescq, 1903), pp. 179–182.

37. E. Levasseur, *L'enseignement de l'économie politique au Conservatoire des Arts et Métiers* (Paris: Chevalier-Marescq, 1901).

Quarter, but, located in a working-class section of Paris, it developed a following of artisans, skilled workers, and especially office employees seeking to advance their careers. Courses gradually multiplied, and in 1854 a chair was created in Administration and Industrial Statistics. The first incumbent was Burat, whose lectures overlapped with those in economics. A. de Foville held the same chair from 1882 to 1893, and was succeeded in turn by André Liesse. A book by Liesse based on his Conservatoire lectures includes the historical development of formal statistics, measures of central tendency, and the use of indicators and indices.[38]

In 1875 Louis-Adolphe Bertillon taught a demography course at an annex of the Ecole de Médecine. Some of the published course material shows him presenting vital statistics one by one, and minutely examining differences in rates of birth, death, crime, and the like, region by region within France and other European countries. However, most interpretations of differences in rates were ad hoc and superficial.[39] In close contact with Broca and the Société d'Anthropologie, after 1876 Bertillon taught at the Ecole d'Anthropologie as incumbent of the chair of Demography.[40] Other extra-university courses in statistics were offered by Emile Levasseur after 1871 and later Liesse at the Ecole Libre des Sciences Politiques,[41] by Emile Cheysson in the early 1890's at the Ecole des Ponts et Chaussées,[42] and by Jacques Bertillon in a course on demography at the Collège Libre des Sciences Sociales after 1896.[43]

Emile Levasseur also covered statistical questions in his

38. André Liesse, *La statistique* (Paris: Guillaumin-Alcan, 1905). The discussion of indices deals largely with the economic index numbers in use at the time for production, standard of living, etc.

39. *Annales de démographie internationale*, I (1877), 517–540; II (1878), 494–506.

40. *L'Ecole d'Anthropologie de Paris* (Paris: Félix Alcan, 1907), p. 60. Attendance was not as great as at some courses of the Ecole d'Anthropologie, which occasionally numbered 200; but about 60 students listened to Bertillon, half of whom were serious enough to take extensive notes. Cf. *Annales de démographie internationale*, IV, 1880, 5–8.

41. See the section on the Ecole Libre des Sciences Politiques in Chapter 3.

42. Paul Melon, *L'enseignement supérieur et l'enseignement technique en France* (2d. ed.; Paris: Armand Colin, 1893), p. 72.

43. May, *L'enseignement social à Paris.* On the Collège Libre, see chap. 5.

courses at the Collège de France in the 1880's.[44] Between 1889 and 1893, he published a massive three-volume study, *La population française*,[45] which reviewed statistical methods in the social sciences and contained a thorough history of the growth and distribution of the French population (still widely used by historians and demographers), plus a consideration of population theories from Malthus to the Bertillons, rigorously examined using cross-national and historical materials.

One of the first textbooks in statistics was written by Jacques Bertillon. The *Cours élémentaire de statistique administrative*[46] grew out of his work with the Conseil Supérieur de Statistique. In 1899 the Conseil recommended that governmental ministries require some of their officials to be trained in statistics.[47] The response was minimal, however, and several ministries complained of the inadequacy of instruction and the lack of a text with which candidates could prepare for an examination. Bertillon consequently drafted the *Cours,* which was, in fact, quite an impressive treatise.[48]

Entering the University System

As statistics developed largely outside the university, the pattern of entry involved more diffusion from without than differentiation from within. The precise date and location of entry depend on the definition of statistics used, but the major steps were taken between 1870 and 1900.

Statistical instruction began with political economy. Three extra-university chairs in political economy were founded in the first half of the nineteenth century: in 1819 at the Conservatoire National des Arts et Métiers (entitled industrial economy and first occupied by J.-B. Say), in 1830 at the Collège de France (also occupied by Say), and in 1846 at the Ecole des Ponts et Chaussées (occupied by Garnier). Individual courses were

44. R. Marjolin, "La statistique," *Les sciences sociales en France, Enseignement et recherche* (Paris: Centre d'Etudes de Politique Etrangère, Publication No. 5, 1937), p. 205.

45. (Paris: Arthur Rousseau, 1889, 1891, 1893.)

46. (Paris: Société d'Editions Scientifiques, 1895.)

47. *Bulletin du Conseil Supérieur de Statistique,* 1895, pp. 103–105.

48. See Clark, "Discontinuities in Social Research."

created at the Faculties of Law of Paris and Toulouse in 1864 and 1865, and a third at Lyon in 1875. Then, shortly after 1877, when a section of the licence in law was devoted to political economy, courses were offered at most Law Faculties in France. Many of these courses developed into chairs, but the considerable integration of instruction in the Law Faculties and recruitment for all chairs via the same agrégation[49] led this political economy to emphasize institutional and legal elements. Such "deforming" of political economy upon entering the Law Faculties was criticized by the few French economists at the time, most of whom held to a theoretical conception closer to their British counterparts. The division became especially evident in 1887 when the institutional economists in the Law Faculties created the *Revue d'économie politique* to oppose the older *Journal des économistes.*[50] Thus, although chairs of political economy were increasing near the end of the nineteenth century, their incumbents seldom built on classical economic theory or utilized systematic quantitative analysis.[51]

Throughout the late nineteenth century, the appropriate university niche for the social sciences occasioned many a debate. While proposals were made for a separate faculty of social sciences, as in certain American universities, they came to naught. The major alternatives thus became the Faculties of Law and of Letters. Since the Faculties of Law attracted future civil servants, since statistics were mainly collected through the ministries, and since statistical data appeared as relevant to policy-oriented lawyers as to social scientists, the Faculties of Law were as much or more congenial to statistics than the Faculties of Letters.

Instead of considering total reorganization, decisions of this sort were made piecemeal; separate fields were gradually institutionalized in different sectors of the university, depending on demands of the moment, temporary budget surpluses, and avail-

---

49. See Chapter 1.
50. See Hauser, *L'enseignement des sciences sociales,* pp. 144ff. and Charles Gide, "France," in Lester F. Ward, "Sociology at the Paris Exposition of 1900," *Annual Reports of the Department of the Interior, Report of the Commissioner of Education,* Vol. 2, House of Representatives, 55th Congress, 2nd session (Washington: Government Printing House, 1901), pp. 1463–1470.
51. Cf. Charles Gide's remarks on the problem, quoted at the beginning of the chapter. Gide himself followed a career as a political economist in the Faculties of Law.

ability of potential staff meeting institutional requirements. This last point was particularly difficult for statisticians: with chairs at a Faculty of Letters contingent on a Doctorat d'Etat and those at a Faculty of Law on an agrégation en droit, even with full-time study it was difficult to meet either requirement before age thirty-five. Consequently, few persons following the conventional statistical career — that of ministerial official and statistical bureau director — could simultaneously complete the academic degrees. Moreover, since many statisticians were trained in medicine, engineering, or one of the natural sciences, they had the requisite background neither for the Faculty of Law nor the Faculty of Letters. Persons seeking a university chair in social science or statistics were consequently forced to complete degrees in a more traditional discipline, to assume a chair in that specialty, and then to attempt to change the orientation of courses and the title of the chair.

This pattern of differentiation was followed by Fernand Faure, who became the first professor of statistics in the French university system.[52] After completing the agrégation en droit in 1878, Faure spent two years at the Faculty of Law in Douai, and was named to the Bordeaux Faculty of Law in 1880 where he assumed a chair of political economy in 1883.[53] A man of action as much as a scholar, Faure ran for the Chamber of Deputies, was elected in 1885 and resigned his chair; defeated in the next election, however, he returned to Bordeaux, and in 1889 taught a course on statistics. In 1892 he was named professor of statistics at the Paris Faculty of Law,[54] where he remained until 1924.

Statistics thus penetrated the university to a minimal degree, but what its first professor did not do in the thirty-two years he held the Paris chair was perhaps more impressive than what he did. His only book was a thin little *manuel, Eléments de stati-*

52. On Faure, see particularly H. Truchy, "Fernand Faure," *Bulletin de l'Institut International de Statistique,* XXIV, no. 1 (1929), pp. 360–361; but also Edouard Julia, "Fernand Faure," *Revue politique et parlementaire* (1929), pp. i–ii.

53. Cf. Fernand Faure, "Sur l'enseignement de la statistique et les programmes d'examens d'admission dans les administrations publiques; 1 ère Partie, — Sur l'organisation de l'enseignement de la statistique présenté au Conseil supérieur, au nom de la Commission," *Bulletin du Conseil Supérieur de Statistique* (1894–1897), p. 99.

54. Virtually no information is available on details of the appointment.

stique,[55] which reviewed the history of statistical bureaus in the ministries and summarized elementary concepts of formal statistics. As the university representative for statistics, he was invited to sit in governmental councils, to present papers at professional meetings, and to contribute to various memorial volumes. Such rituals Faure performed satisfactorily; but he did virtually nothing to advance basic statistical theory or to extend quantitative analysis in the social sciences. The situation could have been considerably different if a more dynamic figure had been appointed to the chair. An incumbent with the creativity of a Léon Walras or a Vilfredo Pareto, or even an organizer with the skills of a René Worms, should have made a considerable impact on French social statistics. But Walras and Pareto, lacking academic credentials, languished in Lausanne, and the less gifted Worms, who would have loved to become a *grand patron*, remained outside the university.

Faure himself admitted that his lectures were too elementary to train statisticians for the ministries;[56] without a distinct examination series, almost no students learned enough to utilize quantitative tools creatively. A few persons, such as the young philosophers François Simiand and Maurice Halbwachs, were still enthusiastic enough about statistics to complete doctorates at the Paris Faculty of Law analyzing quantitative materials.[57] Guided by a more creative statistician, they, and others like them, could have moved further toward correlation, regression, and other multivariate procedures than they ever did.[58]

The development of statistics, like that of sociology, was hampered by the lack of state examinations and university posts. Persons following the traditional career still had to learn statistics largely through individual reading and apprenticeship in a Ministry. They remained correspondingly divorced from social science in the universities. Those inside the university — political econ-

55. (Paris: Larose, 1906.)
56. Fernand Faure, in "Procès-Verbal de la séance du 21 décembre 1892," *Journal de la Société de Statistique de Paris,* XXXIV (1893), 15–20, and "Observations sur l'organisation de l'enseignement de la statistique," pp. 25–29.
57. François Simiand, *Le salaire des ouvriers des mines en France* (Paris: Société Nouvelle de Librairie et d'Edition, 1904); Maurice Halbwachs, *Les expropriations et le prix des terrains à Paris* (Paris: Félix Alcan, 1909).
58. Raymond Boudon, *L'analyse mathématique des faits sociaux* (Paris: Plon, 1967), pp. 11ff.

omists, historians, and others potentially receptive to quantification — received little illumination from *le professeur* Faure. If Faure had brought statistics to bear on adjoining fields as Durkheim did for sociology, the results could have been impressive. But Faure attracted few colleagues or disciples, and in 1924 he abandoned the Faculty of Law for the Senate, where he remained until his death in 1929.

In 1923 an Institut de Statistique was created under the auspices of the Paris Faculties of Law, Science, Medicine, and Letters. It offered several courses, a certificat, and a diplôme, but the degrees were not integrated with those of the Faculties and there were very few serious students.[59] Scattered individuals may have conducted interesting work,[60] but from an institutional standpoint statistics continued to languish through the interwar years, and the social sciences proceeded largely without the input which statistics might have provided, and did provide in England, Italy, and the United States.[61] The case of Faure and the statistics chair nevertheless remains interesting to compare with that of Durkheim and sociology. Faure was a striking demonstration of how little could be done from a university chair. The case of Durkheim was quite different.

59. R. Marjolin, "La statistique," in *Les sciences sociales en France,* pp. 200–223. Lucien March, *Les principes de la méthode statistique* (Paris: Félix Alcan, 1930) is a summary of the basic course presented at the Institut de Statistique.

60. Marcel Lenoir, for example, completed an important study of prices, *Etudes sur la formation et le mouvement des prix* (Paris: Giard and Brière, 1913). See George Stigler's discussion of the work in *Essays in the History of Economics* (Chicago: University of Chicago Press, 1965), pp. 222ff.

61. Cf. Joseph Ben-David, "The Universities and the Growth of Science in Germany and the United States," *Minerva,* VII (Autumn–Winter 1968–69), 14–18, and Helen M. Walker, *Studies in the History of Statistical Method* (Baltimore: Williams and Wilkins, 1929), especially chap. 7, on statistics in other countries.

Chapter 5

The International Sociologists

Ross to Ward, Stanford University, California, October 14, 1900
I can't tell you how glad I am that the Institute elected you President.
We just whooped when we read it . . . I guess Giddings *et al.* won't
think they are the whole thing now . . . How Small will chortle though!
— Bernard J. Stern, "The Ward-Ross Correspondence, II. 1897–1901,"
American Sociological Review, XI (December 1946), 741.

Ward to Ross, Villa Stanislas, Paris, July 16, 1903
And now I must tell you about the *dinner* . . . Sir John Lubbock, the
first president of the Institute in 1894, set a precedent which has never
yet been departed from. He gave a dinner to all the members of the Congress in attendance . . . Of course such dinners are costly things, for
champagne flows as free as water, but I would not for ten times the cost
have been the first to depart from the custom. The Wormses helped me
and we found a somewhat more moderate priced hotel which was not less
perfectly respectable . . . My dinner did not fall below any of the preceding ones and was a grand success. Lest I scare you about the cost, let
me say that the whole thing only netted me 110 francs ($42.00). — Ber-
nard J. Stern, "The Ward-Ross Correspondence, III. 1902–1903," *American Sociological Review,* XII (December 1947), 713–714.

Professional Activities

The Revue internationale de sociologie and
the Institut International de Sociologie

In the last two chapters, the involvement of several groupings
in social scientific activities was discussed: the official positivists,
the two strands of Le Playists, the anthropologists, and the social
statisticians. However, a scattering of persons gradually emerged
that was only loosely attached to any grouping. Some were dilet-
tantes in the worst sense of the term: part of the Latin Quarter
flotsam and jetsam that might appear in any conference hall
heated or out of the rain. But others were more serious; if far less

147

professional than the Durkheimians, they still devoted considerable time to social science and, stimulated by existing activities, were ready to support more.

One of the most important of these persons was René Worms (1869–1926). Son of Emile Worms, professor of political economy, from his early years René Worms sought to synthesize the emerging knowledge dealing with man and society. He began to follow a standard academic career: Ecole Normale Supérieure, agrégation in philosophy, Doctorat-ès-Lettres. But he also acquired a Doctor of Law, Doctor of Science, and agrégation of economic science. Even before obtaining these degrees, however, when still only twenty-four, Worms was convinced of the need for further structures to support the social sciences. He thus founded the *Revue internationale de sociologie* (*R.I.S.*) and the Institut International de Sociologie (IIS). The year was 1893. Worms asked dozens of social scientists in France and abroad to serve on the editorial board of the *R.I.S.* and to enroll in the IIS. There is no record of the refusals (Durkheim was very likely one), but the list of acceptances was impressive. In France, they included Alfred Espinas, professor at Bordeaux; Gabriel Tarde, then probably the best-known French sociologist outside the university; Jacques Bertillon and Emile Cheysson, the social statisticians; Charles Gide, the economist; and two leading academicians and journal editors: Gabriel Monod, Ecole Normale professor and editor of the *Revue historique,* and Théodule Ribot of the *Revue philosophique* and the Collège de France. Foreigners included Louis Gumplowicz at the University of Graz, Carl Menger at Vienna, Alfred Marshall at Oxford, Georg Simmel and Ferdinand Toennies in Germany, and Thorstein Veblen and Franklin Giddings in the United States. The cover of the first *R.I.S.* noted that it was published "avec la collaboration et le concours de . . . ," and listed forty-two persons including these men and others less well known. The numerous foreigners in institutions organized by Worms makes the designation "international sociologists" appropriate even for the French members.

Many of these collaborators contributed to early issues of the *R.I.S.,* but further discussion will be postponed to the appendixes, where the social background of *R.I.S.* contributors and the content of their articles will be considered. Here it is enough to establish that the *R.I.S.* became the central journal of the international sociologists.

The Institut International de Sociologie included provision for one hundred members and two hundred associates, who would meet annually "for the common study of sociological questions." [1] The core of the membership was the same as the editorial board of the *R.I.S.* Each year the members elected a bureau including a president and four vice-presidents; a secretary general was elected for a term of ten years. Worms became secretary general the first year and held the post until his death in 1926. Other bureau members, however, changed almost every year, and although the president would make a general address and preside over congress sessions, the driving force remained the secretary general.

Certainly, the bureau included an outstanding sample of social scientists, with such presidents as Albert Schaeffle, Alfred Fouillée, Paul Lilienfeld, Carl Menger, Lester Ward, E. B. Tylor, Gustav Schmoller, Emile Levasseur, Maxime Kovalevsky, Franklin Giddings, and Ferdinand Buisson. Among the vice-presidents were Gabriel Tarde, Louis Gumplowicz, Lujo Brentano, Alfred Espinas, Alfred Marshall, Ferdinand Toennies, Georg Simmel, Wilhelm Wundt, Albion Small, Thorstein Veblen, E. A. Ross, James Bryce and Woodrow Wilson.

In early years the Institut's only funds came from the nominal membership fee, which just covered the publication of congress papers.[2]

The first congress was held in October 1894. Nonmembers could attend only with a ticket from the secretary general.[3] A

1. "L'Institut International de Sociologie," *R.I.S.*, I (1893), 561–562. Cf. also Francesco Paolo Cerase and Adriano Varotti, "L'Institut International de Sociologie, 1893–1969: Fatti e tendenze," *R.I.S.*, Series II, 5 (1969), 159–174.

2. As the Ward-Ross correspondence indicated, the president customarily offered a banquet. Virtually all other costs, however, seem to have been met by individual congress participants.

3. Although as Worms explained, "pour qu'il fût nettement entendu que l'on ne voulait priver personne de la lumière qui pouvait sortir de ces études, le secrétariat général ne refuse aucune des cartes qui lui furent demandées." Thus, in addition to the 20 IIS members, some 50 to 100 persons attended the sessions, "sensiblement plus nombreuses à celles du soir qu'à celles du matin." Le Secrétaire Général, "Le premier congrès de l'Institut International de Sociologie," *Annales de l'Institut International de Sociologie*, I (Paris: Giard & Brière, 1895).

second congress was held in 1895 and another in 1897; subsequently they were held every three years until World War I. The first five took place in Paris, the rest in London, Bern, and Rome. Some twenty to thirty members would generally attend, and perhaps a dozen more would send papers. A few congresses followed a single theme, such as the evolution of political forms, crime as a social phenomenon, social conflict, or social solidarity; but, typical of the international sociologists, there was considerable variety in both orientation and quality.

A report by Worms to the second congress suggested that most members tended toward one of three general conceptions of sociology. A first "tendance pratique" sought to formulate principles for "social art," oriented toward solving economic, legal, and moral problems. Second was a historical conception, which sought generalizations transcending any single historical period; by comparing demographic, economic, moral, and legal phenomena, it sought to develop a "comparative ethnology of societies." A third philosophical conception was more deductive in approach, constructing general theoretical systems from a few basic principles. Worms characteristically stressed the complementarity and communality of the three tendencies. Such benign eclecticism, despite ridicule from cartesian *universitaires*, at least guarded against premature closure. What he lost in theoretical coherence he regained in his ability to distinguish weak points in his more systematic contemporaries. In their measure and balance, many passages from Worms appear closer to the mid-twentieth-century sociologist than those of more illustrious contemporaries, such as Durkheim or Tarde.[4]

In assembling social scientists from such different countries and institutions, the IIS was no mean accomplishment. Discussions were held after most papers, and occasionally these were quite animated. But members often talked past each other. Beyond extending a spirit of international and intellectual tolerance, any results of the congresses were difficult to observe. Perhaps the most striking exception was the debate over organicism at the 1897 congress.

Comparisons between societies and biological organisms were

4. See Terry N. Clark, "René Worms," *International Encyclopedia of the Social Sciences* (New York: Macmillan and Free Press, 1968).

used by Comte, and developed by Herbert Spencer, Schaeffle, and dozens of others in the nineteenth century. Worms presented highly detailed comparisons between biological and social organisms in his *Organisme et société* (1897)[5] Aware of increasing criticisms of such analogies, however, Worms arranged several sessions to deal with the subject at the IIS congress that same year. The sessions marked a turning point in the history of sociology and demonstrated the value of a congress meeting.[6]

Favorable comments on the analogy by Ludwig Stein and R. Garofalo generated an exchange involving Tarde, Jacques Novicow, and others. Tarde was one of the most forceful critics of the analogy. René Worms, the Dane C. N. Starcke, N. Kareiev, historian from Saint Petersburg, and A. Espinas continued at another session; discussion went over the time allocated, continued privately, and emerged in other sessions throughout the four days.

Although many remained committed to their positions, a few younger participants gradually abandoned the organismic analogy. René Worms was an impressive case, for though he was the author of an extreme statement of the analogy, he included only passing mention of it in subsequent writings. Indeed, he spent the next decade on a three-volume work providing what he considered a more successful, although less systematic, theoretical statement: his *Philosophie des sciences sociales.*[7] In it Worms sought to synthesize the most important social scientific knowledge of the period. Considering such phenomena as economic institutions, scientific institutions, and the family, he sought above all to formulate what he termed "partial syntheses" — ultilizing an approach essentially similar to what has since been termed, among other things, "middle range theory." [8]

At IIS sessions, as in other activities arranged by Worms, a

5. Worms's defense of the work as a Doctorat-ès-Lettres at the Sorbonne was attended by "plusieurs centaines de personnes." *R.I.S.,* IV (1896), p. 166.

6. Cf. the discussion of the organismic analogy, and the 1897 congress, in Pitirim A. Sorokin, *Contemporary Sociological Theories* (New York: Harper & Row, 1928), pp. 195–218.

7. See his comments on the matter in *Les Principes biologiques de l'évolution sociale* (Paris: Giard & Brière, 1910), p. 10, and *La sociologie* (Paris: Giard & Brière, 1921), p. 55.

8. For further discussion, see Terry N. Clark, "Marginality, Eclecticism, and Innovation: René Worms and the *Revue internationale de sociologie* from 1893 to 1914," *R.I.S.,* Series II, 3 (December 1967), 12–27.

151

constant effort was made to involve leading university and governmental officials, by inviting them to present speeches, attend receptions, and so forth. Such efforts led to official recognition of the IIS by the French government in 1909, and eventually a subsidy in 1931.

The Bibliothèque des Sciences Sociales

When he founded the *R.I.S.* and the IIS in 1893, Worms also launched the Bibliothèque des Sciences Sociales. Like the *R.I.S.* and *Annales* of the IIS, it appeared with the law-oriented publisher Giard and Brière. Simply in terms of volumes published (eventually over fifty), the Bibliothèque was one of the leading sociological series in the world. Works included *Organisme et société* by René Worms (1897) as well as his three-volume *Philosophie des sciences sociales* (1903–1907). A volume of essays by Gabriel Tarde entitled *Etudes de psychologie sociale* (1898) was the first in the world with "social psychology" on its cover.[9] Nearly half the works were by foreign associates, often collections of essays or translations, such as Louis Gumplowicz, *Sociologie et politique,* Lester Ward, *Sociologie pure,* or Robert Michels, *Amour et chasteté.* For foreigners who had difficulty publishing in their own countries, such as the Russian Maxime Kovalevsky, the Bibliothèque was an important outlet: he published four volumes in the series.[10]

The Société de Sociologie de Paris

The eminent social scientists that Worms attracted to Paris impressed many of his Parisian associates. But several found it incongruous that the Parisians met only with an international organization. As no Parisian sociological society had existed since Littré's organization in 1872,[11] after the 1895 IIS meeting several

9. See Borgatta's comment on this matter, correcting Gordon Allport's assertion that Ross and McDougall were first. Edgar F. Borgatta, ed., *Social Psychology: Readings and Perspectives* (Chicago: Rand McNally, 1969), p. vii.

10. Giard and Brière was subsequently acquired by the Librairie Générale de Droit et de Jurisprudence. Unfortunately no sales records for the Bibliothèque were preserved, but sales were considerably less than the number of volumes printed, for many pre-1914 volumes were still available in the publisher's warehouse in 1966.

11. René Worms pointed out in a note on Littré's society that there were four common members of the two societies. "La première Société de Sociologie," *R.I.S.,* XVIII (1910), 202–206.

persons suggested that IIS members residing nearby Paris assemble at more frequent intervals. The result was the Société de Sociologie de Paris.[12] It first met on December 11, 1895, and thereafter convened monthly except for summers. It had no formal association with the IIS, but was organized in similar fashion: Worms became the secretary general, and continued year after year; other officers, generally elected annually, left most details to the secretary general.[13] An annual membership fee of 5 francs supported the organization. As in the IIS, there were a president, vice-president, and general secretary; but by 1898 there were also a treasurer, three secretaries, an archivist-librarian, and five "conseillers." The many positions indicated Worms's taste for formal organization and efforts toward co-optation, even if the titles were largely honorific.

Considered strictly as an organization, the Société was a clear success: officers were renewed regularly, meetings were held almost every month from 1895 until 1914, and attendance ranged from one hundred to two hundred. The participants were enthusiastic and the discussions animated. Some officers were quite distinguished; for example, the first president was Gabriel Tarde. But he was succeeded by Beaurin-Gressier, as much administrator as social scientist, Adolphe Coste, part-time journalist, statistician, and economist, and Ernest Delbet, deputy and prophet of orthodox positivism. Most members were amateurs at best. Their participation often brought down discussions to an abysmally low level.[14]

Efforts were clearly made to attract men of wealth and power. In one illustrative case Prince Tenichef, general-commissioner for Russia at the 1900 World's Fair, was made a member of the IIS and Société de Sociologie de Paris. He was led to contribute 5,000

12. See the discussions at the time in the *R.I.S.*, as well as in René Worms, "Pour le 25e anniversaire de la Société de Sociologie de Paris," *R.I.S.*, XXIX (1921), 38–45.
13. As one president remarked, "M. René Worms est en quelque sorte l'âme de la Société; c'est lui qui prépare les sujets de discussion, qui récrute les orateurs, qui sollicite l'assiduité des auditeurs. Le succès de nos séances est en grande partie le résultat de ses efforts." Ernest Levasseur, "Allocution," *R.I.S.*, XIV (1906), 149.
14. See appendixes I and II for discussion of their social backgrounds and the content of the meetings. (Minutes of Société meetings were published in the *R.I.S.*)

francs as a prize for a scholarly monograph. But the subject had to be "Threats to the Social Order," and it was only after many months of publicity that a few young and hungry social scientists were cajoled into participation.[15]

The Prince Tenichef episode was all too exemplary of Worms's eagerness to flatter the influential and the affluent. A few careers may have been advanced thereby, and the Worms organizations unquestionably attracted the public eye. It may be that the public relations effects of these activities included more benefits than losses for social science. But some doubted even this; the Durkheimians were especially critical of the verbal meanderings that passed for analysis at Société de Sociologie de Paris meetings. Tarde and a few others were of unquestionable quality, but the general impressions left by Worms and his many activities were far from entirely favorable.

Teaching Institutions

In the last part of the nineteenth century, as has been discussed, social scientific instruction was offered by several sectlike groupings; but this frequently dogmatic inculcation dismayed even many would-be enthusiasts. Alternatives began to emerge in the 1890's, especially in *cours libres*. Free in that auditors could attend without a registration fee, and the lecturer would receive an equal amount for his efforts, most French Faculties offered *cours libres* during the evening hours. These often appealed to a general public which found the increasingly specialized lectures by Faculty professors unappetizing; the professors were generally delighted to be rid of the general public, and as no salary or academic privileges were accorded professors of *cours libres,* the Faculty lost little. Finally, in *cours libres* potential innovations could obtain a first airing.

Concerned with the public reputation of the Caen Faculty of Law, its Dean, E. Villez, instituted three *cours libres* in 1894: he himself taught a course on Suffrage (women were an important audience for *cours libres*), a M. Le Fur a course on Parliamentary

15. See the notes at the end of the monthly issues of the *R.I.S.*, mainly during 1906, and H. Monin, "Rapport sur le concours Tenichef," *Annales de l'Institut International de Sociologie,* IX (1907), 539–555.

Government, and René Worms a course on The Doctrine of Le Play in Social Economy. Many other social scientists offered *cours libres* in these years, as was mentioned in the case of Pierre du Maroussem at the Paris Faculty of Law, and a few years earlier, the courses in political economy cited by Duruy. Other courses were offered outside of any Faculty. For example, after 1893, the Conseil Municipal de Lyon supported a course on Sociology, taught by A. Bertrand.[16] There were soon to be imitations.

The Collège Libre des Sciences Sociales

One especially enthusiastic participant in such activities was a Mademoiselle Jeanne Weill, who wrote under the pseudonym of Dick May. Like René Worms, she was concerned with the fragmentation of efforts, and sought to do for teaching institutions what Worms had done for professional organizations. Intellectually and personally attractive, she came to know leading social scientists inside and outside the university. She was in especially close institutional and personal contact — according to reliable informants, as his mistress — with Alfred Croiset, Dean of the Paris Faculty of Letters, professor of *Eloquence grecque,* and Member of the Institut. For influencing the Sorbonne, as well as various academic commissions and the Ministry of Education, she could scarcely have chosen better. A request for cooperation from Mademoiselle Weill was considered seriously when it was known that word of it might reach the Sorbonne.

If in Croiset Mademoiselle Weill enjoyed the perfect contact with the university, she simultaneously cultivated the most important private philanthropist in the social sciences: the Comte de Chambrun. As his personal secretary,[17] she seems to have influenced the allocation of considerable sums. Chambrun endowed the Musée Social, as discussed, as well as several chairs at leading institutions.

In 1895, two years after René Worms created the *R.I.S.* and the IIS, and the same year he founded the Société de Sociologie de

16. Marcel Bernès, "Quelques réflections sur l'enseignement de la sociologie," *R.I.S.,* III (1895), 629–643.

17. Mademoiselle Weill had a lively pen, and published several novels dealing with themes such as the proper position of women and the role of science in modern society before she edited and prepared introductions for essays and poetry by the Comte.

Paris, Mlle. Weill was central in establishing the largest social science teaching institution in France: the Collège Libre des Sciences Sociales.[18] The formal director was Théophile Funck-Brentano, a mildly Le Playist professor at the Ecole Libre des Sciences Politiques.[19] Mademoiselle Weill and he persuaded twenty-five persons to offer courses.

The faculty members exhibited the same diversity as the professional organizations of Worms; the eclecticism, for certain observers, was one approaching chaos. The Collège was reorganized more than once, but initially there were two major sections: Methods, and Doctrines and Social Applications.

The Methods section included courses by several persons who have already been encountered: Jacques Bertillon taught Demography. Pierre du Maroussem lectured on Monographic Methods of Social Enquiry.[20] Like Bertillon and du Maroussem, Arthur Fontaine lectured on his methods in governmental research bureaus; his specialty was economic and labor statistics. There were also courses by two soon-to-be-eminent *universitaires:* Charles Seignobos lectured on Historical Methods Applied to the Social Sciences; and Jean Brunhès offered a course on Geographic Methods: Application to Some Problems of Social Economy.[21] The second section, Doctrines and Social Applications, included representatives of the main currents of ideas considered in earlier chapters. Ernest Delbet taught the Doctrines of Comte, and A. Delaire lectured on Doctrines of Le Play. There were also courses on Doctrines of Marx, Theoretical Socialism, and Labor Questions. But adjoining these courses by socialists and labor organ-

18. Dick May, "L'enseignement social à Paris," *R.I.E.,* XXXII (July–December 1896), 1–29; XXXIII (January–July 1897), 499ff.; XXXIV (July–December 1897), 28–45.
19. See his discussion of the Collège in *La science sociale* (Paris: Plon, 1897), which summarizes his own course there.
20. His volume *Les enquêtes* (Paris: Félix Alcan, 1900) was adapted from courses at the Collège and the Paris Faculty of Law. It appeared in a series, the Bibliothèque Generale des Sciences Sociales, of which Dick May served as *Secrétaire de la Rédaction.* The same series included volumes by the law professor R. Saleilles, the historian H. Hauser, Gabriel Tarde, and the university philosopher E. Boutroux, most of which were presented at least in part as lectures at one of the Dick May institutions.
21. Dick May, *L'enseignement social à Paris,* (Paris: Arthur Rousseau, 1896), pp. 60ff., and "L'enseignement social à Paris," *R.I.E.,* XXXII (July–December 1896), 1–35.

izers were others on Principles of Colonization, by the former governor general of Indo-China, and Catholic Sociology, by the Abbé de Pascal.[22] Apparently many of these courses were highly dogmatic. Given the ideas and personalities of the period, however, it was difficult enough to bring proponents of such contrasting traditions together under a single roof; to ask them to reexamine their assumptions or consider new approaches would no doubt have doomed the venture from the outset.

According to Mademoiselle Weill, in its early years the Collège attracted some two hundred students[23] from institutions as varied as was the faculty: the Sorbonne, Ecole Normale Supérieure, Ecole des Chartes, Institut Catholique, Ecole Coloniale, Ecole Libre des Sciences Politiques, and the Institut Thiers. Most students may have attended only lectures close to their previous conceptions; but, again according to Mademoiselle Weill, a nucleus of some twenty attended "almost every course, collecting lecture notes without regard for doctrine, with a remarkably avid, curious, and almost passionate application." [24] Such students had to be motivated largely by the materials discussed, for there were no examinations, prizes, degrees, or awaiting careers.

The inevitable conflicts from assembling such a motley faculty in an institution with no endowment (there were modest student fees), no official legitimacy, and no traditions were soon enhanced by several outside developments.

First was competition from more established institutions. Although Durkheim was still in Bordeaux when the Collège was founded in 1895, just a year later he launched the *Année sociologique;* work by most persons at the Collège suffered by comparison. Gabriel Tarde offered courses in the 1890's at the Ecole Libre des Sciences Politiques, the Ecole Russe des Hautes Etudes Sociales, as well as the Collège Libre des Sciences Sociales. But with the death of J.-F. Nourisson in 1900, the chair of Modern

22. See the course listings in the *R.I.E.* and the *R.I.S.* Later years included courses by Gabriel Tarde and Robert Michels. Part of Tarde's course on "La sociologie politique" was published in the *R.I.E.,* XXXVII (1899), 19–21; a lecture by Michels was included in "Mouvement social," *R.I.S.,* XXIV (1906); pp. 801ff.

23. May, *L'enseignement social à Paris,* pp. 60–108.

24. *Ibid.,* p. 70.

Philosophy at the Collège de France became vacant, and Tarde's friends urged him to submit his candidacy. He did, simultaneously requesting that the chair be entitled Sociology; the title was not changed, but he was elected and left free to teach as he pleased. He thereby became less interested in such marginal institutions as the Collège Libre.

Another source of pressure might be labeled international criticism and competition. These were especially important following the 1900 Paris World's Fair, where the ever present Mademoiselle Weill arranged several sessions.[25] Reports there included comparisons and criticisms of existing arrangements in the different countries, in which the standards, or absence of same, at the Collège Libre were mentioned more than once.

There were also increasing tensions due to the Dreyfus Affair. As might be imagined, Mademoiselle Weill was an active Dreyfusard.[26] She turned her organizational skills to the cause: in 1899 she created the Ecole Indépendante de Morale, among other reasons, to help formulate and disseminate Dreyfusard ideology, and the Ecole de Journalisme, to train a cadre of committed journalists. Certain professors at the Collège Libre supported her in these projects. Such partisan activities, however, aroused indignation among their anti-Dreyfusard colleagues. A battle ensued. In part to remove the most partisan elements from the Collège Libre, in 1900 Mademoiselle Weill merged the Ecole Indépendante de Morale and the Ecole de Journalisme with a third subdivision, the Ecole Sociale, to form the Ecoles des Hautes Etudes Sociales. Dean Alfred Croiset became its president. The director was Emile Duclaux, Director of the Pasteur Institute. Mademoiselle Weill

25. There were reports from Lester Ward on the United States, Charles Gide on France, Emile Waxweiller on Belgium, Alfredo Niceforo on Italy, and Sidney Webb on England. See *Le premier Congrès de l'Enseignement des Sciences Sociales* (Paris: Alcan, 1901), and Lester F. Ward, "Sociology at the Paris Exposition of 1900," *Annual Reports of the Department of the Interior,* House of Representatives, 56th Congress, 2nd Session, Document No. 5, Report of the Commissioner of Education, Volume II (Washington: Government Printing House, 1901), 1451–1593.

26. Daniel Halévy referred to her as "une agitée du Dreyfusisme," in *Péguy et les Cahiers de la Quinzaine* (Paris: Bernard Grasset, 1941), p. 102.

As a footnote on the importance of Dreyfusard contacts, it might be added that Mademoiselle Weill made space available in the Ecole's building on the rue de la Sorbonne to Charles Peguy, who published there his *Cahiers de la Quinzaine.*

served as secretary general.[27] Almost immediately, the Ecole[28] was accorded state recognition (as was the Collège Libre nearly simultaneously), and a subsidy for operating expenses.

The Ecole des Hautes Etudes Sociales

Despite ideological birth pangs, apparently the Ecole was less dogmatic than the Collège Libre. As its name implied, the Ecole was meant to resemble the Ecole Pratique des Hautes Etudes.[29] As one participant even put it, "as far as possible, it fills the place of the absent section (for social science) at the Ecole Pratique des Hautes Etudes, and at the same time maintains the taste for the scientific study of these questions." [30]

The Ecole shared the EPHE's cooperative research emphasis and arranged several seminars with leading university figures. One of the best known was on "solidarity," presided over by the apostle of solidarity Léon Bourgeois. Outstanding *universitaires* in the seminar included the philosophers Duclaux, Alphonse Darlu, Xavier Léon, and Frédéric Rauh, the political economist Charles Gide, and Ferdinand Buisson, Director of Primary Education at the Ministry and professor of Pedagogical Science at the Sorbonne.[31] Following publication of his *Division of Labor in Society,* Durkheim was one of the acknowledged experts on solidarity. Another seminar at the Ecole was on Pedagogy, directed by Dean Croiset and Ferdinand Buisson; in it they conducted a series of *enquêtes* on the teaching of ethics in primary, secondary, and higher education. Again on this topic Durkheim had written more carefully reasoned and forceful articles than almost anyone in France, and as a forty-one-year-old professor at Bordeaux was

27. The administrative structure, on paper at any rate, was quite complex, involving committees and boards with numerous eminent professors, bankers, governmental administrators, and others siding together in the Dreyfus Affair. See Dom Besse, *Les religions laïques* (Paris: Nouvelle Librairie Nationale, 1913).

28. It was soon referred to simply as the Ecole (singular) des Hautes Etudes Sociales.

29. Another institution with a closely similar name was the Ecole Russe des Hautes Etudes Sociales; it included courses by Gabriel Tarde, Maxime Kovalevsky, and Eugène de Roberty, among others. See Henri Hauser, *L'enseignement des sciences sociales* (Paris: Chevalier-Marescq, 1903), pp. 211ff., and the announcements in the *R.I.S.* after 1901.

30. Hauser, *L'enseignement des sciences sociales,* pp. 209–210.

31. Their various contributions were published together in *La solidarité* (Paris: Alcan, 1902).

eminently suitable for a call to Paris, which came just a year later.

By 1910 student enrollment at the Ecole had grown almost four times since 1900. The increase in the social and moral sections was probably restrained by university competition,[32] but the Ecole still provided a forum for certain issues not treated in the university.

For example, in 1904 Dean Croiset arranged a debate there between Emile Durkheim and Gabriel Tarde.[33] Célestin Bouglé presented a lecture series at the Ecole published as *La nation armée*.[34] There were dozens of other individual lectures and discussions of current issues.

Essentially similar activities were continued at the Ecole during the interwar years; its closest successor is the Sixth Section of the EPHE. The Collège Libre des Sciences Sociales, however, began to decline with the founding of the Ecole des Hautes Etudes Sociales. As the basic social sciences penetrated the university, it increasingly offered vocational evening courses for civil servants and businessmen.[35]

Conclusion

The professional institutions created by René Worms and the teaching institutions animated by Mlle. Jeanne Weill thus brought together representatives of strands of thought that had developed separately. They were brought together in that various positivists, Le Playists, anthropologists, social statisticians, and others became members of the same professional organizations, occasionally published in the same journal, and taught at some of the same institutions.

Certain idealistic observers, such as René Worms and a few

32. In 1910 in Art there were 310 enrolled students; in Journalism, 222; in "Etudes Sociales," 215; and in "Morale et Pédagogie," 136. Dom Besse, *Les religions.*

33. See "A Debate with Emile Durkheim," in Terry N. Clark, ed., *Gabriel Tarde on Communication and Social Influence* (Chicago: University of Chicago Press, 1969), pp. 136–142.

34. (Paris: Alcan, 1909).

35. See *Le Collège Libre des Sciences Sociales et Economiques* (brochure, 1964, 112pp). The final adjective was added in 1946 when the Collège reopened after having been closed by the Nazis, who also destroyed its archives and dispersed its library.

associates, hoped that an intellectual synthesis would emerge from the institutions they had helped to erect. But while these institutions may have represented progress in concentrating social thinking of the period, their influence on the development of ideas was quite limited. Spokesmen of conflicting strands of thought, when brought into closer contact with each other, merely grew more aware of their differences and concentrated on defending their respective positions. Too often they retained a prophetic style and outlook. As much work of the period consisted of programmatic suggestions, compromise was difficult. And of course these fragile structures provided almost no shelter from the strong winds of political ideology, which accentuated specific nonideological disagreements almost beyond recognition. Most listeners were only peripherally interested in the materials discussed; or to put the matter slightly differently, in the absence of regular social science careers, it was virtually essential for students to obtain degrees in fields that would provide regular means of support. Persons studying to become lawyers, civil servants, or lycée professors might thus attend a few lectures out of general interest, but there were few listeners who aspired to university careers.

With mounting interest in social science near the end of the century, however, these various institutions were like soapboxes around the walls of the Sorbonne. Every variety of would-be social scientist could stand upon them and present his wares. Not only were listeners from the Latin Quarter streets attracted, so were a few from inside the university. Then when the *universitaires* themselves participated in the new organizations, the probability increased that the university would find room inside its walls for a few social scientists. How the walls were breached and the university entered is the subject of the next chapter.

Chapter 6

The Durkheimians and the University

Ceux qui sont infiniment dangereux, ce sont ceux qui sont tyranniques, ce sont ceux qui par des moyens temporels dans des situations intellectuelles veulent introduire, veulent établir un gouvernement (absolu, tyrannique) des esprits, ce sont ceux qui veulent enrégimenter les jeunes gens, mener les esprits à la baguette, faire des écoles et des sectes qui soient comme des régiments prussiens, ce sont ces hommes, ces professeurs qui se conduisent dans leurs chaires comme des préfets, de Combes ou de Clemenceau, qui introduisent . . . dans tout l'enseignement, sous prétexte, sous le nom de pédagogie, sociologie . . . — Charles Péguy, *Oeuvres en prose 1898–1908* (Paris: Gallimard, Bibliothèque de la Pléiade, 1959), pp. 1135–1136.

After 1880 a general concern with social questions and increasing public interest in social science exerted definite pressures on the university.[1] There was also a strong demand from inside the educational system: educational administrators looked to social science for a new civic training in the schools; the void left by Catholicism had still not been satisfactorily filled. The time was thus propitious for institutionalization of the social sciences. But first someone had to synthesize earlier advances so that the results, and he himself, met established university standards. When a young lycée professor wrote about a scientific philosophy based on social science, he attracted considerable interest. Unlike many

1. Charles Gide, Professor at the Paris Faculty of Law, observed that "The special schools, which are very numerous in France (much too numerous, since it is their competition that empties our universities, at least in the faculties of letters and of the sciences), almost all inscribe on their schedules courses [in the social sciences] . . . It is certain that this competition has exercised a very salutary influence on the development of these same branches in the faculties of the State." "Advanced Instruction in the Social Sciences in France," in *Annual Reports of the Department of the Interior,* Report of the Commissioner of Education, Vol. 2, House of Representatives, 56th Congress, 2nd session, Document No. 5 (Washington: Government Printing Office, 1901), p. 1465.

162

amateurs in the new private institutions, Emile Durkheim had a proper academic background and wrote with rigor, insight, and intelligence.

Two of Durkheim's important supporters were Alfred Espinas and Louis Liard. Espinas had defended the first sociological Doctorat d'Etat in France, *Les sociétés animales,* in 1877, and became professor of philosophy and then Dean of the Faculty of Letters at Bordeaux. Liard, Director of Higher Education, was firmly convinced of the necessity of studying society with scientific methods. He too had taught at Bordeaux and had been active in local political activities. In 1886 Liard had an important conversation with Durkheim concerning republicanism, science, and secular morality.[2] The next year a Ministry of Education fellowship permitted Durkheim to study with Wilhelm Wundt at Leipzig and at the University of Berlin. Durkheim published several incisive articles on scientific morality in Germany, and in 1887 Liard arranged for him to become chargé de cours in Science Sociale et Pédagogie at the Bordeaux Faculty of Letters.[3] He was reappointed each year for seven years, offering courses on social solidarity, the sociology of the family, suicide, physiology of law and ethics, and other subjects. In 1893 he defended, vigorously,[4] *De la division du travail social* and *Quid Secundatus politicae scientiae instituendae contulerit* as his doctoral theses at the Paris Faculty of Letters, and the next year was given a permanent appointment as professeur adjoint at Bordeaux.[5] At that point, in

2. See Raymond Lenoir, "L'oeuvre sociologique d'Emile Durkheim," *Europe,* XXII (1930), 294.

3. See René Lacroze, "Allocution: Emile Durkheim à Bordeaux (1887–1902)," *Annales de l'Université de Paris,* 30th year (January–March 1960), p. 26, and Harry Alpert, "France's First University Course in Sociology," *American Sociological Review,* II (June 1937), 311–317.

4. On the thesis defense, see L. Muhlfeld, *Revue universitaire,* I (1893), 440–443.

5. The Rector wrote to the Ministry on 19 November 1894 that "J'ai l'honneur de vous transmettre, avec avis très favorable, copie de la déliberation . . . par lequel le Conseil de la Faculté des Lettres de Bordeaux propose à l'unanimité pour le titre de Professeur adjoint M. Durkheim, actuellement chargé d'un cours complémentaire de science sociale et de pédagogie." A footnote added that of eleven titulary professors, one, M. Radel, either abstained or was absent from the meeting. Whether informal influence had been exercised from Paris is thus unclear; all official documents show the initiative coming from the Bordeaux Conseil.

These, other letters, and information about Durkheim's salary advances,

addition to the two theses, Durkheim had published a dozen articles and reviews in Ribot's *Revue philosophique,* criticizing sociological works and outlining the need for a scientific foundation of ethics. The same year that he was given a permanent appointment he published the programmatic *Rules of Sociological Method,* thus defining the ideology for a new cluster. In 1896 he became Professeur de Science Sociale, assuming the first such chair in France,[6] and launched the *Année sociologique.*

In articles, lectures, and conferences, Durkheim distinguished himself as an outstanding university figure and a particularly clear spokesman on ethics and public morality. In the mounting Dreyfus Affair, he was a prominent *intellectuel.* He brilliantly combined the roles of prophet and nascent patron.

In 1902, when Ferdinand Buisson left his Sorbonne chair of Science de l'Education for the Chamber of Deputies, Durkheim was invited to substitute as chargé de cours.[7] This continued each year until 1906 when he was named to the chair. In 1905 *"morale et sociologie"* became one of four possible subjects for the written section of the philosophy licence. In 1906 his course on pedagogy became mandatory for all agrégation candidates in the Faculty of Letters, the only required course in any field in the Faculty. The title of Durkheim's chair was changed to Science de l'Education et Sociologie in 1913; he died four years later.

Sociology, in Durkheimian guise, thus penetrated the university. In the rest of this chapter some of the more important factors contributing to its success will be examined: first how the status of sociologist came to be defined, then the rise of Durkheim inside the university system, the creation of a cluster around the *Année*

---

teaching schedule, and other administrative matters are included in the Dossier Durkheim, compiled by the Ministry of Education. It was transferred to the Archives Nationales and first became available for consultation fifty years after his death, in 1967.

6. The official papers are included in the Dossier Durkheim. The appointment apparently was made as smoothly as that to professeur adjoint two years earlier.

7. Durkheim had earned 4,000 francs annually as chargé de cours after 1888; 5,000 as professeur adjoint in 1894; and 6,000 as professeur in 1896. When he left his chair in Bordeaux, he still received one-half the salary from it. In Paris he earned 9,000 francs as chargé de cours from 1902 to 1904. Salary information after 1904 is not available in the A. N. Dossier Durkheim.

sociologique, and Durkheim's relations with the intellectual community and the broader society.

Professionalism and the Durkheimian Conception of Society

Although existing social science organizations and journals would have welcomed Durkheim, he started his own journal, the *Année sociologique,* drawing to it an intelligent, committed group of young scholars. Another short-lived publication joining the Durkheimians was edited by François Simiand while he served as librarian at the Ministry of Commerce, *Notes critiques: sciences sociales.* For about four years after 1900, *Notes critiques* published monthly "critical notes" on new books similar to those in the *Année.* Contributors were largely the same as for the *Année,* including Durkheim, who published an important review there of Simmel's *Philosophie des Geldes.* Lucien Herr also published several reviews of Durkheim's works in *Notes critiques.*

In their writings and other activities, Durkheim and his colleagues showed great disdain for most persons not collaborating with the *Année;* they thereby contributed to crystallizing French social scientists into outwardly aggressive and inwardly self-satisfied schools.

More will be said of relationships among the Durkheimians presently; here it may simply be noted that, in contrast to the groupings considered thus far, the Durkheimians were not united through a professional organization; Durkheim never created a formal organization as the basis for a cluster. Some Durkheimians occasionally participated in organizations overlapping with their concerns. Thus, Durkheim, Marcel Mauss, and a few others met with Léon Brunschvicg, Elie Halévy, and Xavier Léon in the Société Française de Philosophie. Lucien Lévy-Bruhl, Robert Hertz, Henri Hubert, Mauss, and Durkheim met (infrequently) at the Institut Français d'Anthropologie, founded in 1911.[8] After Durkheim's death, the remaining cluster members continued participating in these organizations, and founded their own Institut

8. Institut Français d'Anthropologie, *Comptes rendus des séances,* I (1911–1913), 129–131.

Français de Sociologie. But by that time the cluster had changed considerably; (discussion of most postwar developments will be reserved for Chapter 7.)

Durkheim and most *Année sociologique* collaborators had impeccable pedigrees for a university career. The ideal type included an outstanding secondary school record and study at the Ecole Normale Supérieure; agrégation in philosophy; teaching philosophy in provincial lycées; fellowship term in Germany; Doctorat-ès-Lettres.[9] Nonacademic but significant personal characteristics were petty bourgeois family origins (ideally with a father as a primary school teacher), passionate devotion to the Republic, militant anticlericalism, and Radical Socialist or Socialist political preferences.[10] The Jewish background of Durkheim and certain associates does not appear to have been directly important inside the university; the overshadowing religious issue was clericalism versus anticlericalism.

Last, but of obviously great significance, was Durkheim's intellect. Even at the Ecole Normale he was viewed as a remarkable student.[11] Although he ranked next to last on the agrégation, this reflected the well-known conservatism of the examining committee — comprised not of his innovative teachers at the Ecole, but of older men from outside.[12] After the turn of the century, he was exceptionally active in national university affairs, wrote indefatigably in general publications, and ranked in the popular eye with such intellectuals as Bergson, Jean Jaurès, or Lanson.[13]

---

9. See Appendix I for further discussion of social backgrounds of the Durkheimians.

10. Paul Gerbod, *La condition universitaire en France au XIXe siècle* (Paris: Presses Universitaires de France, 1965), pp. 535–582.

11. Ecole Normale director Fustel de Coulanges wrote that Durkheim was an "excellent élève, esprit très vigoureux, à la fois juste et original, et d'une maturité remarkable. Véritable aptitude pour les études de philosophie, surtout de psychologie — ses maîtres ont une grande opinion de lui."

Later in the lycée St. Quentin he was evaluated by S. M. Lachelier as having "dehors très graves et un peu froids." A. N. Dossier Durkheim.

12. Cf. Charles Andler, *Vie de Lucien Herr* (Paris: Rieder, 1932), pp. 13–30.

13. When Durkheim was first called to Paris, the normally laconic minutes of the Conseil de l'Université de Paris noted that Buisson was being replaced by Durkheim, "dont le nom et les travaux sont universellement connus." Ministère de l'Instruction Publique et des Beaux-Arts, *Enquêtes et documents relatifs à l'enseignement supérieur*, LXXX (Paris: Imprimerie Nationale, 1902), 11.

The epitome of the brilliant *universitaire,* his magnetic intellect attracted some of the best young *normaliens.* Their combined talents did a good deal to raise the general status of sociology and to facilitate its diffusion.

In sharp contrast to many who merely dabbled in social science, the Durkheimians were thorough professionals. Because they were committed to largely traditional university careers — or, to be more precise, because Durkheim invited only such persons to collaborate — their major activity was creative research. But although full-time self-supporting *universitaires,* generally they were not destined for chairs labeled sociology. Certain Faculties were prepared to modify titles for some chairs, but just how far the system would expand remained unclear at least until the 1920's. The possibility that sociology might become a lycée subject, implying considerable expansion of university posts, seemed quite real for many years. But a realistic young man could not plan his career on that eventuality. In 1900 the only sociological position in France was Durkheim's chair in Bordeaux. In 1914 there was the Bordeaux chair, and at the Sorbonne Durkheim's chair of Science de l'Education and Bouglé's position as maître de conférences in Economie Sociale. But there was still not a single chair entitled sociology. It was therefore necessary, if only temporarily, to develop a specialized competence to be named to existing positions in the system.

This career structure seems to have been significant in leading Durkheim to define sociology as broadly as he did, for in this way, professors of law, education, linguistics, religion, and other subjects could legitimately consider their work sociological. Durkheim was thus able to draw on a pool of talent of up to forty persons; if he had collaborated uniquely with potential professors of sociology, the cluster would have been drastically reduced.

The comprehensive sociological utopias antedated Durkheim: Saint-Simon and his disciples, particularly Auguste Comte, were among the most flamboyant; organismic theorists such as Schaeffle and Fouillée also shared a taste for the grandiose; if Marxists are included, although they seldom claimed the title of sociologist, the choice of themes broadens still further. Indeed, social theorists of the nineteenth century characteristically painted vast frescoes of humanity, postulating fundamental laws for past, present, and frequently the future.

In contrast to these immodest predecessors, Durkheim was a systematic student of very circumscribed phenomena; and, in fact, he saw himself largely in this light. But the ideological stamp of his work was conspicuous next to certain contemporaries as well as later sociologists. He was by no means immune to quasi-utopian pronouncements. The original preface of his first book contains perhaps his best-known passages in this respect:

> This book is pre-eminently an attempt to treat the facts of the moral life according to the method of the positive sciences . . . We do not wish to extract ethics from science, but to establish the science of ethics, which is quite different . . . Although we set out primarily to study reality, it does not follow that we do not wish to improve it; we should judge our researches to have no worth at all if they were to have only a speculative interest . . . for we shall see that science can help us adjust ourselves, determining the ideal toward which we are heading confusedly . . . Finally, comparing the normal type with itself — a strictly scientific operation — we shall be able to find if it is not entirely in agreement with itself, if it contains contradictions, which is to say, imperfections, and seek to eliminate them or to correct them . . . The passage from science to art is made without a break. Even on the ultimate question, whether we ought to wish to live, we believe science is not silent.[14]

Positions more ideological than utopian were taken by disciples in later works aimed at popularizing the faith, such as Georges Davy's *Sociologues d'hier et d'aujourd'hui*[15] and Bouglé's *Bilan de la sociologie française contemporaine*.[16]

Their precise designation was of great concern for the Durkheimians. Followers of Le Play, for example, spoke of "la science sociale" to refer only to contributions from their own grouping. "Sociology," for the Le Playists, included only the doctrines

---

14. Emile Durkheim, *The Division of Labor in Society* (New York: Macmillan, 1933), pp. 32–35. Cf. also *Ibid.,* p. 23, and Durkheim's response to an *enquête* on "L'élite intellectuelle et la démocratie," *Revue bleue,* 5th series, I (June 4, 1904), 705–706.

15. (Paris: Félix Alcan, 1931). Cf. p. 2.

16. (Paris: Félix Alcan, 1935).

of Auguste Comte and writers building on them.[17] The Durkheimians sought to redefine sociology to cover their own work
and significant social science contributions by others, including
many who did not label themselves sociologists. This "imperialism" led to more than one misunderstanding.

Nomenclature for subfields also generated no little debate.
The section in the *Année* entitled "social morphology" contained
works identical with the "human geography" of Vidal de la
Blache and his followers.[18] Much work termed "economic sociology" by Simiand and Halbwachs was claimed by the economist
and historian.[19] "Juridical sociology" overlapped with law and
political science. Much of "moral sociology" was essentially philosophy. Finally, on a conceptual level, ethnology and sociology
remained close to synonymous until the 1930's.[20]

Such terms as "collective conscience," "collective representa-
tions," "collective memory," "social solidarity," and "suicideo-
genic current," among others, became identified with the Durkheimians. These matters of nomenclature were important in defining relationships with adjoining fields.

Less pretentious than Comte's "queen of the sciences," Durkheim's conception of sociology was still more audacious than that
of most sociologists today. His dogmatic proclamations on these
matters also did not help relations with neighboring fields. Probably the most acrimonious disputes were those between sociologists and psychologists. They originated in Comte's failure to in-

17. See the priority claims set forth in Philippe Robert, "Le progrès contemporain, en géographie humaine, en sociologie, en histoire, et l'antériorité des
découvertes de la science sociale," *La science sociale,* Second series, Nos. 100–
01 (January and February 1913).

18. M. C. Elmer, "Century-Old Ecological Studies in France," *American
Journal of Sociology* (July 1933), 63–70; Jean Stoetzel, "Sociologie et démographie," *Population* (1946), 79–89.

19. Some of the polemical discussion is contained in François Simiand,
"Méthode historique et science sociale," *Revue de synthèse historique,* II (1903),
1–157; and Simiand, *Statistique et expérience, Remarques de méthode* (Paris:
Marcel Rivière, 1922).

20. "Anthropology" in France has been used more frequently than in the
United States to refer strictly to physical anthropology. Claude Lévi-Strauss,
"La sociologie française," in Georges Gurvitch and Wilbert E. Moore, eds., *La
sociologie au XXe siècle* (Paris: Presses Universitaires de France, 1947), II,
513–545. See also his "Ce que l'ethnologie doit à Durkheim," *Annales de l'Université de Paris,* 30th year (January–March 1960), pp. 47–52.

clude psychology in his list of sciences, and were sharpened when Durkheim virtually reasserted Comte's position that ultimate principles of human behavior lay in the social, not the individual, realm. These intellectual issues were aggravated by the direct competition between sociology and psychology for the few university positions in pedagogy and "scientific" philosophy. The controversy did not subside until close to World War II.[21] Perhaps less detrimental to ongoing research than the struggle with psychology, territorial disputes with such young disciplines as human geography, social history, and political economy were still far from negligible.[22] More than one philosopher also felt that sociology was only a branch of that august discipline.[23]

For Durkheim, sociology neither claimed a subject matter separate from the individual social sciences, nor did it approach the same subject matter with a distinctive methodology; sociology comprised the "system" or the "corpus" of the individual social sciences.[24] But the total content of every social science was not included, only those elements that were "sociological." Specialists working with economic or political materials unsociologically were not sociologists. But his emphasis on social factors led Durkheim to deny that such nonsociological research was fruitful; he dismissed such specialists as largely misguided or incompetent.[25]

The manifesto and handbook for proselytes was *The Rules of Sociological Method*; it defined the Durkheimian approach to

21. Thorough documentation on the controversy was compiled by Daniel Essertier in *Psychologie et sociologie* (Paris: Félix Alcan, 1927); *Le psychologie* (Paris: Félix Alcan, 1929); and *La sociologie* (Paris: Félix Alcan, 1930).

22. Philippe Robert, "Le progrès contemporain"; Henri Berr, *La synthèse en histoire* (Paris: Félix Alcan, 1911), Part II; Jacques Faublée, "Henri Berr et *l'Année sociologique,*" *Revue de synthèse,* Third Series, XXXV (July–September 1964), 68–74; Robert N. Bellah, "Durkheim and History," in Robert A. Nisbet, ed., *Emile Durkheim* (Englewood Cliffs: Prentice Hall, 1965), pp. 153–176.

23. Cf. Emile Durkheim, *Sociology and Philosophy* (Glencoe: The Free Press, 1953), and the introduction by J. G. Peristiany.

24. See Harry Alpert, *Emile Durkheim and His Sociology* (New York: Columbia University Press, 1939; Russell and Russell, 1961), pp. 163–173, and Durkheim's works cited there; also Guy Aimard, *Durkheim et la science économique* (Paris: Presses Universitaires de France, 1962), pp. 3–114.

25. Emile Durkheim, "Prefaces to *L'Année sociologique,*" republished and translated by Kurt H. Wolff in Wolff, ed., *Emile Durkheim, 1858–1917* (Columbus: Ohio State University Press, 1960), pp. 344–348; "Notre Siècle: La sociologie en France au XIXe siècle," *Revue bleue,* Fourth Series, XIII (May 19, 1900), 648.

sociological analysis, founded on "social facts." The two basic criteria for social facts were exteriority and constraint. Defined as "every way of acting, fixed or not, capable of exercising on the individual an external constraint," [26] social facts are those elements in a society which are more than merely present in individual psyches; they are, as contemporary sociologists would say, institutionalized. Social facts are to be analyzed as external data, *"comme des choses,"* and not introspectively in the consciousness of the observer; complete objectivity is imperative for true science. The efficient cause producing each social fact should be isolated, and the functions specified which it fulfills. In every case, however, the analytical level is social: adopting Boutroux's theory of emergent levels, Durkheim would admit no cause for a social fact except another social fact; similarly, functions performed by social facts are preeminently social. Sociology was thus the study of economic, legal, religious, and other social facts gleaned by specialists, and the summation of principles from these areas into a systematic and integrated theory.

This conception of sociology contrasted with two others of the period. The first, supported by Worms and Tarde, among others, held that sociology was not the aggregate but only the "philosophy" of the social sciences, the body of general principles subsuming the individual disciplines.[27] This conception, they pointed out, did not arouse charges of imperialism by other social scientists. The Durkheimians retorted that such an approach, adequate for grandiose systems of earlier years, was too superficial for an adequate general theory, and too general to be useful to specialists.[28]

The second conception contrasting with Durkheim's held that sociology was parallel to other social sciences, and was distinguished by its formal approach to patterns of social relationships. Although this conception was supported by few French sociolo-

26. Emile Durkheim, *The Rules of Sociological Method* (Glencoe: The Free Press, 1938), p. 13.

27. René Worms, *Philosophie des sciences sociales* (Paris: Giard and Brière, 1903, 1904, 1907), 3 vols.; Gabriel Tarde, "La sociologie," and "Les deux éléments de la sociologie," in *Etudes de psychologie sociale* (Paris: Giard and Brière, 1921), chaps. 3–5.

28. René Worms, *La sociologie; sa nature, son contenu, ses attaches* (Paris: Giard and Brière, 1921), chaps. 3–5.

gists, an outstanding German proponent, Georg Simmel, published a major programmatic paper in the first *Année sociologique*. Durkheim did not conceal his disagreement with Simmel, however, and Simmel never published again in the *Année*.

While engendering conflict with some, the Durkheimian conception was consistent with the goals of career-conscious *universitaires*. A distinction must still be made between employing sociological analysis and becoming a sociologist. Durkheim inspired many persons to apply sociological analysis to traditional fields, but trained only a handful of sociologists without some qualifying adjective. How he brought sociological analysis to these fields had a good deal to do with his role in both national and university politics.

The Dreyfus Affair and the New University

Many potential political issues may have been slighted during the Third Republic,[29] but those that were raised involved public education to a remarkable degree.[30] It was through scholarships created for secondary and higher education in the first decades of the Third Republic that many persons of petty bourgeois, and occasionally working-class and peasant, background completed higher degrees. Many of these became teachers in state institutions, and constituted for many observers the core of active support for the Third Republic.[31] The national educational system thus selected a meritocracy which in many respects became a new "establishment," based not on titles, land, or industry, but on examinations. Represented in the Radical and Radical Socialist parties, its political dominance grew after 1880, and became consolidated during the Dreyfus Affair. The mistrial of a Jewish officer by the aristocratically-oriented military was a perfect symbol around which to mobilize opponents of the tradi-

29. Cf. Stanley Hoffman, "Paradoxes of the French Political Community," in Stanley Hoffman et al., *In Search of France* (Cambridge: Harvard University Press, 1963), pp. 1–117.

30. See the sections by Jean-Marie Mayeur, François Bedarida, and Antoine Prost in *Histoire du peuple français, cent ans d'esprit républicain* (Paris: Nouvelle Librairie de France, 1964); John Edwin Talbott, "Politics and Educational Reform in Interwar France, 1919–1939" (Ph.D. diss., Stanford University, 1966).

31. The standard argument is presented in Albert Thibaudet, *La république des professeurs* (Paris: Bernard Grasset, 1927).

tional order. The rising *professeurs* used the issue to topple their adversaries and continued to dominate the political scene until the 1930's.

It was no coincidence that the success of the Durkheimians paralleled that of the *république des professeurs;* and the Dreyfus Affair was a bench mark for both. Students in the Latin Quarter have a long tradition of street and classroom violence, and during the affair disturbances between Dreyfusard and anti-Dreyfusard occurred almost daily.[32] The leadership of the Dreyfusards was at the Ecole Normale Supérieure, where the socialist librarian Lucien Herr directed his lieutenant Charles Péguy in daily battles, using *normaliens* as shock troops.[33] The Sorbonne as a whole was pro-Dreyfus, but Latin Quarter students were split almost evenly so that conservative, anti-Sorbonne, anti-Dreyfusard critics would spread violence around the Sorbonne and disrupt lectures of Dreyfusard professors. Elaborate quasi-military systems of spies, runners, messengers on bicycles, rowdies, shock troops, and defense guards were organized by both sides and prepared to mobilize on less than half an hour's notice.[34]

Durkheim and his associates were among the most active of Dreyfusards. Simiand and several younger Durkheimians participated in the activities organized by Herr.[35] Durkheim became secretary general of the Bordeaux section of the Ligue pour la

32. Cf. Eugen Weber, *Action Française* (Stanford: Stanford University Press, 1962).

33. Andler, *Vie de Lucien Herr,* pp. 112–150; Romain Rolland, *Péguy* (Paris: Albin Michel, 1944). On Péguy's criticisms of the Durkheimians, see Charles Péguy, *Oeuvres en prose, 1898–1908* (Paris: Gallimard, Bibliothèque de la Pléiade, 1959), pp. 991ff.

34. Péguy would mobilize shock troops by banging on students' doors at the Ecole Normale with a heavy cane that he also used in street fights. See Rolland, *Péguy,* I, 306ff.; Daniel Halévy, *Péguy et les Cahiers de la Quinzaine* (Paris: Bernard Grasset, 1941), pp. 68–80.

35. Herr had been highly critical of *The Division of Labor in Society* when it first appeared, writing in the quasi-official *Revue universitaire,* III (1893), 477–478, that Durkheim had eliminated the sources of acting and feeling from individuals by investing them in the abstraction of society, concluding that "not only do I not adhere . . . but I do not comprehend and I refuse to recognize as scientific anything that could be constructed on such a foundation, with these materials." Herr's strong support for Durkheim and his associates during and after the Dreyfus Affair was presented by critics like Hubert Bourgin as a clear demonstration that Durkheim was called to Paris because of his Dreyfusard activities. Cf. also Pierre Lasserre, "La sociologie de Sorbonne ou l'école du 'Totem,' " *Revue de l'Action Française,* XXXIII (1), 412–414.

Défense des Droits de l'Homme, the main Dreyfusard organization, soon after its founding in 1898.[36] He was a favorite speaker at rallies in the Bordeaux area.[37] In conjunction with his colleague Octave Hamelin, Durkheim founded an association of university teachers and students called "la Jeunesse Laïque," which met weekly. Meetings were ideological discussions with socialist, antimilitarist overtones which stressed the importance of science as an alternative to Christianity. Along with Radical and Radical Socialist deputies, senators, and educational administrators, Durkheim was a leading speaker at the Congrès International de l'Education Sociale, held at the Paris World's Fair of 1900.[38] At the Congrès, at the institutions created by Dick May, and elsewhere, republicanism, Dreyfusard ideology, and the emergence of the new social sciences became combined as a single effort.

Precise information is not available about public opinion concerning the New University, the Dreyfus Affair, and the emergence of romantic nationalism. But from about 1880 to 1900 there appears to have been considerable support among the intellectual public for the ideas, men, and institutional arrangements associated with the New University. These years also saw the greatest activity of the Société de l'Enseignement Supérieur.[39] Numerous articles in the Société's *Revue internationale de l'enseignement* favored the New University and the new social sciences. Contributions were included from Durkheim and Tarde on general intellectual issues and from René Worms and Dick May on organizational questions. These *R.I.E.* discussions provided important links between strictly intellectual debates and organizational changes and appointments.

One issue continually discussed in the *R.I.E.* was pedagogy,

36. Although she was either a very distant relative of Captain Dreyfus or entirely unrelated, the fact that Dreyfus was the maiden name of Durkheim's wife was still of symbolic importance. Lucien Lévy-Bruhl was a cousin of Captain Dreyfus.

37. A Bordeaux newspaper account of a 6 June 1900 meeting of the Ligue spoke of the strong applause for "M. Durkheim, professor at the Faculty of Letters of Bordeaux, whose fiery speeches bring supporters to the Ligue from far and wide." Clipping in Durkheim's dossier, University of Bordeaux, cited in Steven Lukes, "Émile Durkheim: Socialism, the Dreyfus Affair and Secular Education," unpublished manuscript.

38. Durkheim also presented a motion, adopted by the Congrès, that more courses in "social economy" should be created in the universities. Henri Hauser, *L'enseignement des sciences sociales* (Paris: Chevalier Marescq, 1903), p. 165.

39. See Chapter 1.

"la science de l'éducation." Many felt that developments in sociology and psychology bearing on education made university instruction in the area worthwhile. Thus, in 1883 Henri Marion became chargé de cours at the Paris Faculty of Letters, lecturing on Science de l'Education. He was given a chair with the same title in 1887, which he occupied until his death in 1896 when he was replaced by Ferdinand Buisson.[40] In Buisson's lectures and most public debates, *la science de l'éducation* consisted less of educational theories than the social, political, and philosophical beliefs which should inform the general educational process.[41] To teach this mixture of secular morality, republican ideology, and the "art of forming good citizens," the incumbent of such a chair had to remain in close touch with more general political and ideological developments. Buisson clearly did. As Director of Primary Education for fifteen years before assuming the chair, he had been the major individual to enforce the laws of Jules Ferry establishing general secular public education. He later served as president of the Ligue pour la Défense des Droits de l'Homme. After six years in the Sorbonne, in 1902, he was elected deputy and took a temporary leave from the chair; in 1906 he abandoned it definitively. When he left the important chair vacant, it was imperative to find a replacement who had the appropriate ideological, philosophical, and social scientific elements.

The year 1902 witnessed several developments that made Durkheim a logical choice. After a widely publicized campaign for donations, a statue of Auguste Comte was erected which dominated the Place de la Sorbonne. The 1902 reforms were enacted, which led the next year to merging the Ecole Normale with the Paris Faculties of Letters and Sciences, and increasing attention to the nonclassical subjects in the licence sequence. Also in 1902, at Dick May's Ecole des Hautes Etudes Sociales, Dean Alfred Croiset and Ferdinand Buisson were conducting their seminar on pedagogy and their *enquêtes* on the teaching of ethics in primary, secondary, and higher education. Durkheim thus im-

40. See F. Buisson, "Leçon d'ouverture du cours de science de l'éducation," *R.I.E.*, XXXII (July–December 1896), 481–503; also E. Boutroux, "Henri Marion," *ibid.*, pp. 289–311.
41. See Ferdinand Buisson, *Un moraliste laïque* (Paris: Félix Alcan, 1933). The work contains enthusiastic prefatory statements by Edouard Herriot and Bouglé; Bouglé remarks that "il demeura toujours le 'militant,' le propagandiste par excellence," p. 2.

pressed the Dean of the Faculty of Letters and the incumbent of the chair; he seems to have been respected by the professors of philosophy, especially Boutroux, whose student he had been at the Ecole Normale.[42]

When Buisson's chair was declared vacant, six persons presented their candidacies. Durkheim was the unquestioned choice of Buisson, whose opinion was seconded by Boutroux, Professor of History of Modern Philosophy, Brochard, Professor of History of Ancient Philosophy, and Espinas, Professor of Social Economy. Durkheim was elected "first line" candidate.[43]

42. *The Division of Labor in Society* was published with the dedication "A Mon Cher Maître, M. Emile Boutroux, Hommage respectueux et reconnaissant."

43. Here is the exact summary of the meeting from the minutes kept by the Secretary of the Faculty: *Conseil de la Faculté: mardi 24 juin 1902.*

Le Conseil de la Faculté s'est réuni le mardi 24 juin 1902, sous la présidence de M. A. Croiset, Doyen, étant présents MM. Gebhart, Lavisse, Bouché-Leclercq, Cartault, Boutroux, Lichtenberger, Decharme, Luchaire, Aulard, Collignon, Dubois, V. Henry, Brochard, J. Martha, Buisson, Vidal de la Blache, Séailles, Lemonnier, Thomas, Brunot, Beljame, professeurs — Guiraud, Gazier, Espinas, Lafaye, Denis, Dejole, Egger, professeurs adjoints . . .

Par suite de l'élection comme Député de M. le Professeur Buisson, la Faculté avait à dire de quelle façon il convenait, à son avis, de pourvoir aux besoins de l'enseignement dans la chaire de "Science de l'Education." 6 candidats s'étaient mis sur les rangs pour briguer ses suffrages: MM. Durkheim, Lefèvre, Malapert, Mauxion, Payot et Pinloche. Invité par M. le Doyen à donner le premier son avis, M. le Professeur Buisson passe en revue successivement les titres des candidats; il résulte de son exposé que M. Durkheim s'est placé hors de pair par l'ensemble de ses travaux, par la puissance et la justesse de son enseignement, par l'originalité de sa méthode. M. Durkheim est un sociologue de premier ordre, mais la pédagogie n'est-elle pas une province de la sociologie? Aussi, quoique MM. Payot, Pinloche, Lefèvre, Malapart aient aussi à leur actif des titres considérables, M. Buisson n'hésite pas à déclarer qu'à ses yeux M. Durkheim doit occuper le premier rang. Telle est également l'opinion de MM. Boutroux, Brochard, et Espinas, ce dernier rappelant que comme collègue de M. Durkheim, il l'a vu à l'oeuvre à la Faculté de Bordeaux, où le jeune professeur exerçait sur ses auditeurs et ses disciples une véritable maîtrise.

Le Conseil se déclarant suffisamment éclairé procède au scrutin qui donne les résultats suivants:

Votants: 29

— Présentation en 1ère ligne: M. Durkheim : 21 voix —
M. Malapert : 8 voix.
— Présentation en 2ème ligne: M. Malapert : 16 voix —
M. Payot : 10 voix.
M. Lefèvre : 2 voix —
M. Pinloche : 1 voix.

Source: Archives of the Paris Faculty of Letters.

Durkheim's success was a combination of many intellectual and ideological factors. To emphasize the ideological is in no way to denigrate the intellectual, but it is essential to explain how many administrators and faculty evaluated him, and how many of his followers advanced their careers. Critics like Hubert Bourgin, Pierre Lasserre, Charles Péguy, and Henri Massis no doubt exaggerated the ideological elements; the Durkheimians themselves stressed the intellectual qualities; both factors contributed, reinforcing each other so as to make their segregation most difficult.

Clearly, Durkheimians had to be both ideologically and intellectually outstanding to make headway in a system so structurally unresponsive. Nevertheless, several types of positions were amenable to definition, or redefinition, as at least partially social scientific. *La science de l'éducation* was one such field. Another was *"l'économie sociale."* Considered by some as the study of the distribution of wealth in contrast to political economy's focus on the production of wealth,[44] in the 1890's the concept attracted the Comte de Chambrun. Not only did Chambrun found the Musée Social, he also created courses and chairs in "social economy." A course at Sciences Po in 1893 (by Cheysson) was followed by others at the Paris Faculty of Law in 1898 (by Charles Gide) and the Ecole des Ponts et Chaussées in 1900 (also by Gide.)[45] Most important for present purposes, however, was the chair he endowed in the History of Social Economy at the Paris Faculty of Letters in 1894. Alfred Espinas, then professor of philosophy and Dean at the Bordeaux Faculty of Letters, was called to Paris in 1894 as chargé de cours in the area of the chair. He became professeur adjoint in 1899 and *titulaire* in 1904. But in 1907 he took a leave of absence for reasons of health. The ambiguous nature of the chair then became evident in discussions of the Conseil. Following an interesting debate, Bouglé was elected to the chair.[46]

The case of Bouglé illustrates well the role of ideology in ad-

44. See the discussion of the concept in Hauser, *L'enseignement des sciences sociales,* pp. 155, 170, 198.

45. See Dick May, *L'enseignement social à Paris* (Paris: Arthur Rousseau, 1896), pp. 53ff.; *R.I.E.,* XXXI (1896), 89; and scattered announcements in the *R.I.S.*

46. See the quotation in Chapter 2.

vancing a career. Older than most other Durkheimians, he had attended the Ecole Normale in the early 1890's, placed first in the agrégation for philosophy in 1893 and consequently spent the next year with a fellowship in Germany.[47] He became maître de conférences at the Montpellier Faculty of Letters in 1898. The next year he defended his most important work, *Les idées égalitaires,* as his thesis and became chargé de cours (1900) and then professor (1901) of social philosophy at the Faculty of Letters of Toulouse. He completed several insightful articles in the *Année,* in particular on the Indian caste system. But with the Dreyfus Affair, he began publishing more ideological works (*La crise du libéralisme,* 1902; *Solidarisme et libéralisme,* 1902; *Le solidarisme,* 1907). His publicist reputation derived from these works, frequent lectures and debates, and his activities as journalist and editor of the important leftist newspaper *La dépêche de Toulouse.* By 1907, when he entered the Sorbonne, his ideological activities had almost supplanted the scientific; these continued while he substituted in the chairs of Espinas and later Durkheim until 1919, when he became professor of History of Social Economy.

Durkheim and Bouglé were the two central members of the cluster before 1914, although they were increasingly supported by Lucien Lévy-Bruhl.[48] Durkheim's other collaborators remained outside the Sorbonne before 1914, but nevertheless increased in numbers and advanced quite impressively in their careers (see Tables 5 and 6).

When the first volume of the *Année* appeared in 1898, it included as collaborators (there was never an editorial board) Georg Simmel; Emmanuel Lévy, and Célestin Bouglé in junior university positions; Gaston Richard, who had completed his Doctorat but still was awaiting an appointment; and eight agrégés, most in lycée posts.[49] The last prewar issue included contributions from nine of the original thirteen collaborators. Durkheim and Bouglé were then at the Sorbonne; Paul Lapie and Emmanuel

47. A summary of his observations was published as *Les sciences sociales en Allemagne* (Paris: Félix Alcan, 1895).
48. See Chapter 7.
49. Details about the social backgrounds of these and subsequent *Année* collaborators are presented in Appendix I, their intellectual contributions in Appendix II, and their postwar careers in Chapter 7.

Table 5. Number and Rank of *Année sociologique* Collaborators, 1898–1913

Rank	I 1898	II 1899	III 1900	IV 1901	V 1902	VI 1903	VII 1904	VIII 1905	IX 1906	X 1907	XI 1910	XII 1913
Chairholders in Faculties or Collège de France; EPHE												
Directors	1	1	1	2	4	5	5	5	6	7	5	5
Nonchairholders in Faculties; EPHE Staff below												
Directors	2	3	2	3	3	4	4	4	4	2	4	4
Administration (Inspectors, Librarians)	–	–	–	–	–	1	1	2	2	2	2	2
Agrégé or Docteur	9	8	8	8	8	5	7	8	7	8	12	12
No Agrégation	–	–	–	–	–	–	–	–	–	–	–	–
Foreigners	1	–	4	–	–	–	–	–	–	–	2	2
Total	13	12	15	13	15	15	17	19	19	19	25	25

Source: *Année sociologique.*

Table 6. New Collaborators of *Année sociologique*, 1898–1913

I	
1898	Durkheim, Professor of Social Science, Bordeaux Faculty of Letters
	Lévy, chargé de cours, Toulouse Faculty of Law
	Bouglé, maître de conférences, University of Montpellier
	Fauconnet, Hubert, Lapie, Mauss, Milhaud, Muffang, Parodi, Simiand, Richard, *agrégés*
	Simmel, a.o. professor, University of Berlin
II	
1899	Foucault, *agrégé*
III	
1900	Ratzel, professor, University of Leipzig
	Sigel, professor, University of Warsaw
	Steinmetz, professor, University of Utrecht
	J. T. Stickney (Harvard)
IV	
1901	Charmont, professor, Montpellier Faculty of Law
	Aubin, H. Bourgin, *agrégés*
V	
1902	Meillet, Director, EPHE
	Hourticq, E.-Cl. Maître, *agrégés*
VI	
1903	Huvelin, professor, Lyon Faculty of Law
VII	
1904	Lalo, *agrégé*
VIII	
1905	Halbwachs, Hertz, Vacher, *agrégés*
	G. Bourgin, *archiviste-paléographe*
X	
1907	Bianconi, *agrégé*
XI	
1910	David, Davy, Gernet, Ray, Reynier, *agrégés*
	de Félice, Lafitte

Source: *Année sociologique.*
Note: There were no new contributors in 1906.

Lévy had become Faculty professors; Henri Hubert and Marcel Mauss were directeurs adjoints at the EPHE; Paul Fauconnet was chargé de cours at Toulouse; François Simiand and Dominique Parodi were still listed as agrégés; Gaston Richard, Georg Simmel, H. Muffang, and Albert Milhaud no longer collaborated. Additional contributors included Antoine Meillet, professor at the Collège de France; Paul Huvelin, professor of law at Lyon; A.

Aubin, Inspecteur; Georges Bourgin, *archiviste-paléographe;* Bianconi, Hubert Bourgin, Maxime David, Georges Davy, Louis Gernet, Maurice Halbwachs, Robert Hertz, R. Hourtig, Jean Ray, and Jean Reynier, agrégés; and Ch. de Félice and J. P. Lafitte, who had not completed an agrégation. What did collaboration with the *Année* mean to these persons?

The *Année sociologique* as a Research Institute

The *Année sociologique,* to use Durkheim's mot, was a phenomenon sui generis. Félix Alcan, the enterprising publisher of the *Revue philosophique* and Durkheim's books, apparently decided that the material on "scientific philosophy" in the *Revue philosophique* was sufficient to warrant separate publication. Alfred Binet and H. Beaunis were thus asked to edit an *Année psychologique,* and Emile Durkheim an *Année sociologique,* each of which was published in the same format. But the organizations of the two journals were strikingly different. The *Année psychologique* included considerable material by Alfred Binet, who remained isolated in his EPHE laboratory, and contributions by a wide range of persons whom he had difficulty attracting.[50] The *Année sociologique* became instead the center of a powerful cluster. How did the *Année sociologique* develop in this distinctive manner?

The research institute, as found in many German universities, was one organizational model which inspired it. While a student at the University of Leipzig, Durkheim had been impressed by Wilhelm Wundt's famous institute.[51] The general association of research in Germany with the research institute[52] lent this structure considerable prestige. Durkheim did not however adopt that institution closely allied with the research institute in Germany — the seminar. While the ideal of collective research was greeted with enthusiasm,[53] the form it assumed in the *Année* was more

50. See Theta Wolf, forthcoming study on Alfred Binet.
51. Alpert, *Emile Durkheim and His Sociology,* p. 35.
52. Friedrich Paulsen, *The German University,* (New York: Macmillan, 1894), pp. 126–173.
53. The visit to Germany by some of Durkheim's collaborators helped to socialize them to collective research, not a negligible task given the traditional individualism of French intellectual life. Bouglé writes apropos of his trip to Germany: "What I was able to see of German intellectual organization made

rigidly hierarchical than in Germany. The more authoritarian professor-student relations in the French university,[54] and Durkheim's authoritarian personality,[55] reshaped the research institute from the German model.

The model for a seminar had existed even closer to home: in 1891, Léon Duguit, professor at the Bordeaux Faculty of Law, had organized a seminar on sociology. But Durkheim apparently had nothing to do with Duguit's seminar.[56] Nor did he ever organize a seminar of his own.[57]

---

me clearly understand the degree to which a collective effort could be useful to French sociology, an effort in groups [note Bouglé's use of the plural] that Durkheim would guide. I was thus fully prepared to offer him my collaboration, to recruit collaborators for him, in order to swell the ranks of this 'Ecole de Bordeaux' that he had formed." C. Bouglé, "L'oeuvre sociologique d'Emile Durkheim," *Europe,* XXII (1930), 283.

54. Paulsen contrasted the German situation with the French: "Only a few years before, in 1808, Napoleon had reorganized the French universities, consistently following the opposite principle . . . The professors were teachers and examiners rather than scholars, and all individual initiative was restricted to the smallest minimum . . . The fact that, two generations afterwards, the French people began to reorganize their universities on German lines would seem to afford a strong proof of the superiority of the idea of liberty as compared with the principle of rules and regulations." Friedrich Paulsen, *German Education, Past and Present* (London: T. Fisher Unwin, 1908), pp. 185–187.

55. His nephew Marcel Mauss experienced such authority most directly. He began with a unique education: not at the Ecole Normale, but the Bordeaux Faculty of Letters, where he prepared the agrégation directly under the surveillance of his uncle. But Mauss never quite internalized the Durkheimian moral education. Durkheim frequently had to lock him in his room to keep him at his books. Even when Mauss was a grown man, Durkheim remained a very external and highly constraining social fact. For example, one hot summer day not before 1909 (Mauss was thus at least thirty-seven), he and Georges Davy stopped work for a beer in a café on the Place de la Sorbonne. Durkheim then walked out of the Sorbonne courtyard, to the horror of his nephew, who immediately whispered to Davy, "Quick, hide me! Here comes my uncle!" He escaped behind an orange tree decorating the café, and at least that time evaded the eye of the stern taskmaster. (Personal communication, M. Georges Davy).

56. "I use . . . [the term 'seminar'] instead of some other because my goal has been to follow as closely as possible the method and procedures of German seminars." It brought together a small number of advanced students, one of whom would present a paper at each meeting which would be discussed by the other participants.

Léon Duguit, "Un seminaire de sociologie," *R.I.S.,* I (1893), 201–208, quotation at p. 201.

57. Every faculty member submitted an annual report to the Ministry indicating the subjects and scheduling of courses and the number of students attending. To these reports, the Rector would occasionally add a few comments. Durkheim's reports from Bordeaux between 1888 and 1902 indicated that from nineteen to forty students attended his one-hour course on pedagogy. He also offered a one-hour *conférence d'agrégation,* generally attended by fewer than ten students. These first two courses were scheduled in mornings or afternoons

The *Année* was thus far more than a journal. It shared many goals and performed many functions of a modern social research institute. As a collectivity it could — and did — realize two of Durkheim's basic ideals: scientific objectivity and intellectual excellence. As a firmly established social fact, the *Année* provided both exteriority to minimize subjective bias, and constraint from association with hypercritical minds, to maintain standards at a consistently high level. These two goals overshadowed the others.

The principal manifest goal of the *Année* was still compilation of sociologically useful contributions of the previous year. Between 1895 and 1912, out of what might easily have become a mechanical abstracting service, however, Durkheim and his collaborators produced twelve of the most significant volumes in the history of sociology. Like contemporary research institutes specialized in secondary analysis, they synthesized studies of such varied subjects as French industrial plants, Bavarian peasant villages, Australian tribes, New York slum dwellers, and Sicilian criminals, as well as theoretical contributions from practically every country in the world. From this heterogenous clay, the Durkheimians molded a vigorous and proud sociology, unsurpassed in many respects for years to follow.[58]

In this collective enterprise, Durkheim also achieved another ideal essential to transcend earlier superficiality: specialization of

during the week. The third course, on some aspect of sociology, was on Saturday at 5:30 P.M. in 1902, and was attended by thirty students. There were almost no comments by the Rector in earlier years, but in 1901 he noted that "Il est animé d'éveiller d'un proselytisme ardent et militant." (A blue pencil, presumably in the Ministry, underlined the comment and added a line in the margin next to it.) He wrote in 1902 that "Il entend son enseignement comme une sorte d'apostolat, qui doit s'étendre sur ses élèves au dehors de la Faculté et les suivre dans la vie et dans la société. Intelligence supérieure . . ." A. N. Dossier Durkheim. The reports after 1902 are not included in the Dossier.

For (incomplete) listings of Durkheim's courses, see *R.I.S.*, XXIII (1915), 468–469, and Alpert, *Emile Durkheim and His Sociology*, pp. 65–66.

58. Their success may have surpassed Durkheim's own expectations. In 1902 he wrote to Simiand about publishing the *mémoires* separately. "Ce dernier principe me paraît tout à fait excellent. Je n'ai pas besoin de vous dire combien il m'en a coûté de publier certaines choses. Je le faisais, d'abord parce que, dans le principe, je n'osais espérer l'homogénéité morale qui s'est établie entre nous et que je ne songeais à faire de *l'Année* qu'un recueil où il suffirait pour entrer d'être scientifiquement honnête. Je le faisais aussi parce qu'il n'y avait pas moyen de faire autrement. Mais il est clair que cet éclecticisme, si limité qu'il ait été, nuit à l'impression d'ensemble. J'ajoute que dans ce qui a été publié, il n'y a que ce qui vient de nous qui ait de la valeur." Letter of 15 February 1902 in Salle des Manuscrits, Bibliothèque Nationale.

task through division of labor. Individual specialization was complemented by a common master scheme. Durkheim's methodological works, especially *The Rules of Sociological Method,* were basic guides; the *Année* itself promoted further unity. Its *mémoires originaux* amalgamated major advances of specialists.

Beyond these manifest goals — reviewing the literature, enforcing scientific objectivity, maintaining high intellectual standards, promoting specialization, and providing integration into an overall pattern — the *Année* performed four more latent functions: recruitment, training, social integration, and the exercise and legitimation of authority.

Reviewing a single book or article was a simple enough task to delegate to a student in one of Durkheim's courses or to others that *Année* collaborators might contact. A young man thus could try his hand at a limited task and learn about the cluster. In this way Durkheim created a channel for recruiting new talent.[59]

Providing external checks for advanced collaborators, collective activity also facilitated evaluation of younger men. Weak points could be remedied through suggested reading, direct instruction and criticism, and informal example. Apprenticelike training thus complemented more didactic lessons of formal lectures. Such activities reinforced informal relationships; these in turn furthered social and intellectual integration.

Finally, Durkheim's authority was extended and legitimated through the *Année.* Group pressures against deviance are generally stronger than those of even an eminent individual. Division of labor led to elaboration of Durkheim's ideas by others who in turn enforced the master's authority. He was thus freed for other tasks.

Compilation of the Année sociologique

Durkheim still played a considerable role in compilation of the *Année.* He had no office for the *Année* except his personal study, and no administrative assistance except from his wife, who assumed numerous menial tasks; Alcan provided only minimal support in these matters, although they did provide a modest honorarium.[60]

59. See Hubert Bourgin's quotation in Chapter 1 on being recruited to the *A.S.*

60. In 1902 the honoraria totaled 950 francs. Letter from E. Durkheim to F. Simiand, 11-3-02, Salle des Manuscrits, Bibliothèque Nationale.

The standard procedure for compiling the *Année* was as follows.[61] Bibliographies from publishers, newspapers, and various professional journals were scanned for appropriate titles; more came from associates in France and abroad. After this stage Mauss took most responsibility for the religious section and Simiand for the economic, but Durkheim still had the greatest burden. All three would write to publishers for review copies of the works. Upon arrival, they were examined briefly and sent to specialized collaborators, or the director of the section would review it himself. Individual reviewers sent manuscripts to the section directors, who would edit them and perhaps return them for revisions.[62] Eventually manuscripts were assembled and sent to Alcan for printing. Proofs were sent to the director of each section, who sometimes returned them to individual authors for final editing. Durkheim, aided by Mme. Durkheim, would go over almost every page, critically.[63] When proofs had been corrected by various authors and section directors, they were returned to the publisher for final printing. As Durkheim was in Bordeaux from 1896 until 1902, these activities took place through the mails. Even after that time, however, with collaborators scattered throughout France,[64] most communication remained confined to the mails.

Only Durkheim assured coordination among the many collaborators. In keeping with his authoritarian preferences, no staff meetings were held; he would see people one at a time. Certainly informal contacts emerged between collaborators of similar age and specialty, but for many — particularly younger men in provincial lycées — most work was done in isolation. Mauss and

61. In addition to the published accounts of the *Année,* this section draws on conversations with MM. Georges Davy and André Davidovitch.

62. This continual reworking of manuscripts led to more jointly written articles than was typical of other journals. Of every other article sampled from four volumes between 1886 and 1914 of each of three other journals — the *Revue internationale de sociologie,* the *Science sociale,* and the *Journal de la Société de Statistique de Paris* — there was not one jointly written paper. In just the 1912 issue of the *Année sociologique,* however, a total of 334 articles included 6 by two authors and 1 by three.

63. M. Georges Davy recalled one instance when he had written a critique of just one short article. Durkheim returned it with a note to reread the article and rewrite his own contribution, as an argument had been misinterpreted.

64. In later years, Hertz, Fauconnet, Bouglé, Davy, and Halbwachs also took on some of the responsibility for subsections of the *Année.* Personal communication, M. Georges Davy. See also Georges Davy, "Emile Durkheim," *A.S.,* 3rd series (1957–58), pp. vii–x, and H. Lévy-Bruhl, "Marcel Mauss," *A.S.,* 3rd series (1948–49), pp. 1–4.

Simiand each led subclusters, but despite the cluster's remarkable *intellectual* integration, *social* integration was much less developed. Many contemporary descriptions of the *Année* reflect the background from which it developed: as advanced collective work remained infrequent, the relative integration of the *Année* understandably impressed outside (and inside) observers.[65] When there was finally one meeting of the entire staff in 1912 — a unique occasion in the prewar period — it was a collective ritual charged with all the emotion that Durkheim had described in the totemic ceremonies of Australian aboriginals. Cognizant of the importance of religious symbols and rituals, the tribe would have found the ceremony incomplete without erection of a totem. There was no disappointment that day, for a bust of Durkheim had been executed especially for the occasion!

Integration of the Cluster:
Socialism and the Durkheimians

It is interesting to inquire how Durkheim coordinated the many persons around the *Année,* with no professional organization or editorial board meetings, minimal funds to dispense, no

65. Perceptions of cohesiveness still varied with the observer's vantage point. Alfred Espinas, for example, saw the group around Durkheim as "a militia organized for the propagation of political theories or an engine of politics, and also as a secret society . . . having its mysteries to cover its ambitions, and its police, its reports, its admissions, its white and black lists." Quoted in Hubert Bourgin, *De Jaurès à Léon Blum, l'Ecole normale et la politique* (Paris: Arthème Fayard, 1938), p. 91.

Davy, in contrast, asserted that "There were, in effect, certain persons around him who formed a sort of spiritual family, united by the tie of common method and of a common admiration for their master. [Note that Davy does not mention ties among individuals.] They constituted . . . the clan of the *Année sociologique.* Durkheim created and maintained the spirit of unity of this little society, without the least tyranny, leaving to each his entire liberty. He only acted through the enormous supremacy of his mind and of his method. Everyone liked to go see him to receive his advice and experience the affectionate interest he had for all. But there were no court sessions, no meetings, no slogans. How many have been wrong in having thought to see in him the apostle of tyranny and the despiser of the individual . . .

"If Durkheim was thus the chief of a school, it is because he instituted a new doctrine. It is he who in fact was, despite illustrious predecessors such as Montesquieu and Auguste Comte, the true founder of French sociology." Georges Davy, "Emile Durkheim," *Revue de métaphysique et de morale,* XXVI (1919), 194–195.

seminars, and no research institute in the traditional sense. Most groupings discussed in earlier chapters consciously strove toward integration — employing these and other mechanisms for institutionalization that Durkheim eschewed — but they largely dispersed within a decade or two, and almost none achieved the intellectual integration of the Durkheimians.

One major factor integrating the Durkheimians was, of course, the centralized structure of the national educational system: for the reasons outlined in Chapter 2, the system tended to generate clusters. Even lacking direct support for the *Année,* Durkheim's missionary zeal for sociology led him to devote time to lectures, public debates, committee meetings, and other activities that made him into a leading *patron universitaire.* He thus assisted his collaborators in obtaining positions throughout the educational system. There was also, of course, Durkheim's unquestionable intellect. In addition, he had a remarkable ability to formulate problems strategic both for sociological theory and pressing moral and political concerns. His prestige with both his collaborators and the general public was enhanced by the timeliness of his theoretical works for definition of a secular morality, development of a theory of solidarity, and isolation of causes of social deviance. The Durkheimians shared a common training and career pattern. They were brought together again by a series of important political experiences.

Their militant pose and internal cohesion were strengthened by serving in the Dreyfusard army. When attacks on the master took the form of loud jeers, thrown objects, and manhandling of students at the lecture hall entrance, his defenders understandably closed ranks and assumed a belligerent pose. Political continuity after the Dreyfus Affair came through socialism. National transformations were doubtless important in this metamorphosis, but a major influence must be attributed to Lucien Herr.

A graduate of the Ecole Normale in philosophy (four years after Durkheim), Herr began research for a possible thesis (never completed), and in 1888 was named librarian at the Ecole Normale. Long fascinated by politics, Herr eventually joined the relatively undogmatic "possibiliste" socialists led by Jean Allemane. He attended weekly cell meetings and wrote a weekly article for the party organ *Le parti ouvrier.* His role in the Dreyfus Affair achieved legendary proportions.[66] As a bachelor Herr lived for many years near the Ecole, usually dining with students in residence; he was also in frequent contact with them through the library. These close relationships with students led to a considerable number of converts to socialism (including Jaurès himself).[67] By the late 1890's, the Ecole had become a citadel of socialism. And many leading converts came to collaborate with Durkheim.[68]

For many at the time, socialism, social science, and sociology were related closely enough to make confusion a frequent occurrence.[69] This tendency was facilitated by the active socialism of the majority of *Année* collaborators. Marcel Mauss, François Simiand, and Lucien Lévy-Bruhl were all involved with Herr and Jaurès in founding *l'Humanité,* and they, Halbwachs, and Fauconnet contributed to the paper for many years.[70] In the Ecole

66. In one climactic incident, a letter from Herr describing police brutality in 1899 was quoted by Edouard Vaillant in an address to the Chamber of Deputies; it led to the collapse of the Dupuy ministry. Waldeck-Rousseau's government which followed ordered the retrial of Dreyfus. See *Vie de Lucien Herr,* pp. 143–147.

67. "Jaurès began to set his thought in order, to organize his social theories systematically. His petty bourgeois republicanism had succumbed to disappointment, and he was ready for socialism. In a crucial interlude in 1889, he struck up a friendship with the erudite librarian of the Ecole Normale Supérieure, Lucien Herr, who guided him toward a new affirmation . . . Equipped with a staggering mastery of sources and endowed with a great personal warmth, Herr, who had become socialist by 1889, directed successive generations of *normaliens* to the important treatises on socialist theory. 'Here was the man, whom the public did not know,' Léon Blum once exclaimed, 'yet under whom the socialist *universitaires* were formed, from Jaurès to Déat, including my generation and that of Albert Thomas.'" Harvey Goldberg, *The Life of Jean Jaurès* (Madison: The University of Wisconsin Press, 1962), p. 62.

68. Mauss noted in an obituary of Herr in the *Année* that "Jusqu'à ses derniers jours et y compris cet actuel volume, il a été pour nous tous un conseiller constant et écouté . . . Son autorité personelle, son enthousiasme, ses encouragements ont decidé de la vocation de nombre d'entre nous." "Notices biographiques," *A.S.,* New Series, II (1927), 9.

69. Until as late as 1925, there was a combined heading of "Socialisme; Science Sociale" in Otto Lorenz, *Catalogue générale de la librairie française,* the major bibliography of books published in France.

70. Andler, *Vie de Lucien Herr,* pp. 169–182. A particularly compelling but little known case of the influence of socialist ties was that of Maurice Halbwachs during his fellowship term in Germany. After about three months in Berlin, Halbwachs, acting as correspondent for *l'Humanité* while collecting material for his thesis, published an article in *l'Humanité* criticizing the brutality of the Berlin police at a mass demonstration. The Prussian authorities saw the article, and, following a perfunctory interrogation, gave Halbwachs one week to leave Prussia. He was forced to complete his fellowship term in Vienna.

Socialiste, founded to instruct workers in socialist doctrines, Emmanuel Lévy, Simiand, Mauss, and Fauconnet all served as teachers.[71] Simiand and Hubert Bourgin sat with Herr, Mario Rocques, and Léon Blum on the board of a socialist publishing house founded by Herr and managed by Péguy;[72] thirteen contributors to the *Année* became stockholders in subsequent years.[73] Henri Hubert and Robert Hertz were also socialists.[74]

The closeness of the Durkheimians' scholarly work to socialism was underlined when sections of their academic writings were republished with fiery introductions in a series of socialist tracts.[75] Bouglé spent a good deal of his time with socialist activities, and edited an annotated version of the works of Proudhon.[76]

Durkheim's own relations with socialism were extremely com-

The affair aroused attention in France, and was criticized by Jaurès in *l'Humanité*, 23 December 1910, and in *Le Temps* of 2 January 1911. The *Humanité* of 15 February 1911 carried an article by Liebknecht denouncing the affair, although Halbwachs affirmed that he had not been in personal contact with Liebknecht, being closer to the socialism propounded by Bernstein. The entire affair is discussed in a four-page closely written document by Halbwachs, entitled "Une expulsion." It was written just a few months before he was deported in 1944, not, however, because of his family background, but because he, and even more his son, had been deeply involved in underground activities during the war. The two were sent to Buchenwald, and although neither was put to death, the father did not survive the miserable living conditions. (Personal communication from Madame Maurice Halbwachs and André Davidovitch). I am extremely grateful to Madame Halbwachs — herself a sociological researcher at the Centre d'Etudes Sociologiques in former years — for her hospitality and patience in going through her husband's papers and files, filling in many unpublished details.

71. Andler, *Vie de Lucien Herr*, p. 163.

72. *Ibid.*, pp. 151–168.

73. The complete list of stockholders is in the Archives Nationales, 40 AQ 1, 2, and reproduced in Robert John Smith, "The Ecole Normale Supérieure in the Third Republic" (Ph.D. diss., University of Pennsylvania, 1967).

74. Hubert Bourgin, *Le socialisme universitaire* (Paris: Delamain and Boutelleau, 1942), p. 107.

75. The series, Les Cahiers du Socialiste, was founded by François Simiand, Robert Hertz, and Hubert Bourgin a few years before World War I. Bourgin, *Cinquante ans d'expérience démocratique*, p. 85. Halbwachs published an abridged version of his law doctorate on population movements in the series, Maurice Halbwachs, *La politique foncière des municipalités* (Paris: Les Cahiers du Socialiste, No. 3, 1911).

76. Bouglé tells us: "In fact, the majority, the near totality of the collaborators of the *Année sociologique* — the most moderate among them can affirm it — great friends of the celebrated librarian of the Ecole Normale named Lucien Herr, were enrolled in the socialist party, and more than one was also a collaborator of *l'Humanité*." C. Bouglé, *Humanisme, sociologie, philosophie: remarques sur la conception française de la culture générale* (Paris: Hermann, 1938), p. 34. Apparently Bouglé himself never joined a socialist party.

plex and have been the subject of considerable scholarly controversy.[77] His original thesis topic had been the relation of individualism to socialism, and although changed to the individual and society, socialism was never far below the surface of *The Division of Labor in Society*; nor was it in *Suicide* or several other works.[78] He planned a history of socialist thought, although he completed only the section on Saint-Simon.[79] Jaurès came to Durkheim's home for Sunday dinner several times[80] and he was in close contact with Lucien Herr, who first directed him to Sir James George Frazer's work on religion. Durkheim was known to arrive at lectures and to walk out of the Sorbonne conspicuously carrying *l'Humanité,* a political act in itself.[81] He never joined a socialist party, however, nor did he participate in partisan activities with his younger collaborators. Repelled by the emotion and lack of rigor of most socialist writers, he remained deeply concerned with many phenomena they treated. But to many less concerned with these subtleties, there was no doubt that Durkheim was a socialist.[82]

The Reaction Against the New Sorbonne

The combination of petty bourgeois family origins, the Ecole Normale, philosophical training, collaboration on the *Année,* common career lines, the Dreyfus Affair, and socialism bound the Durkheimians to one another and to the national university system. But such cohesion also helped unite their opponents. The many reforms leading to the New University were not made with-

77. See Jean-Claude Filloux, "Durkheimism and Socialism," *The Review,* X (1963), 66–85.

78. See *Suicide* (Glencoe: The Free Press, 1951), pp. 361–392.

79. Emile Durkheim, *Socialism* (Yellow Springs, Ohio: The Antioch Press, 1958).

80. Personal communication, M. Georges Davy. Jaurès also attended the tenth anniversary celebration of the *Année.* Goldberg, *The Life of Jean Jaurès,* p. 85.

81. Personal communication, MM. Georges Davy and Armand Cuvillier.

82. See Filloux, "Durkheimism," and Raymond Aron, "Sociologie et socialisme," *Annales de l'Université de Paris,* 30th year (January–March 1960), pp. 30–37. Aron's thesis — ". . . in a simplified formula that we will seek to rectify, one could say that he conceived sociology as the scientific counterpart of socialism" (p. 33) — is similar to that of Bourgin in *Le socialisme universitaire,* pp. 72–79.

out considerable resistance. The very criticisms, however, illuminate the Durkheimians' success.

Four types of critics of the New University may be discerned. Traditional Catholics, incensed by abolition of the Faculty of Theology, regarded the new secularism as undermining religious values. Second, upper-class groups abhorred the left-of-center orientation of most Sorbonne professors and students;[83] upper-class children consequently preferred the Faculties of Medicine or Law, a Grande Ecole, or the Ecole Libre des Sciences Politiques. Third, humanistic *littérateurs* resented the intrusion of scientific attitudes into fields which traditionally favored intellectual flair and intuitive brilliance.[84] This was one element of the aristocratic heritage which opposed the bourgeois style — calculating, rational, and unpolished.[85] Petty bourgeois students at the Ecole Normale and the Sorbonne were assailed as *Berufsmenschen*. Finally, superpatriots attacked the reforms as imports from an alien and barbaric foreign culture, woefully lacking the effervescent *esprit latin*.[86] The old tensions between cartesianism and spontaneity were quite clear.

83. "The real grief against the Sorbonne, that which united against her so many different passions, is not in fact, whatever may be said, either literary or pedagogical. It is political. It is religious. She has against her conservatives and clericals of every shade . . . She is an alarming specter for those who want to subject youth to the old political and religious dogmas . . ." *Le Temps,* June 16, 1911, quoted in Eugen Weber, *The Nationalist Revival in France* (Berkeley: University of California Press, 1959), p. 81.

84. "This scientific preoccupation . . . has swept away our Faculties of Letters. Professors of literature no longer base their judgments on precisely observed facts. They are doing the work of historians, thus of scholars . . .

"Philosophy in turn has followed this same evolution. Metaphysics occupies a modest place in our Faculties . . . Disciplines are also developing here that were formerly confused with general philosophy. Psychology, pedagogy, sociology, have their chairs and their laboratories. The teaching of the Faculty of Letters is becoming penetrated by the same mentality as the Faculty of Science." Theodore Steeg, "Ancienne et Nouvelle Sorbonne," *Revue bleue,* XLVIII (1910), 64ff. Steeg cites three major "promoteurs" of this movement: Lavisse, Lanson, and Durkheim.

85. See Priscilla P. Clark, "The Bourgeois in the French Novel 1789–1848" (Ph.D. diss., Department of French, Columbia University, 1967), for a discussion of these and related themes.

86. The Sorbonne had sided with the British during the Hundred Years' War, thus opposing Joan of Arc. Péguy, in whose works Joan was a recurrent subject, at one point presented an image of her trial where such "Sorbonnards" as Durkheim and Lanson mingled with their fifteenth-century predecessors, dressed in the same robes, and condemned the undisciplined girl. Halévy, *Péguy et les Cahiers de la Quinzaine,* p. 287.

The *Geist* of the Sorbonne also opposed that of the Collège de France, at least as then expressed from certain chairs in philosophy. Facing each other across the Rue Saint Jacques, the two buildings housed sharply contrasting philosophies, personalities, and styles. This temperamental conflict was reflected in many facets of the notorious debates between Durkheim and Gabriel Tarde. Tarde had been elected to the chair of modern philosophy at the Collège in 1900, defeating Henri Bergson by only a few votes.[87] Upon Tarde's death four years later, Bergson acceded to the chair, and in the decade before 1914 came to symbolize for many all that the Sorbonne lacked.[88] Georges Sorel, the *polytechnicien* turned revolutionary, drew heavily on Bergson in his mystique of violence. He would come into Paris from his suburban residence on Friday afternoons, stop by the *Cahiers de la Quinzaine* to meet Charles Péguy, Daniel Halévy, Julien Benda, Berth, and Peslouän, whence they would proceed past the Sorbonne to the Collège de France to attend Bergson's weekly lecture.[89]

87. Bergson also submitted his candidacy for Sorbonne positions in 1894 and 1898; he was defeated both times. See the file of unpublished documents on Tarde in the library of the Centre d'Etudes Sociologiques. The competition with Bergson is treated in the "Dossier Bergson," consisting largely of documents from the Collège de France.

The mutual sympathy of Bergson and Tarde is well known. See, for example, Gabriel Tarde, *The Laws of Imitation* (New York: Henry Holt, 1903), p. 145, and the preface by Bergson to the memorial volume on Tarde, Gabriel Tarde, *Introduction et pages choisies par ses fils* (Paris: Louis-Michaud, 1909).

88. "Certainly Sorbonne professors no longer take account of the intimate life of *chefs-d'oeuvre*. They wish to reduce history, literature, philosophy to some sort of dead and dry knowledge . . .

"One well understands the animosity they feel for M. Bergson. It is a pleasure to note, during lectures, during thesis defenses, unfavorable allusions to 'outside influences,' in general, and to that great thinker in particular." "Les tendences de la nouvelle Sorbonne, lettre d'un etudiant," *l'Action*, n.d., signed Jacques Jary, student in philosophy at the Sorbonne. Cf. also Rolland, *Péguy*, I, 35, and Henri Chevalier, *Henri Bergson* (New York: Macmillan, 1928).

89. Georges Goriely, *Le pluralisme dramatique de Georges Sorel* (Paris: Marcel Rivière, 1962), pp. 172–182. Sorel was a major influence in turning Péguy toward Bergson and away from Lucien Herr and the Durkheimians. Sorel detested the university and its "pretentions of furnishing, through sociology, a new and definitive foundation for the Republic . . . It is Durkheimian sociology which appeared to constitute the major arm of this 'parti intellectuel,' which, thanks to Dreyfusism, had conquered certain high university posts . . ." *Ibid.*, pp. 175–177.

Bergson, in contrast, fascinated them: "Seated on the higher benches of the

Among others frequenting the crowded lecture hall were Gabriel Tarde's son (who, unlike his father, insisted on the aristocratic particule), Guillaume *de* Tarde, and a close friend, Henri Massis. Using the nom de guerre of Agathon, the two collaborated on several pamphlets and books in which the four criticisms already mentioned were combined in lashing diatribes against the Sorbonne, and especially that diabolical figure and family enemy, Emile Durkheim.[90] It was also at the Collège de France that Jean Izoulet was professor of social philosophy, the Izoulet who wrote the damning phrase so widely quoted by Durkheim's adversaries: "the obligation of teaching the sociology of M. Durkheim in 200

---

room [an amphitheater], we would listen to the fascinating words, subtle, precise, always simple and always creative. All ears, all eyes too, for the teaching of Bergson had to be watched as well as listened to. The philosopher worked alone in front of his audience like an artisan alone at his bench. The whole man applied himself in front of us. Concentrating intensely, he would bend forward, straighten up again, sometimes as if overwhelmed with the difficulties in rising. To a meticulous analysis he would add, as if he had received an inspiration, an image. What marvelous lectures!" Halévy, *Péguy*, p. 111. See also Georges Sorel, "Les théories de M. Durkheim," *Le devenir social,* I (1895), 1–26, 148–180.

90. Several articles published elsewhere were reprinted as *L'esprit de la Nouvelle Sorbonne: la crise de la culture classique, la crise du français* (Paris: Mercure de France, 1911). One passage on Durkheim is the following: "Would it be M. Durkheim that M. Liard has charged with elaborating the new doctrine? The powers that he has conferred to him in the organization of the New Sorbonne leave us with some basis to fear that this is the case. He has made of him sort of a *préfet d'études.* He has given him his entire confidence and had him called, first to the Conseil of the University of Paris, then to the Comité Consultatif, which permits M. Durkheim to survey all appointments within the field of higher education. The case of Durkheim is a victory of the new spirit. Charged with university pomp, he is the regent of the Sorbonne, the all-powerful master, and it is known that professors in the section of philosophy, reduced to the role of humble civil servants, follow his every order, oppressed by his command. One is forced to recall Cousin, who spoke to the professors of philosophy as 'my regiment' and of his doctrine as 'my banner.' But Cousin, although fanatical in his way, had suppleness, capriciousness, and a persuasive eloquence.

"Dogmatic, authoritarian, M. Durkheim . . . has created his own domain, *pedagogy.* This is the grand creation (should we say the great thought?) of the New Sorbonne . . . The importance attributed to this subject is proven by a simple fact: it is the *only obligatory course* for all students preparing the agrégation, and those who miss two or three lectures are not permitted to pass exams. Does he in this way have as his goal the rational formation of a future professor? . . .

"M. Durkheim has firmly established his intellectual despotism. He has made of his teaching an instrument of domination." *Ibid.,* pp. 98–100. Similar diatribes continue for pages. Cf. also Agathon, *Les jeunes gens d'aujourd'hui,* pp. 77ff.

Normal Schools in France is the gravest national peril that our country has known for some time." [91]

Over a period of twenty years, Durkheim and his thought thus rose from near obscurity to dominate the university system to the extent that for critics he symbolized its very essence, with all the advantages and problems that this implied. If at the outset Durkheim had been in harmony with the music of the university, by the end of his career he became one of its major composers.

Relations with the Intellectual Community and the Broader Society

Although Durkheim published most scientific work in the *Année sociologique* and in separate books, he also wrote about seventy-five articles for magazines and journals of more general circulation, such as the *Revue bleue,* and the *Revue des deux mondes.*[92] His ideas on scientific ethics were widely debated by philosophers, educators, and the general public.[93] At meetings of the French Philosophical Society he debated the epistemological and ethical aspects of sociology.[94] Several polemics, including those with Tarde, took place in more popular publications. This was especially true of social problems involving legislative action, such as the causes of crime, suicide, divorce, depopulation, and the effects of the press on public morality.[95] Durkheim's role in the Dreyfus Affair has already been discussed.

91. Cited in M. Goyau, *Comment juger la "sociologie" contemporaine* (Marseilles: Editions Publioror, 1934), p. 184.

92. The most complete published bibliography is in Harry Alpert, *Emile Durkheim and His Sociology,* pp. 217–224. Steven Lukes has prepared a more complete listing which is to be published shortly.

93. A volume attacking Durkheim's secular morality was written by a professor at the Catholic university in Louvain, Simon Deploige, *Le conflit de la morale et de la sociologie,* second edition (Louvain and Paris: Alcan, 1912). The second edition contains two letters by Durkheim attacking Deploige's work. See also Ferdinand Brunetière, *La science et la réligion* (Paris: Firmin-Didot, 1895); and Georges Weill, *Histoire de l'idée laïque en France au XIXe siècle* (Paris: Alcan, 1925), especially chaps. 7–14.

94. See D. Parodi, *La philosophie contemporaine en France* (Paris: Félix Alcan, 1920), pp. 113–160; and Durkheim, *Sociology and Philosophy.*

95. Emile Durkheim, "Crime et santé sociale," *Revue philosophique,* XXXIX (1895), 518–523, is an incensed reply to an article by Tarde of the same title. Then Durkheim, "Suicide et natalité," *Revue philosophique,* XXVI (1888), 446–463, and Durkheim, "Le divorce par consentement mutuel," *Revue bleue,* 5th series, X (1906), 549–554, were attacks on such statisticians as Bertillon.

The impact of the Durkheimians on the Latin Quarter climate, their influence on the ideological tenor of the educational system,[96] and their success in promotions and appointments must still be sharply distinguished from structural change of the system. The success of the Durkheimians, for the most part, took place within established structures. Before 1914, only one chair was created in the entire system for them, that of Durkheim in Bordeaux; those assumed by Durkheim and Bouglé in the Sorbonne, and most assumed by Durkheimians in later years, had existed for some time. Attacked as ideologues by political critics outside the university, inside it they were more often condemned as academic imperialists. The internal criticisms were enhanced as the Durkheimians did not try to create new posts and fail, but because they were named over non-Durkheimian philosophers, historians, and others who sought the same existing chairs.[97] Such imperialism made possible a large and powerful cluster; but without a licence-agrégation foundation it remained structurally insecure. The constraints of the national system prevented creation of full-fledged examinations and chairs in sociology, even with administrators as sympathetic as Paul Lapie in the Ministry of Education.[98] Lacking the foundation on which other fields built, the Durkheimians were forced to maintain leadership through moralizing and political debate. This they did with considerable success, for a time.

96. A 1907 questionnaire survey of philosophy professors in secondary schools led Alfred Binet to conclude that "La plupart des correspondants nous assurent, en des termes divers, que la 'sociologie inspire à leurs élèves un intérêt passionné.' C'est un des faits les mieux mis en lumière par notre questionnaire. La désaffection pour la métaphysique, l'intérêt pour la psychologie pathologique, et surtout pour la sociologie sont les traits marquants de la génération actuelle." "L'évolution de l'enseignement philosophique," *Année psychologique*, XIV (1908), 210.

97. One Gilbert Maire (pseudonym?) suggested that Bouglé's biography might be entitled *La carrière d'un arriviste*, or *De Montpellier à Paris par Dreyfus*, which would include a central chapter on *De l'usage du faux en philosophie*, or *Les moyens de parvenir*. Indeed, he suggested, opportunism was too mild a characterization for Bouglé: "On le prend pour un professeur; c'est plutot une espèce d'agent électoral . . . je crois qu'il mettra au service de chaque régime le même zèle inlassable, mais nous saurons nous tenir en méfiance, car à l'avènement de Philippe VIII, il nous proposerait un Rousseau monarchiste." "Un politicien en Sorbonne: M. Bouglé," *Revue critique des idées et des livres*, XIX (1912), 161–180.

98. See Chapter 7.

Part III

Continuities and Discontinuities

Introduction

The Durkheimians, up to 1914, seemed remarkably successful in penetrating the university. When developments after 1914 are examined, however, the precariousness of their success becomes increasingly apparent. Neither sociology nor the other social sciences achieved a secure niche in the lycées; they correspondingly remained outside the licence-agrégation sequence. The role of sociologist thus remained loosely defined and retained a strong philosophical element. Ideological associations in turn took on great importance for sociological careers; two fundamental reference points were the Ministry of Education and the Latin Quarter climate.

A shift in Latin Quarter climate after 1905 hampered the Durkheimians. The cartesianism dominant since the 1880's gave way to a more spontaneous orientation. Students, publicists, and others mounted attacks on the cartesian university and the Durkheimians in particular. The Durkheimians in turn grew more dogmatic and ideological, even though they continued to advance in their careers. Some time series for French sociological productivity even suggest a decline before 1914. Then the war took the lives of several younger cluster members, and shortened the lives of others. With the death of Durkheim in 1917, morale of the cluster reached a low ebb.

At the end of the war the cluster also faced a severe succession crisis. No one member combined the intellectual, temperamental, and administrative skills of Durkheim, and leadership correspondingly differentiated. Lévy-Bruhl remained in a central position to influence university appointments, and helped Bouglé and Fauconnet be named to the Sorbonne. Most others, however, remained in marginal positions: Halbwachs in Strasbourg, and Mauss, Simiand, Hubert, and Granet at the EPHE. Fauconnet and Halbwachs held positions with sociology in their titles, but most others did not. To integrate activities as diverse as economic history, sinology, and the history of religion was thus crucial if a sociological perspective was to be maintained.

The force of Durkheim's personality, the structure of the university system, and the compilation of the *Année sociologique* had provided such integration in earlier years. Efforts were made to revive the *Année,* but only two issues appeared before it faltered again. The Institut Français de Sociologie was then organized in 1924 to hold meetings and publish a *Bulletin.*

The problem of recruitment still remained, and was not facilitated by the establishmentarian activities of many Durkheimians. When forced to choose between appealing to the Ministry or the Latin Quarter, the Durkheimians clearly chose the former: Lapie became Director of Primary Education; Bouglé, director of the Ecole Normale; and Davy, Inspecteur Général and agrégation examiner in philosophy. Thus, although certificats were created in *sociologie générale* and *ethnologie* in the 1920's, these were outside the required sequence for the licence d'enseignement. With most university students still oriented toward careers in lycées, the Durkheimians had to depend on extra-lycée support to attract full-time followers. This became possible in the late 1920's when their contacts brought funds for fellowships; these helped create two new subclusters.

One formed around Mauss, Lévy-Bruhl, and Paul Rivet at the Institut d'Ethnologie. Its young ethnologists remained distant enough from ideological debate in the Latin Quarter to perpetuate and extend the Durkheimian legacy. The second subcluster was associated with Bouglé at the Ecole Normale. The sociologists it attracted, however, were largely alienated by the Durkheimian heritage; they groped toward alternatives.

Non-Durkheimian alternatives in France were most dismal. The war ended most foreign contacts for the Worms institutions and few new French associates were attracted. Gaston Richard succeeded Worms at the *R.I.S.* and IIS in 1926, and continued a tradition of benign eclecticism, as did his students Daniel Essertier and Emile Lasbax. But their intellectual drive was not impressive even by declining Durkheimian standards, and with the Le Playists dispersed and the social statisticians increasingly isolated, the generation of the 1930's was forced to seek most inspiration abroad.

Communism, fascism, and world depression again heightened a concern among talented students with social issues in the 1930's, and in those years Raymond Aron went to Germany and Georges Friedmann to the Soviet Union. Jean Stoetzel was led to the United States. Georges Gurvitch came from Central Europe. Claude Lévi-Strauss undertook field work in Brazil. Each returned to Paris with new intellectual acquisitions. After the Second World War, it was around these men that major clusters took shape. Sharing only a minimal core of beliefs, however, they created neither the intellectual consensus that the Durkheimians had achieved, nor the looser sort of professional community found in the United States and to some degree in Germany. The continuing involvement of the university in Latin Quarter life, and the intense ideological debates there in the 1940's and early 1950's, further accentuated disagreements among social scientists.

Increasing support for social scientific laboratories and research activities from the CNRS and the Sixth Section of the EPHE, especially after 1960, made the traditional cluster arrangements unmanageable. EPHE instruction broadened considerably, and with expansion of research posts, traditional career patterns and administrative arrangements broke down. At the beginning of the 1970's, however, despite tensions in several conflicting directions, no clear new alternatives had succeeded the old patterns.

Chapter 7

French Social Science Since 1914

> I must force myself to recognize the merits, however splendid, of Durkheim, whereas Max Weber never irritates me even when I feel most remote from him.—Raymond Aron, *Main Currents in Sociological Thought* (New York: Basic Books, 1967), II, 8.

Historical Fluctuations in Productivity

Crucial for continuing success of a field is attracting a talented *Nachwuchs;* such attraction derives in part from the field's performance relative to its past and to developments in the same field abroad. French enthusiasm for sociology at the turn of the century was associated with French leadership in the subject. International leadership attracted both young Frenchmen and foreigners to sociological activities in Paris and facilitated expansion into the university.[1] Being first in one's field, nationally and internationally, creates a confidence and drive that is generically different from being almost first.[2]

Problems in later years were due partly to the difficulties of sustaining such leadership. Precise judgments on such matters, however, are extremely difficult. One source of evaluation is the historical accounts of observers, at the time and in subsequent years. These accounts generally suggest a decline with World War I, modest activity in the 1920's, a renaissance in the 1930's, and continuing progress from 1945 through the 1960's.[3]

1. Comparisons with adjoining fields are also clearly important; but these seem more crucial at the stage of selecting a field than in formulating one's contributions to it. The Latin Quarter climate seems to have been fundamental at the earlier stage for post-Durkheimians, international comparisons entered a few years later in their careers.

2. Cf. Joseph Ben-David, *The Scientist's Role in Society* (Englewood Cliffs, N. J.: Prentice-Hall, 1971) and my "The Rise and Decline of France as a Scientific Centre," *Minerva,* VIII (October 1970), 599–601.

3. Emile Durkheim, "La sociologie," in *La science française* (Paris: La-

International comparisons, however, are limited in such accounts. A second approach was thus employed. The attention accorded French sociology by foreign observers whose judgments were less fully explicated, but more precisely recorded, was examined. Three series were prepared, which supply at least crude quantitative measures of continuing judgment: classification by country of volumes acquired by the British Museum since creation of its *Subject Index* (1880) and then *Catalogue* (1901); second, acquisitions of the various libraries of the University of London; third, reviews of books in the *American Journal of Sociology*.[4]

Slightly more sensitive than library acquisitions are reviews in professional journals, since, within limits, large libraries continue acquisition even if the quality of books may decline. Jour-

---

rousse, 1913). Gaston Richard, "Nouvelles tendances sociologiques en France et en Allemagne," *R.I.S.*, XXXVI (1928), 647–649. Georges Davy, *Sociologues d'hier et d'aujourd'hui* (Paris: Félix Alcan, 1931). C. Bouglé, *Bilan de la sociologie française contemporaine* (Paris: Félix Alcan, 1935). Paul Fauconnet, "The Durkheimian School in France," *Sociological Review* (1927), 15–20. Daniel Essertier, *Psychologie et sociologie* (Paris: Félix Alcan, 1930). Henri Lévy-Bruhl, "The Social Sciences as Disciplines: France," *Encyclopedia of the Social Sciences* (New York: Macmillan, 1930). A. Joussain, "Les deux tendances de la sociologie française," *R.I.S.*, XXXIX (1931), 266–70. René Marjolin, "French Sociology — Comte and Durkheim," *American Journal of Sociology* (1937), 693–704. Raymond Aron, "La Sociologie" in R. Aron et al., *Les sciences sociales en France* (Paris: Centre d'Etude de Politique Etrangère; Travaux des Groupes d'Etudes, Publication No. 5, 1937). Pitirim Sorokin, *Contemporary Sociological Theories* (New York: Harper, 1928). Jean Stoetzel, "Sociology in France: An Empirical View," in Howard Becker and Alvin Boskoff, eds., *Modern Sociological Theory* (New York: Dryden, 1957). Claude Lévi-Strauss, "French Sociology," in Georges Gurvitch and Wilbert E. Moore, eds., *Twentieth Century Sociology* (New York: Philosophical Library, 1945). See also the listing of accounts in Jean Viet, *Les sciences de l'homme en France* (Paris: Mouton, 1966).

4. The University of London source was *A London Bibliography of the Social Sciences*. Books in its first volume (1931) were tabulated back to 1800. The category for British Museum acquisitions was "Social Science: Sociology"; that for the University of London libraries was "Sociology." Despite limitation to sociology, the range of titles under this heading in the indexes gives weight to overlapping fields.

These two sources were used for several reasons: the French bibliographies for the same years changed categories several times. The German bibliographical sources consulted either started very late or shifted categories. But French, American, and German sources were biased to the extent that they were from centers of social science at different periods. A small but active country, such as Switzerland or one of the Scandinavian countries, might have supplied an ideal source, but no such source was located. The two English bibliographical guides were thus used.

nals, on the other hand, ideally review important works, irrespective of a country's total production. But few sociology or social science journals have been published continually since the nineteenth century. The oldest such sociological journal is the *American Journal of Sociology,* founded in 1895; it was therefore used for these purposes. Clearly the *A.J.S.* is biased for comparisons between the United States and other countries, although historical changes remain interesting; it would seem less biased as a measure of the relative importance of the various European countries.

Three different sources were used so that they could be compared for reliability. They showed impressive consistency. All indicated a rise for France in the 1880's and 1890's to a peak soon after the turn of the century. Sharp decline came with the war years, and stagnation continued to the late 1920's. An upsurge followed in the late 1930's, but in both library sources it was minor compared with Germany and the United States. The same pattern appeared even more striking in *A.J.S.* reviews, which indicated almost continual decline from 1904–05 to 1934–35, with an improvement only for the 1949–1950 period.[5] The two library sources indicated both relative and absolute declines for France after World War II. The great upsurge since about 1960 was too recent for these sources. (In most periods and sources, the most important "other" country was Italy.)

All three indicators document the turn-of-the-century predominance of French sociology and subsequent decline; this general trend is corroborated by the historical accounts, although they emphasize post–World War II recovery more than the time

---

5. The overall position of France was weaker in 1950 than in 1925 according to one other source: entries for books and journal articles on sociology in a sample from the *Bibliographie der Sozialwissenschaften,* published by the Statistisches Reichsamt:

Items for	1925	1950
Germany	77	73
France	5	3.5
England	7	2.5
United States	8	20
Other	2	1
Total	99%	100%
(N)	(658)	(200)

series. Interestingly, however, as in sociology, more new titles were published in every field in France before 1914 than during the 1950's (see Figure 7).

The *A.J.S.* series suggests that decline began even before 1914. If valid, the wartime loss of Durkheim and many young associates would appear an incomplete explanation of the decline, although these figures refer to aggregate national output. In any case, given their central position for sociology and related

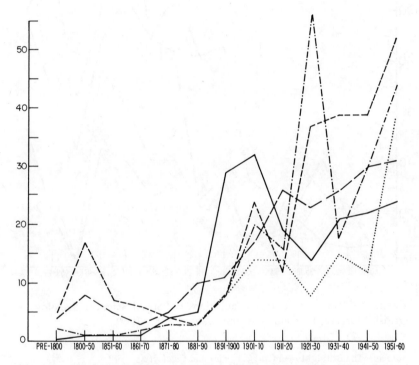

Figure 4.   Sample of library acquisitions in sociology, University of London Libraries, by country of publication, pre-1880 to 1960.

Source: A London Bibliography of the Social Sciences.

France — — — — — —
Germany — · — · — · —
Great Britain —— ——
United States ————
Other · · · · · · · · · · · · · · ·

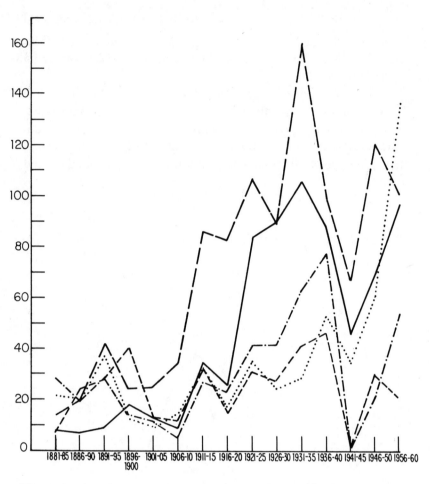

Figure 5.   Sample of library acquisitions in "Social Science: Sociology,"
British Museum, by country of publication, 1881–1960.

Source: The British Museum *Subject Index* and *Catalogue.*

France — — — — — —
Germany — . — . — . —
Great Britain —— ——
United States ————
Other ················

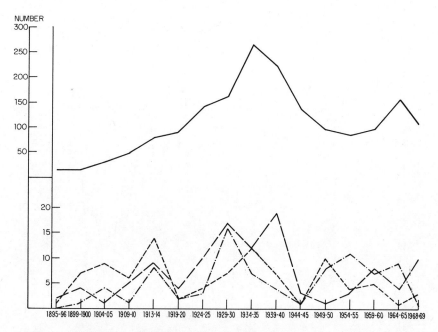

Figure 6. Sample of books reviewed in the *American Journal of Sociology,* by country of publication, 1895–1969.

Source: American Journal of Sociology.

France — — — — — —
Germany — . — . — . —
Great Britain ——— ——
United States ————

fields, consideration of reasons for decline begins logically with the Durkheimians.

Succession Crises of the Durkheimians

In the spring of 1914 the Durkheimians seemed destined to perpetuate their views well into the future. Durkheim, at fifty-six, was a leading figure in French academic life. A decade or so younger were five men who were well into university careers. Bouglé, forty-four, had been chargé de cours at the Sorbonne since 1907 and in academic circles was perhaps the most respected after Durkheim. Lapie, forty-six, had become professor

207

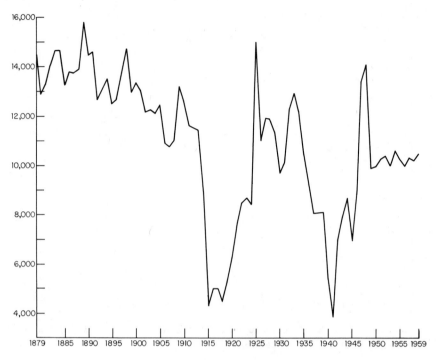

Figure 7.   Number of books published in France in all fields, 1879–1959.

Source: Annuaire Statistique de la France (Paris: Imprimerie Nationale, 1961), p. 72.

and Rector at Toulouse. Also at Toulouse, Fauconnet, at forty, was maître de conférences and had written, although not yet defended, his thesis on responsibility. Mauss, at forty-two, was writing important articles, as was Hubert, just the same age; both held positions at the EPHE, as did Simiand, forty-one, who was also professor at the Conservatoire National des Arts et Métiers. Slightly younger than these five were Halbwachs, who at thirty-seven had just received his Doctorat-ès-lettres; Georges Bourgin, thirty-six, and his brother Hubert Bourgin, thirty-nine, had brought out several monographs on economic history. Others in their early thirties looked most promising — Hertz was thirty-two; Davy and Bianconi were both thirty-one — and only a few years behind were about a dozen who seemed destined to continue the cluster.

But then came the war. Too old to be mobilized, Durkheim threw himself into patriotic activities.[6] Lucien Lévy-Bruhl took part in many of the same activities. Lapie had been named Director of Primary Education in the Ministry in 1914, a post too important to abandon even in wartime. Others in their forties and late thirties volunteered or were drafted for a few months, but with creation of wartime agencies, several were called back to Paris. The most important agency for the Durkheimians was the Ministry of Armaments, led by Albert Thomas, *normalien,* socialist, and great personal friend of Lucien Herr and many Durkheimians.[7] Simiand, Halbwachs, Hubert Bourgin, Mario Rocques, and occasionally Lucien Lévy-Bruhl worked in his Ministry.

In contrast to the brief period of battle in World War II, the French remained in the field for four long years; the military casualties were approximately seven times those of the second war.[8] The losses of young university men were overwhelming: over half the class entering the Ecole Normale in 1913 was killed, as were eighteen of the class of 1911, including Durkheim's only son, André. *Année* collaborators lost were Robert Hertz, Bianconi, Maxime David, Jean Reynier, and R. Gelly. Others were seriously wounded, and lived only a few years after the war: A. Vacher, J.-P. Laffitte, R. Chaillié, Claude Maître, and Maurice Cahen. Beuchat had perished on a field expedition to Alaska in 1914. Durkheim died in 1917.

By 1918 the cluster thus had lost many promising members and faced a serious succession crisis. The difficulties of maintaining leadership will now be considered, then problems of integrating institutions of the cluster, and, finally, recruitment of new members.

6. He was secretary of the Committee for the Publication of Studies and Documents on the War, and for its series wrote *Qui a voulu la guerre?* and *Deutschland Ueber Alles.* He was secretary of the Committee of Publication of Letters to All Frenchmen, and served on committees and boards of Franco-American Fraternity, University Rapprochement, For the Jews in Neutral Countries, and the Republican League of Alsace-Lorraine. See Georges Davy, "Emile Durkheim," *Revue de métaphysique et de morale,* XXVI (1919), 72–76.

7. See B. W. Schaper, *Albert Thomas: trente ans de réformisme social* (Paris: Presses Universitaires de France, n.d.), pp. 22ff.

8. If deaths in World War II of war prisoners, labor deportees, and civil victims are added to the military losses, the figure (about 600,000) is still less than half that for the military losses of World War I. See Warren S. Thompson, *Population Problems* (New York: McGraw-Hill, 1953), p. 66.

Only sixty at the time of his death, Durkheim had not experienced gradual aging during which time a dauphin had been groomed. There was no clear candidate in terms of intellectual abilities, temperament, and stage of career; there were several contenders. Leadership of the cluster thus became differentiated. Lucien Lévy-Bruhl had been centrally placed for some years, but his philosophical career set him apart from the others. Born in 1858 (the same year as Durkheim), he followed the traditional career to the Sorbonne,[9] where in 1899 he was named maître de conférences in philosophy. He simultaneously became directeur d'études for philosophy at the Paris Faculty of Letters. He was thus charged with the program of courses and examinations for all philosophy students, and with inviting Sorbonne professors or others to lecture on material for the program.

Concerned with making philosophy more scientific, he published several works on Auguste Comte. Continuing the same themes,[10] after the turn of the century he took up increasingly "Durkheimian" topics.[11] After he succeeded Boutroux in the chair of History of Modern Philosophy in 1907, Lévy-Bruhl was in a very strong position to influence university appointments.

Durkheim's chair was abolished at the time of his death. Bouglé had been *suppléant* to Espinas and Durkheim since 1907, however, and even after depletion of funds donated by the Comte de Chambrun for the History of Social Economy chair, funds were made available, thanks in part to Lévy-Bruhl, to create a state-supported chair in the subject in 1919.[12] Its first incumbent was Bouglé.

Who should be helped next was more problematical. Mauss and Simiand never completed their Doctorats, and thus remained

9. See Marcel Mauss, "Maîtres, Compagnons, Disciples," in *Oeuvres* (Paris: Editions de Minuit, 1969), Vol. 3, and Jean Cazeneuve, *Lucien Lévy-Bruhl* (Paris: Presses Universitaires de France, 1963).

10. Durkheim stressed his attachment to the Comtean tradition — "au fond la Philosophie positive est tout entière sociologie" — in a 1900 letter to Lévy-Bruhl (provided by M. Georges Davy) and elsewhere.

11. After *La morale et la science des moeurs* in 1903 he focused on comparing "primitive mentalities" with those of more civilized cultures. Although *Les fonctions mentales dans les sociétiés inférieures* appeared in the *Travaux de l'Année sociologique* in 1910, he had not published in the *Année* itself. He collaborated instead with Ribot and the *Revue philosophique* (replacing Ribot as its director in 1920).

12. Minutes of Paris Conseil de la Faculté des Lettres.

ineligible for leading university positions. In 1919, Halbwachs taught briefly at the University of Caen, and later the same year was named to a position in Pedagogy and Sociology at Strasbourg. Fauconnet was three years the senior of Halbwachs, even though he did not become Docteur until 1920. (Halbwachs had completed his Doctorat in 1913.) The next year, however, Fauconnet was named maître de conférences in Pedagogy and Sociology at the Sorbonne; the title was that of Durkheim's former chair. He became professeur sans chair in 1926, and the first professor of Sociology at the Sorbonne in 1932. Why Fauconnet should have been appointed instead of Halbwachs is not entirely clear. Halbwachs had already made more important intellectual contributions, but although he completed an agrégation in philosophy, his work was more empirical than that of Fauconnet. Furthermore, Fauconnet's *thèse principale* was entitled *La responsibilité,* while that of Lévy-Bruhl had been *L'idée de responsibilité.* How important a role was played by personal contacts and other less intellectual matters is difficult to say, but in any case, Fauconnet remained in the most important sociology position in France until his death in 1938.

Most other cluster members held positions without sociology in their titles. If they were to continue sociological activity, it could only be through adding a sociological perspective to other subjects. Earlier this had been accomplished through the charisma of Durkheim and collaboration with the *Année sociologique.* No one could claim Durkheim's charisma, but efforts could be made to channel it into more solid structures. As Durkheim's nephew and longtime collaborator, Mauss was an important symbol of the cluster. But he remained marginal to the university: not a *normalien,* not a Docteur, not the author of a single weighty volume, he was at the EPHE until a chair (in Sociology!) was created for him at the Collège de France in 1931. His distinctly nonprophetic temperament, his egalitarian camaraderie, and his gourmandise inclined him to convene meetings in carefully selected restaurants.[13] Such meetings could provide undeniable integration for the cluster, but more formal organiza-

---

13. Paul Honigsheim, "Reminiscences of the Durkheim School," in Kurt H. Wolff, ed., *Emile Durkheim, 1858–1917* (Columbus: Ohio State University Press, 1960), pp. 309–316.

tions were necessary to perpetuate its collective consciousness. Mauss played a leading role in maintaining these institutions.

A first and natural choice was continuation of the *Année sociologique*. All prewar issues were out of print, and Alcan was not prepared to continue the earlier arrangements. However, the cluster now had friends in important positions. The Confédération des Sociétés Scientifiques made available support from Parliament. The ASMP (of which Lévy-Bruhl and Meillet were members) made a special research award to Mauss and Hubert. Private donations came from affluent friends.[14] These funds permitted launching the New Series of the *Année* in 1925. Only two volumes appeared in the New Series, however, in 1925 and 1926, and these only with considerable effort on the part of Mauss.

Given the crucial role of the *Année* in earlier years, its demise warrants examination. Most important were the age and career stage of cluster members. No longer bright young men preparing theses, they were now professors in established institutions. Collaboration on the *Année* had created their common orientation. But once it was formed, they did not feel the same need to search quantities of literature for new ideas. They did need continuing documentation for their research; but the painstaking earlier efforts to organize raw materials were too demanding for most *professeurs* (as well as EPHE *directeurs*). Making revisions or meeting deadlines under a director was not congruent with the status of a mature scholar. In 1925 the average age of *A.S.* collaborators was fifty, whereas before the war it had ranged from twenty-nine to thirty-six. Compiling such an annual was a useful exercise for younger men; the absence of such collaborators brought the *Année* to a second halt.

With the disappearance of the *Année,* the main integrating institution became the Institut Français de Sociologie. Mauss served as its first president (1924–1927) and was succeeded in four-year intervals by Lévy-Bruhl, Simiand, Granet, Fauconnet, and Halbwachs. The Institut's *Bulletin,* the official cluster publication from 1926 to 1934, included papers presented at the Institut's monthly sessions and subsequent discussions. This for-

14. Max Lazard, David Weill, Mme. Alfred Gans, and from London, Victor Branford. Cf. *A.S.,* New Series, I (1925), 1–5.

mat was better adapted than the *Année* to the cluster's new egalitarianism.

With leading members aging, and younger ones lost in the war, new talent was essential for the cluster's survival. Restaurant meetings and Institut Français de Sociologie sessions were too exclusive for attracting young collaborators. Two new structures were thus created, financed through connections of the cluster, in which for the first time ethnology became institutionally differentiated from sociology.

Students in philosophy would still be exposed primarily to Lucien Lévy-Bruhl, who offered courses for the certificat in *morale et sociologie.* An additional certificat in *sociologie générale* was created at the Paris Faculty of Letters in 1921, but it attracted fewer students.[15] Bouglé's ideological pose may have appealed to students about 1900, but as he grew older, he attracted more followers through his institutional activities. In 1927 he became *directeur adjoint* of the Ecole Normale Supérieure, and in 1935 *directeur,* continuing until his death in 1940. He sought to play a role similar to Lucien Herr's at an earlier period. He created a Centre de Documentation Sociale, where, like Herr, he built up an excellent library. His views, and those of persons with whom he sympathized, were presented in seminars at the Centre. Such *normaliens* as Raymond Aron, Georges Friedmann, Jean Stoetzel, and René Marjolin, as well as certain non-*normaliens,* were to benefit from Bouglé's support in Paris as well as in obtaining traveling fellowships.[16]

A second subcluster was less oriented toward political ideology and contemporary society than the circle around Bouglé;

15. When the system of four certificats comprising a licence was instituted in 1920, the section of the licence from prewar years on *morale et sociologie* became one of the four required certificats for the licence d'enseignement in philosophy offered at all Faculties of Letters in France. (The other three were *histoire générale de la philosophie, psychologie,* and *philosophie générale et logique.*) In 1921 a certificat on *sociologie générale* was created at the Paris Faculty of Letters, but as it could not be substituted for required certificats of the licence d'enseignement, it attracted few students interested in secondary school teaching. See *Guide pratique et programme du certificat d'études littéraires générales* (Paris: Croville, 1962), and Armand Cuvillier, *Où va la sociologie française?* (Paris: Marcel Rivière, 1953), pp. i–viii.

16. Cf. E. Sicard, "Célestin Bouglé," *Proceedings of the 14th International Congress of Sociology* (Rome: Società Italiana di Sociologia and Institut International de Sociologie, 1950), pp. 120–121.

its concerns were more ethnological than sociological. Like the *normaliens* around Bouglé, most ethnology students began with a licence in philosophy, and after 1927 they could also prepare a certificat in ethnology.[17] Mauss offered the main course for the new certificat; in this way, although still at the EPHE, he had a repectable number of students channeled to him for the first time. His course was offered at the Institut d'Ethnologie, created in 1925 by Mauss, Lévy-Bruhl, and Paul Rivet, with a budget coming largely from the Ministry of Colonies. These funds provided fellowships so that career alternatives to the lycée became available to young agrégés. In this way, serious field work was undertaken for the first time by trained French ethnologists. Young scholars associated with the Institut included Marcel Griaule, Mme. Dieterlen, André Leroi-Gourhan, Michel Leiris, Denise Paulme, Jacques Soustelle, and Claude Lévi-Strauss.[18]

By 1934 enough young scholars were attracted to these subclusters to launch a continuation of the *Année,* the *Annales sociologiques.* Rather than a single integrated volume, the *Annales* included five separately published series; each contained original articles and reviews under the direction of a different Durkheimian.[19]

A niche in the examination program, research centers, fellowships, and a new publication could draw some students, but many of the best young minds were led to different specialties as a function of the Latin Quarter climate. This was a variable over which the Durkheimians had little control, and one which operated to their distinct disadvantage for a number of years.

Elsewhere three periods have been isolated, distinguished largely by shifts in cultural ideals of leading Latin Quarter figures.[20] The first grew in strength through the 1880's and extended

17. Although like the certificat in *sociologie générale,* it was not required for the licence d'enseignement.

18. See the annual reports on the Institut in the *Annales de l'Université de Paris.*

19. A. General Sociology — Bouglé
    B. Religious Sociology — Mauss
    C. Juridical Sociology — J. Ray
    D. Economic Sociology — Simiand
    E. Social Morphology, Technology, Esthetics — Halbwachs

20. See Priscilla P. Clark and Terry N. Clark, "Writers, Literature, and Student Movements in France," *Sociology of Education,* XLII (Fall 1969), 293–314.

until about 1905; students selecting careers in this period constituted the bulk of the prewar Durkheimians. *Secular rationalism* was the predominant cultural pattern: its principal components were rationalism, a civic lay morality, internationalism, and social solidarity. This was the same blend of cartesian ideas that penetrated the university after the Franco-Prussian War, was defended in the streets by young Durkheimians in the Dreyfus Affair, written about in the pages of *l'Humanité* and taught enthusiastically in the *universités populaires*. Lucien Herr, in his glory during these years, helped guide some of the best *normaliens* to Durkheim, a near-perfect incarnation of the period's ideals.

But after about 1905 the mood began to change. The cartesianism receded with a reemergence of spontaneity. The ideals of social solidarity were sullied when the Dreyfusards took office: they unmercifully repressed their adversaries and used confiscated Church property for patronage. The internationalism and ties with German universities and German socialism receded with preparations for war. The civic lay morality was no longer an ideal of republican underdogs; it was offered as legitimation by a victorious majority. The rationalism immeshed with these other ideals eroded with them as a *spontaneous nationalism* became dominant; its major components were irrationality, Catholicism, nationalism, and individualism. The leading *normalien* Dreyfusard, Charles Péguy, underwent a crisis, and by 1908 was an antisocialist and ardent defender of Catholicism. Durkheim and Lucien Herr gave way to Barrès and Bergson as dominant Latin Quarter figures. The shift in climate was soon felt inside the Ecole Normale: in 1905 only three or four students were practicing Catholics; seven years later they numbered about forty, or one-third of the school. A student recounted that in earlier years the *Internationale* could be heard in the hallways, but if it became audible in 1911, it would be drowned by a *Marseillaise*.[21]

Immediately after the war, vestiges of both secular rationalism and spontaneous nationalism could be found in Latin Quarter activities and publications, but they were only vestiges: the dominant mood, if any, seemed to be a rejection of all that had preceded and generated the absurd war. Both previous ideals suf-

21. Agathon, *L'esprit de la Nouvelle Sorbonne* (Paris: Mercure de France, 1911), p. 172.

fered guilt through association.[22] The Surrealists' nihilism opposed previous ideologies, but at the outset had little else to offer.[23] As various Latin Quarter movements confronted one another in the early 1920's, many observers declared themselves unable to assume any commitment. The pompous rhetoric of the Durkheimians, which seemed to echo wartime slogans, was simply abhorrent.

When major changes did take place, it was already the early 1930's. The world-wide depression and political turmoil saw the growth of more powerful forms of leagues and of fascism. The new concern of Latin Quarter intellectuals with politics, the creation of new journals and political groupings, and the constant street fights again heightened the interest of students in careers involving political and social questions. Their ideological legacy, however, made it extremely difficult for the Durkheimians to profit from the new situation.

At this point a brief international comparison is in order. Certain developments in Germany and the United States in these years deserve mention because of their absence in France, namely, the differentiation of social scientific roles and the definition of ethical neutrality. The relative detachment of the German and American universities from their societies has been contrasted with the involvement of the French. In each country nascent social sciences in their preuniversity stages were inextricably associated with social problems. But as they entered the German and American universities, the social sciences gradually became detached from social problems and tended toward elaborating their distinctive paradigms. General factors behind such professionalization have already been considered; of most importance here is that in contrast to France, professional organiza-

---

22. In a novel about *normaliens,* Paul Nizan presents a scene at a 1924 reception celebrating the transfer of Jaurès's body to the Panthéon. Lucien Herr, attending the occasion with Lucien Lévy-Bruhl, comes over to the students and asks if they would like to meet Léon Blum. They coolly agree to do so, but leave the ceremony early, overwhelmed with revulsion for the Establishment and its past. They did not begin committed political action until 1929. See *La conspiration* (Paris: Gallimard, 1938).

23. One Surrealist later remarked, "Notre doctrine de base était: Table rase." Philippe Soupault in response to " 'Qu'as-tu fait de ta jeunesse?' Une grande enquête de Gilbert Ganne sur les mouvements intellectuels d'avant-guerre," *Arts,* 21–27 March 1956, p. 8.

tions in Germany and the United States helped reinforce and extend the roles defined at leading universities. Intellectual byproducts in Germany were such variations of relativism as the economic *Methodenstreit,* the debate about historicism, Max Weber's formulations on objectivity and ethical neutrality, and *Wissensoziologie.*[24] In America the social reformism of the early social scientists began to give way to more detached, scientific concerns.[25]

In France the centralized educational system and its associated characteristics discouraged professional organizations as in Germany and the United States. Furthermore, lacking full university status, most social sciences remained more involved with the society around them. This was generally true for psychology, economics, and political science, but particularly so for the Durkheimians and sociology. Despite his important reflections on professional organizations[26] and the relationships between philosophy and social science, Durkheim consistently resisted separation of the scientific and moral components of his work.[27] This provided an ideological impetus[28] for careers of his immediate disciples, but as the times changed, the aging Durkheimians came to

24. See Fritz K. Ringer, *The Decline of the German Mandarins: The German Academic Community, 1890–1933* (Cambridge: Harvard University Press, 1969).

25. An important step was marked by the election of W. F. Ogburn to the presidency of the American Sociological Society in 1929. His presidential address was one of the strongest statements on ethical neutrality to come from an American sociologist. Affirmations such as "sociology as a science is not interested in making the world a better place to live," and "it will be desirable to taboo ethics and values (except in choosing problems)" would have been inconceivable only a few years before. William F. Ogburn, "The Folkways of a Scientific Sociology," *Proceedings of the American Sociological Society,* XXIV (1930), 2–10, quoted in Anthony Oberschall, "The Institutionalization of American Sociology," unpublished paper, Yale University, September 1968.

26. Emile Durkheim, *Professional Ethics and Civic Morals* (Glencoe: Free Press, 1958), chaps. 1–3; *Suicide* (Glencoe: Free Press, 1951), pp. 361ff.; *The Division of Labor in Society* (New York: Macmillan, 1933), pp. 1–49. The English "occupational group" is a more correct rendering of Durkheim's concern, which was really not with "professions" as defined by contemporary sociologists.

27. See *The Rules of Sociological Method* (Chicago: University of Chicago Press, 1938), especially chap. 4.

28. Bouglé, and to some degree, Halbwachs, nevertheless harbored doubts about linking science and ethics, which occasionally became explicit. See Maurice Halbwachs, "Célestin Bouglé sociologue," *Revue de metaphysique et de morale,* XLVIII (1941), 24–47.

be viewed by the young as ponderous members of a decaying establishment.

Young men, and bright young men, were again attracted to sociology in the 1930's, and they read in Bouglé's new library, enjoyed fellowship support, and began publication in the *Annales sociologiques*. But while surrounded by the men and institutions of the Durkheimian cluster, in the main they rejected its ideas. The Durkheimian legacy was not elaborated in France, but in the Department of Sociology created at Harvard in 1930 (by Talcott Parsons, George Homans, Robert Merton, Kingsley Davis, and others). The analytical core of Durkheim's work was the focus of attention at Harvard, and the point of departure for new investigations; in Paris the ideological and moral concerns remained more salient to the young philosophers, who looked elsewhere for new ideas.

What did students confront that did not inspire them? As was true from the 1880's to the 1960's, most began with philosophy. Those preparing a certificat in *morale et sociologie* could hear Lévy-Bruhl speak of the glories of Comte and the Durkheimian inheritance of positivist philosophy. This course on Comte reputedly had a decisive positive influence on some early Durkheimians, such as Simiand, but in later years it served merely to link Durkheim to what was seen as a superannuated past.

Another basic course for the certificats of *morale et sociologie* and *sociologie générale* was offered by Fauconnet. In the 1930's it consisted of a superficial and dogmatic review of research strategies used by Durkheimians.[29] One critical *normalien* perceived that Fauconnet in these years "prepared for reirement." [30] Bouglé remained a dynamic lecturer and writer throughout his life, but the more than one hundred books he wrote or edited, and the innumerable articles, contained little original sociology after the early years. In his necrology of Bouglé,[31] the amiable Halbwachs explicitly limited discussion to works published from 1894 to

---

29. *Observation et analyse des faits sociaux* (Paris: Les Cours de Sorbonne, Centre de Documentation Universitaire, n.d.).

30. Jean Stoetzel, "Sociology in France: An Empiricist View," in Howard Becker and Alvin Boskoff, eds., *Modern Sociological Theory* (New York: Holt, Rinehart, and Winston, 1957), pp. 623–657.

31. Halbwachs, "Célestin Bouglé sociologue," pp. 24–47. See also *Annales de l'Université de Paris,* XV (1940), 1–29.

218

1908, and took pains to recall that Bouglé had been a creative sociologist in these years before the efflorescence of political ideology, textbooks, and speeches.

The most creative Durkheimians in the interwar years were either outside Paris or outside the central teaching institutions. Halbwachs remained in Strasbourg (where in 1927 he became the first professor of Sociology in the university system), and when he finally came to the Sorbonne in 1935, his mild personality did not predispose him to the role of *grand patron* or Latin Quarter ideologue. If the quality of his work distinguished him from other Durkheimians, he remained associated with them for the young. Still, his ideas probably found greater resonance through Gurvitch and Stoetzel than did those of other Durkheimians with the exception of Mauss.

Mauss continued his specialized courses in the religious sciences section of the EPHE, adding the course in ethnology for philosophy students, and others at the Collège de France after his appointment there in 1931. Granet was directeur of Religions de l'Extrême Orient in the EPHE Fifth Section with Mauss, but although his publications were respected, he attracted few students.[32] Henri Hubert was directeur of Religions Primitives de l'Europe at the EPHE until his death in 1927. In the EPHE historical sciences section, Simiand continued detailed analyses of time series, publishing his massive *Le Salaire* in 1932. The same year he was named professor of History of Labor at the Collège de France;[33] he died three years later.

For further evidence of establishment contacts of the Durkheimians, students observed their administrative positions. In 1914 Paul Lapie became Director of Primary Education in the Ministry, where he remained until his death in 1926. Dominique Parodi served as Inspector General of Public Instruction through the interwar years. Emmanuel Lévy served simultaneously as

32. Two years of Chinese were essential to understand most of his *explications de text*. Personal communication, M. Georges Dumézil.

33. Drawing on the *procès verbaux* of meetings at the Collège de France, Rose-Marie Mossé-Bastide affirms that Bergson supported a 1905 proposal by Pierre Janet for a chair in Sociology (probably for Lévy-Bruhl), as well as creation of a chair in Sciences Economiques et Sociales for Simiand in 1912, although neither proposal was successful. *Bergson éducateur* (Paris: Presses Universitaires de France, 1955), pp. 67–68.

professor at the Lyon Faculty of Law, and as deputy mayor of Lyon under Edouard Herriot. Jean Ray followed a career in the foreign service and as legal adviser to the League of Nations and other groups. Bouglé, of course, directed the Ecole Normale. Georges Davy, however, held the most varied administrative posts of any Durkheimian. Dean at Dijon in 1922, during the interwar years he served as Inspector General of Public Instruction and Rector of the Academy of Rennes; soon after entering the Sorbonne as professor in 1944, he became Dean of the Paris Faculty of Letters. From the interwar years until the 1950's, he was chairman of the agrégation committee in philosophy, where he earned a reputation as a most demanding examiner. He was also a member and president of the ASMP, and long active in UNESCO, the CNRS, and boards of numerous journals and international associations.

How is this affinity for administration to be explained? The Durkheimians were talented *normaliens,* patriots, and republicans of precisely the sort sought out by the *république des professeurs.* Their wartime experiences interrupted academic careers and brought them into contact with higher administrators. But although aspiring sociologists, they could not, for the most part, follow university careers in sociology.

One administrative activity that might have brought considerable expansion of sociology chairs simultaneously pleased the establishment republicans while alienating critical youths. This was the effort to institutionalize sociology in the primary and secondary schools.

As early as 1900 François Simiand had presented a careful report on civic and moral training in the primary schools.[34] He urged that the Congrès International de l'Enseignement des Sciences Sociales recommend more social scientific instruction for both primary school teachers and students, but he was opposed by Charles Guieysse, Georges Renard, and Henri Hauser.[35] They felt that students were too young and teachers inadequately

---

34. "De l'enseignement des sciences sociales à l'Ecole primaire," in *Le premier Congrès de l'Enseignement des Sciences Sociales* (Paris: Alcan, 1901), pp. 163–185.
35. The Congrès was largely organized by Mlle. Dick May, who acted as secretary general. *Ibid.*, pp. 19ff.

trained for serious social science — in contrast to civics, history, and geography, which they recommended continuing. No vote was taken on Simiand's propositions. Only fragmentary information is available on subsequent efforts in the same direction. During the rest of the prewar period the Durkheimians earned a reputation of being academic imperialists, although no clear details remain concerning efforts toward institutionalization in the schools. A few hours on "sociological methods" were introduced into the lycées, apparently in conjunction with the addition of the sociological section to the philosophy licence.[36] Immediately after the war, a strong effort was made to enter the basic curriculum of the schools. In 1920 Lapie, as Director of Primary Education, quietly suggested revisions in the civics curriculum of the Ecoles Normales Primaires. The word sociology was not used. His recommendations were passed with almost no discussion by the Conseil Supérieur de l'Instruction Publique. When Lapie subsequently wrote out specifications for the required curriculum to be sent to each teacher, however, the word sociology and certain Durkheimian concepts figured prominently.[37] The initial protests seem to have come from administrators and teachers in the Ecoles Normales Primaires.[38] They complained that the teachers they were training were not equipped to deal adequately with such abstract concepts, and that primary school students would not have sufficient knowledge of basic facts necessary to understand sociological interpretations. It was decided that the director of each Ecole Normale Primaire should be responsible for teaching this material himself, and to acquaint the directors with the new materials, they were brought to Paris for special training courses offered mainly by Bouglé and Fauconnet. Davy also wrote a textbook[39] and Bouglé subsequently published a collection of readings.[40] It was suggested by some critics that the program in

36. Albert Binet, "L'évolution de l'enseignement philosophique," *Année psychologique,* XIV (1908), 152–232.
37. *Journal officiel de la République Française,* 52nd year, No. 284 (October 31, 1920), 17073–17074; A. Albert-Petit, "La déviation de l'enseignement primaire," *La revue de Paris,* XXXI (1924), 408–426.
38. M. Hébert, "La sociologie dans les Ecoles normales," *Revue pédagogique,* LXXX (1924), 325–340.
39. Georges Davy, *Eléments de sociologie* (Paris: Vrin, 1924).
40. C. Bouglé and J. Raffault, eds., *Eléments de sociologie* (Paris: Alcan, 1926).

sociology had passed unnoticed only because most members of the Conseil Supérieur were minimally concerned with primary school matters.[41] Suggested revisions in the lycée curriculum would have been more carefully scrutinized.[42] With time, however, the indoctrination efforts of the Durkheimians became more generally known, and increasingly opposed. The extent of resentment in educational circles became clear in 1923 when Lapie proposed to the Conseil Supérieur that sociological instruction be expanded to replace *la morale* in the Ecoles Normales Primaires. It was apparently a heated session, in which Henri Bergson (a member of the Conseil) participated.[43] Not only was the request refused, but sociology was eliminated altogether. The debate then expanded to official publications of the Ministry.[44] The subject was even taken up by the ASMP, where both opponents and supporters of the Durkheimians and of sociology expressed opinions.[45] By this stage, however, the Durkheimians seemed slightly embarrassed by the whole affair, and became rather defensive.[46] Most subsequent discussions of sociology in the primary and secondary schools seemed to be strongly anti-Durkheimian.[47] Certainly the Latin Quarter climate was unfavorable. After the death of Lapie in 1926 the Durkheimians apparently concentrated their efforts on higher educational levels.

The Dismal Non-Durkheimian Alternatives

Some persons dissatisfied with the Durkheimians in earlier years affiliated themselves with the grouping around René

41. Albert-Petit, "La déviation."

42. Léon Berhard, *Pour la réforme classique de l'enseignement secondaire* (Paris: Colin, 1923), and minutes of the Conseil Supérieur de l'Instruction Publique, A. N. J12737.

43. Mossé-Bastide, *Bergson éducateur*, p. 267.

44. Hébert, "La sociologie"; C. Bouglé, "Sur les rapports de la sociologie avec la morale," *Revue pédagogique*, LXXXIII (1923), 157–177; F. Gazin, "Quelques vues sur la morale dans l'enseignement primaire supérieur," *Revue pédagogique*, LXXXIII (1923), 178–188.

45. *Séances et travaux de l'Académie des Sciences Morales et Politiques*, LXXXV (1925), 114–147.

46. C. Bouglé, "La sociologie enseignée dans les écoles normales," *ibid.*, 143–147.

47. Jean Izoulet, *La métamorphose de l'église* (Paris: Albin Michel, 1928), especially 304ff.

Worms. By the interwar years, however, this alternative did not attract talented young men. Most of Worms's associates had been too old for service in the war, but growing international tensions after 1905 were as disastrous for the *R.I.S.* and IIS as war losses for the Durkheimians. Resignations increased until the war, when Worms was compelled to remove the entire list of "collaborateurs" from the *R.I.S.* The IIS held its last prewar meeting in Rome in 1912 and did not reconvene until 1927. The sparse meetings of the Société de Sociologie de Paris were devoted largely to political and geographic questions bearing on the war.

His efforts always diffused, Worms continued teaching in marginal positions as well as engaging in various governmental activities.[48] Before the war Worms had carried on these many activities, along with the *R.I.S.*, IIS, and the Société, and would still publish continual articles and a book every few years. His last significant work, however, was the *Philosophie des sciences sociales,* the third and last volume of which appeared in 1907. A few inflated brochures came after that, and a little *manuel* in 1921, but nothing of consequence. He continued his organizational activities as best he could until his death in 1926.

Worms was succeeded as director of the *R.I.S.* and secretary general of the IIS by Gaston Richard. Richard had been an ostensibly sympathetic Durkheimian when he acceded to Durkheim's Bordeaux chair in 1902. But as Durkheim grew more nationalistic and remained intractable toward adjoining disciplines, Richard, with others, resented his rigidity. As Protestant *croyant,* Richard was especially alienated by comparisons of Australian totemism with modern Christianity. In 1910 he stated his criticisms forcefully in four articles in a journal called *Foi et vie.* With the onset of war the French government and Conseil d'Etat were transferred to Bordeaux, where Richard developed a close association with Worms. While Worms was less outspokenly critical, both agreed that the dogmatism of Durkheim and most other

48. Teaching: an annual course on History of Sociology after 1907 at the Ecole des Hautes Etudes Sociales; a *cours libre* on sociology at the Paris Faculty of Law. Then in 1913 he became chargé de cours for the Philosophy of Commerce at the Ecole des Hautes Etudes Commerciales, and in 1919 was appointed to a chair there in the same subject.

Government: he rose in the Conseil d'Etat hierarchy from 1893 to 1924, when he was named Conseilleur; "Correspondent" of the Académie d'Agriculture de France after 1901, in 1922 he became a full member.

groupings precluded important insights.[49] Although a former philosophy student and *normalien,* near the end of his life Richard was not ashamed to admit full agreement with Parodi's denial of unity to his works: he claimed himself a student of the schools of Le Play, Tarde, Comte, Wundt, Simmel, Spencer, and Giddings. His autobiography records frequent studies undertaken at publishers' requests or for competitions.[50] This eclecticism made him one of the clearest critics of the Durkheimians, but prevented him from developing any subject into a substantial contribution.

Just before World War I, Richard trained two disciples at Bordeaux: Daniel Essertier and Emile Lasbax.[51] The two were also influenced by Bergson through the philosopher Théodore Ruyssen. Their subsequent works were efforts at synthesis. Lasbax defended his doctorate in 1918 (on *Le problème du mal*) and was named to a philosophy chair at Clermont-Ferrand. He brought out subsequent studies on philosophy of social science and a work recording his debts to Ruyssen and Bergson: *Les origines du Bergsonisme sociologique.* Lasbax succeeded Richard as director of the *R.I.S.* in 1934. Essertier completed a thesis on types of explanation and then several volumes of eclectic summaries of work in sociology and psychology, quite in the tradition of Worms's philosophy of the social sciences. Essertier was one of few competent young sociologists in the immediate postwar period, and his concern with integrating conflicting currents appeared promising. His relationships with the Durkheimians were better than those of his *maître* Richard, and he collaborated on the 1923–24 issue of the *Année sociologique.* He was named professor of philosophy at the University of Poitiers and then at Cairo, but in 1930 he died in an automobile accident.

In Cairo a few years before Essertier, René Maunier had de-

49. In his generally laudatory necrology, Worms regretted Durkheim's "attitude dogmatique, intransigeante, et combattive, vraiment trop dédaigneuse," René Worms, "Emile Durkheim," *R.I.S.,* XXV (1917), 561–568.

50. Gaston Richard, "Avant-Propos inédit," published in 1935 in a special issue of the *R.I.S.* devoted to Richard's work.

51. Gaston Richard, "Le nouveau directeur de la *Revue internationale de sociologie,*" *R.I.S.,* XL (1934), 341–347; Emile Lasbax, "Daniel Essertier," *R.I.S.,* XL (1932), 183.

veloped a tradition of applied sociological research.[52] Completing a doctorate in law in 1909, he was chargé de cours at the Lille Law Faculty for a year before becoming professor in Cairo. There he led field expeditions and organized statistical surveys in the Egyptian Ministry of Justice. He continued his field studies while professor in Algiers, publishing numerous monographs on Arab life and what he called the sociology of colonization. He was named to the Paris Faculty of Law in 1924. Maunier's ethnographic interests brought him in contact with Mauss, Lévy-Bruhl, and Paul Rivet, and he met with the Institut Français de Sociologie and published in the *Annales sociologiques.* Simultaneously, however, he remained in close contact with the international sociologists, publishing frequently in the *R.I.S.,* serving on its Comité de Direction, and participating in the IIS, of which he was elected president just before World War II. In work on ritual exchanges, Maunier was close to Mauss's exchange theory of *The Gift,* and he drew on certain Durkheimian ideas in comparing legal institutions in North Africa and elsewhere. He thus appeared as a possible link between the Durkheimians and international sociologists; but during the war he collaborated with the Germans and afterward withdrew from all scientific activities. He died in 1948.

Closer to Worms and the *R.I.S.* than René Maunier was Guillaume-Léonce Duprat, a Bordeaux student from an earlier period.[53] He defended his doctoral theses at the Sorbonne in 1899 (on mental illness and Greek philosophy) and joined René Worms the next year as *secrétaire de rédaction* of the *R.I.S.* He contributed frequent book reviews and articles to the *R.I.S.,* supporting himself in lycées until 1922, when he became professor of Sociology and Social Economy at the University of Geneva. As the more outstanding members of the IIS withdrew or died, Duprat was a loyal follower who remained: he assisted

52. Santi Nova, "René Maunier: sociologue de la colonisation." *R.I.S.,* XLVII (1939), 177–184; H. Mauss, "René Maunier" in Wilhelm Bernsdorf, ed., *Internationales Soziologen Lexikon* (Stuttgart: Enke Verlag, 1959), pp. 366–367.
53. See "In Memoriam, Guillaume-Léonce Duprat," *Actes du XVIIe Congrès International de Sociologie* (Beyrouth: Institut International de Sociologie, 1958), pp. 787–794.

Gaston Richard and then served as vice-president in 1927 and
secretary general from 1930 until 1937 when he withdrew from
professional life. Like several other international sociologists,
however, Duprat spread himself over many subjects but contributed little original to any of them. He was a reliable mainstay of
the Worms organizations, however, and his detachment occasionally produced the balanced insights which Worms and Richard could also show.

Also very loyal to Worms and then Richard was Achille Ouy,
who followed a career teaching philosophy in various lycées. He
performed many day-to-day tasks that held the *R.I.S.* and IIS
together from 1919 to 1940, and occasionally contributed book
reviews, necrologies, and minor review articles to the *R.I.S.*

The last figure to participate actively with Richard, Lasbax,
Essertier, Maunier, and Duprat was Gaston Bouthoul. He shared
their eclecticism after studying in Geneva under Duprat, although he sought to integrate sociology more with economics and
statistics rather than with philosophy as had most of the others.
In the 1920's and 30's he published articles in the *R.I.S.* on population growth, the theories of Thorstein Veblen, and relationships between population and technological change. He subsequently brought out several studies on war. He served as IIS
treasurer from 1928 until the 1950's and remained on the Comité
de Direction of the *R.I.S.* until its last issue in 1939. Bouthoul
did not follow an academic career, but served in administrative
posts in various international organizations.

The eclecticism of the international sociologists might have
led them to consolidate advances of narrower groupings, and
through their organizations to create a professional community
of French sociologists. Certainly Worms tried valiantly, but failing to secure cooperation of the Durkheimians and most Le
Playists, he relied instead on amateurs and foreigners. His success in attracting eminent foreigners brought a wide range of
ideas to French sociology near the turn of the century, and gave
an indirect boost to the Durkheimians. Worms made plans for
a congress of the IIS just before he died in 1926, and Gaston
Richard, already sixty-six when he took over from Worms, did
not have the energy a younger man might have had. The several
hundred persons who would squeeze into meetings of the Société

de Sociologie de Paris near 1900 no longer attended and the organization gradually withered and died. The Institut Français de Sociologie, which might have succeeded the Société, remained dominated by the Durkheimian cluster until after World War II.[54]

A national professional community should have incorporated elements of the Le Playist tradition, but these were rapidly disappearing. Paul de Rousiers sought to keep the *Science sociale* grouping alive, but solid research reports appeared in *La science sociale* only in 1925–26; for the rest of the interwar years the journal was devoted largely to activities of the Ecole des Roches. Irregular meetings of the Société Internationale des Sciences Sociales seem to have been mainly concerned with raising funds and recruiting students for the Ecole des Roches. *La réforme sociale* increasingly turned to problems of agricultural organization on the one hand and bitter criticism of French socialism on the other. In 1935 the two declining journals merged in *Les études sociales,* which continued following the war. The one active researcher after de Rousiers was Paul Descamps, who completed monographic studies on Belgium and England before World War I, and during the interwar years served as professor at the University of Coimbra in Portugal, where he continued field work with students. His summary volume, *La Sociologie expérimentale,*[55] was the most important statement by a Le Playist for some time: it sought to integrate the newer theoretical and methodological advances of the Durkheimians and French human geographers, and to adapt traditional Le Playist ideas to criticism from the Durkheimians, Worms, and others. That Descamps participated regularly in the *R.I.S.* and IIS in the interwar period was a clear sign of convergence, but as both the Le Playists and international sociologists were declining, there were few cumulative results. In the same years, the official followers of Auguste Comte dispersed, while the Durkheimians became identified as the principal heirs of positivism. What remained of the Broca grouping lost all vitality after the Institut d'Ethnologie was

54. In a letter to G. Lutfalla, secretary of the postwar continuation of the Institut, the Société Française de Sociologie, Raymond Lenoir noted that "elle perd le caractère de groupe fermé voulu à l'origine et au lendemain de sa résurrection . . ." (Letter dated 16 September 1952, Archives of the Société Française de Sociologie, Centre d'Etudes Sociologiques).
55. (Paris: Marcel Rivière, 1933).

formed. The statisticians grew more isolated from developments in the social sciences. Virtually no one from these earlier traditions brought new ideas to the institutions created by René Worms.

This decline of the French contingent of international sociologists led to filling the *R.I.S.* with IIS congress papers from foreigners. Certain Germans, such as Leopold von Wiese, returned to the IIS after World War I, but after 1933 few contributions came from Germany. Then although L. T. Hobhouse served as vice-president of the IIS in 1922–23, the English barely participated. Foreign contributions came increasingly from Americans: Robert MacIver, F. Stuart Chapin, William F. Ogburn, E. A. Ross, and Pitirim Sorokin were regular IIS members, and Howard Becker, Robert McKenzie, Howard Odum, Robert Park, and Louis Wirth associate members. After 1930 there were frequent contributions from these men and their students, as well as summary articles and book reviews of their work.[56] Despite this burst of energy, politics soon brought the demise of the international sociologists.

As late as 1939 Achille Ouy published review articles seeking to reconcile differences among French sociologists,[57] but René Maunier as president and Emile Lasbax as secretary general of the IIS had already been making plans for the next congress. It was to be held in Bucharest under the presidency of D. Gusti. The growing isolationist tendencies of the Americans and the fascist sympathies of the congress organizers led to numerous contributions from persons in fascist countries. With the spread of the war, the congress was never held, although Gusti published some of the papers.[58] The *R.I.S.* suspended publication after 1939.

During the war Corrado Gini, IIS vice-president, visited Gusti and arranged to transfer certain IIS materials to Rome. When Maunier, as IIS president, and Lasbax and Ouy, as secre-

56. See G.-L. Duprat, "La sociologie américaine au sein de l'Institut International de Sociologie," *R.I.S.*, XLIV (1936), 307–311.

57. "Les sociologues et la sociologie," *R.I.S.*, XLVII (1939), 245–275.

58. *Travaux du XIVe Congrès International de Sociologie* (Bucharest: Institut International de Sociologie, Institut des Sciences Sociales de Roumanie, 1940).

228

taries, made no efforts to continue the IIS or the *R.I.S.*, Gini took the initiative, and following extended preparations held a congress in 1950 in Rome.[59] However, after the International Sociological Association was founded in 1949, despite protests from Gini and others, it drew the more active sociologists of the world to its meetings. The IIS continued with some prewar associates, as well as new Italian and Latin American members. Gini initiated a new series of the *R.I.S.* in 1954, and by the late 1960's the IIS and *R.I.S.* seemed to be taking on new life for the first time in many years.

The Generation of the 1930's

As has been illustrated, most Durkheimians became too dogmatic to incorporate new ideas into the *patrimoine;* but non-Durkheimian alternatives were far more dismal. When the depression, Communism, fascism, and the Popular Front revived the political and social consciousness of the Latin Quarter, capable persons found little social science stimulation anywhere in France. The time series used here indicates that there may have been objective grounds to their reactions. Younger men reviewing foreign works in the *Annales sociologiques* thus did not seek to integrate ideas into an established framework; these were preparatory forays in altogether new directions.

The generation of the 1930's followed several quite different lines. One began with Marxism. A few scattered individuals had read Marx in earlier years, but there was no serious French tradition of Marxian scholarship as in Germany or Italy. One precipitating event was the arrival in Paris of certain Russian and then German émigrés in the 1930's: Maurice Merleau-Ponty, Henri Lefevbre, and a handful of others developed a philosophical approach to Marx after attending Alexandre Kojève's lectures on Hegel at the EPHE.[60] The Frankfort Institute for Social Research

59. See the account of the transfer of the IIS from Paris and Bucharest to Rome in "Comptes rendus des séances," *Proceedings of the 14th International Congress of Sociology* (Rome: Società Italiana di Sociologia, 1950).

60. George Lichtheim, *Marxism in Modern France* (New York: Columbia University Press, 1966), chap. 3; H. Stuart Hughes, *The Obstructed Path* (New York: Harper and Row, 1966), pp. 153–226.

of T. W. Adorno, Max Horkheimer, Herbert Marcuse, Erich Fromm, et al. was in Paris for part of the 1930's, but did not have a significant impact.

Raymond Aron and Georges Friedmann studied Marx seriously in these years and developed certain themes in Marx by building on advances of others abroad: Aron went to Germany and brought back Max Weber to the French public,[61] as well as a more sophisticated interpretation of Wilhelm Dilthey, Heinrich Rickert, Georg Simmel, and Karl Mannheim than was previously available inside France.[62] Friedmann went to the Soviet Union and returned with a heightened concern for technology and industrialism.[63] Aron and Friedmann both began academic careers which were interrupted by the war: Aron became associated with the Gaullists in London, while Friedmann participated in the metropolitan Resistance movement. After the war, Marxism and associated ideological concerns (defining proper political involvement: inside or outside the Communist party, which petitions to sign, and so forth) were among the most widely debated issues in the Latin Quarter. Maurice Merleau-Ponty and Jean-Paul Sartre had many common experiences with Aron and Friedmann (Ecole Normale, philosophy, study of Marx, the Resistance), and the debates waged among them in *Les temps modernes* and various polemical volumes dominated much of the Latin Quarter and French sociology until the mid-1950's.[64] Assuming a new Sorbonne chair in sociology in 1955, Aron devel-

61. *La sociologie allemande contemporaine* (Paris: Alcan, 1935). Although a relative of Mauss and Durkheim, Aron commented some years later on the dogmatic character of Bouglé and expressed the hope that he was not too unjust toward Durkheim in *Les étapes de la pensée sociologique* (Paris: Gallimard, 1967), pp. 20–21.

62. *Essai sur la théorie de l'histoire dans l'Allemagne contemporaine* (Paris: Gallimard, 1938); *Introduction sur la théorie de l'histoire dans l'Allemagne contemporaine* (Paris: Gallimard, 1938).

63. Georges Friedmann, *Où va le travail humain?* (Paris: Gallimard, 1959); Alain Touraine, *Sociologie de l'action* (Paris: Seuil, 1965), Part III.

64. Raymond Aron, *L'opium des intellectuels* (Paris: Calmann-Lévy, 1955); Herbert Lüthy, "The French Intellectuals," *Encounter* (August 1955), pp. 5–15, and in George B. de Huszar, *The Intellectuals: A Controversial Portrait* (New York: Free Press, 1960), pp. 444–458; Pierre Bourdieu and Jean-Claude Passeron, "Sociology and Philosophy in France since 1945; Death and Resurrection of a Philosophy without Subject," *Social Research*, XXXIV (Spring 1967), 162–212.

oped his non-Marxian approach to industrial society in greater detail in several lecture courses.[65]

A second line of development led Jean Stoetzel to the United States in the late 1930's. His contact with Halbwachs was partly responsible for both a theoretical concern with collective social psychology and a methodological interest in quantification. But whereas Halbwachs never combined the two, Stoetzel did through attitude theory and public opinion measurement as they had emerged in the United States. At his Institut Français d'Opinion Publique and later the Centre d'Etudes Sociologiques, he developed an important following of persons interested in survey research. Some observers suggest that this tendency dominated in the mid-1950's after disillusionment with Marxian-inspired ideology,[66] although there were occasional efforts to combine the two.

A third line that spread out in many directions was that of Georges Gurvitch. Born in 1894, he was about a decade older than other members of the 1930's generation, although he formulated many of his ideas with them. After studying law in Russia, he emigrated to Prague (1921–1924) and then to France, becoming a French citizen in 1928.[67] His works in the late 1920's grappled with German phenomenology, but in the 1930's he worked through the legacy of the Durkheimians; his earlier legal studies merged with the Durkheimian tradition of the sociology of law in a Doctorat d'Etat. After spending most of the war in New York, Gurvitch brought back a mild sympathy for empirical work,[68] returning to Strasbourg (1945) and then the Sor-

65. Raymond Aron, *Dix-huit leçons sur la société industrielle* (Paris: Gallimard, 1962); *La lutte des classes* (Paris: Gallimard, 1964); *Démocratie et totalitarisme* (Paris: Gallimard, 1965). These three courses were presented between 1955 and 1958. See also *La société industrielle et la guerre* (Paris: Plon, 1959).

66. Jean Stoetzel, "Sociology in France: An Empiricist View," pp. 623–657; Lucien Goldmann, *Sciences humaines et philosophie* (Paris: Gonthier, 1966), pp. 5–16. See Viet, *Les sciences de l'homme en France* for a useful listing of further sources, which are not cited here individually.

67. Myrtle Korenbaum, "Translator's Preface," Georges Gurvitch, *The Spectrum of Social Time* (Dordrecht: D. Reidel, 1964); René Toulemont, *Sociologie et pluralisme dialectique: Introduction à l'oeuvre de Georges Gurvitch* (Louvain: Nauwelaerts, 1955).

68. See *Renaissance* and the *Journal of Legal and Political Sociology*, pub-

bonne (1948) where, in keeping with the times, he focused on Marxian-inspired themes.[69] He became one of the leading interpreters of the young Marx, and continued work on social class relationships and the sociology of knowledge; in both of these latter areas he combined Durkheimian themes with phenomenology as well as Theodor Geiger, Mannheim, and Georg Lukács.[70] His work on social time drew on Halbwachs as well as Bergson. But despite influences from the French, like his counterpart Sorokin in America, he never became integrated into French sociology.

The fourth line of development contrasted sharply with the others; this was the ethnological tradition of students of Mauss. Unlike the *normalien* philosophers Aron, Friedmann, and Stoetzel, Lévi-Strauss and many French ethnologists seem to have had a less traditional academic background. Associated less often with Bouglé than with Mauss and Rivet at the Institut d'Ethnologie and the Musée de l'Homme,[71] they avoided the ideological hothouse of the Latin Quarter during long periods of field work. Their integration into an international professional community was also greater than that of the more politicized sociologists.[72] When they listened to Mauss, it was at the EPHE and the Collège de France (and on his famous walks home through the Latin Quarter), rather than at the Sorbonne or the Ecole Normale. Their ancillary work often took them into highly

---

lished through the Ecole Libre des Hautes Etudes, directed by Gurvitch, which included such French émigrés as Alexandre Koyré, Claude Lévi-Strauss, and Jacques Maritain.

69. When a retired lycée professor of philosophy offering a *cours libre* on sociology at the Sorbonne asked if abandoning the Durkheimian tradition really represented progress (Cuvillier, *Où va la sociologie française?*), he received a telephone call from le Doyen Davy informing him that Professor Gurvitch had requested that the *cours libre* be discontinued. Personal communication, M. Armand Cuvillier.

70. See especially Georges Gurvitch, *La vocation actuelle de la sociologie* (Paris: Presses Universitaires de France, 1950), 2 vols., and my "Comments on the Sociology of Georges Gurvitch," *American Journal of Sociology,* LXXIV (1969), 537.

71. Although often referred to as the circle around Marcel Mauss, the organizational leader of the subcluster was Paul Rivet. Despite his intellectual leadership, Mauss performed few activities of a traditional *grand patron*.

72. An intermediate case was Jacques Soustelle, *normalien* philosophy student who worked with Mauss and became an "americanist," but in the Resistance and postwar years, followed de Gaulle into national politics, even though continuing his ethnological work at a reduced level.

specialized courses in linguistics, history, and area studies at the EPHE, Collège de France, or the Ecole des Langues Vivantes Orientales. Here they came into contact with professionally eminent if less politically involved figures, like the linguist Antoine Meillet, the Indologist Sylvain Lévi, or the Sinologist Marcel Granet — all of whom had collaborated on the *Année sociologique*. Initial temperamental differences, field work, and study in less central institutions seem to have generated a certain detachment from the dominant Latin Quarter mood. Then, too, Mauss remained a supple and creative thinker until the end of the 1930's, while Bouglé had become rigid and ideological even before 1914.[73] Mauss was by no means the oratorical professor that other Durkheimians could be; indeed, in later years he sought to differentiate himself from them as well as from the philosophical legacy of his uncle.[74] He never had a large following.[75] However, his followers remained personally devoted and spent their lives developing ideas which he passed on. Through a certain detachment from their national traditions, they were able to build on the strongest at home and integrate the best from abroad, rather than rejecting their training and starting almost from scratch without the support of a professional critical mass.

73. See Claude Lévi-Strauss, "French Sociology," in Georges Gurvitch and Wilbert E. Moore, eds., *Twentieth Century Sociology* (New York: Philosophical Library, 1945), pp. 503–537, and *Tristes tropiques* (New York: Atheneum, 1965); also Louis Dumont, *Homo hierarchus* (Paris: Gallimard, 1966), pp. 7ff., where Dumont criticizes Bouglé, but asks the reader to look twice if he seems to deviate from Mauss, for "en tout cas que ce serait affaire de capacité insuffisante et non d'intention."

Lévi-Strauss would note, for example, that greater cooperation among the social sciences would have been facilitated if "sociologists had not assumed the attitude of a conceited mother witnessing the first paces of her young children and helping them with advice." "French Sociology," p. 506.

74. In doing so, he mentioned Durkheim's name so seldom that students, on reading Durkheim, were occasionally surprised to learn how many of Mauss's ideas could be found there. Personal communication, M. Claude Lévi-Strauss. It was as late as 1958 when his *Structural Anthropology* (New York: Basic Books, 1962) carried the following dedication: "May an inconstant disciple dedicate this book which appears in 1958, the year of Emile Durkheim's centenary, to the memory of the founder of the *Année sociologique*, that famed workshop where modern anthropology fashioned part of its tools." (p.v.)

75. Only about a half a dozen students regularly attended his EPHE and Collège de France courses in the late 1930's. Personal communication, M. Louis Dumont. M. Georges Dumézil reports that some twenty students would attend Mauss's EPHE courses in the mid-1920's. However, there were 171 students associated with the Institut d'Ethnologie in 1935. See Paul Rivet, *L'espèce humaine*, Vol. 7 of *Encyclopédie Française* (Paris: Larousse, 1957), p. 8.

There were of course other areas of French social science — linguistics, various area studies, law, geography, history of religion, and so forth — which bore the impact of the Durkheimians. Without pursuing these, mention should at least be made of the case of economic and social history.[76] Lucien Febvre and Marc Bloch had been professors at Strasbourg in the late 1920's and 30's while Maurice Halbwachs and then Georges Gurvitch were there. These were the years when their important *Annales d'histoire économique et sociale* was launched (in 1929), and Halbwachs from the outset was a member of the Comité de Rédaction and frequent contributor.[77] Much of French history had been close to social science since the turn of the century, but the *Annales* group was an especially important combination of social science and history. By creating and leading the Sixth Section (Economic and Social Sciences) of the EPHE in 1948, the *Annales* historians provided an important institutional structure for the continuing development of French social science. François Simiand also established a model for quantitative historical research with his painstaking reconstructions of economic time series. In the 1950's, Ernest Labrousse developed an important cluster of researchers utilizing many such quantitative procedures.

Structural Changes Since 1945

Ironically, of the Durkheimians who had done so much to bring German ideas to France, Bouglé committed suicide when the Germans entered Paris, Halbwachs died in Buchenwald, and Mauss became too distraught to continue his work after about 1940. The post–World War II period thus witnessed the end of Durkheimian dominance. Friedmann, Gurvitch, Stoetzel, Aron, and Lévi-Strauss developed further the lines of thinking begun in the 1930's. Other social scientific traditions continued in quite varied ways. André Siegfried and his students François

76. Fernand Braudel, "Histoire et Sociologie," in Georges Gurvitch, ed., *Traité de sociologie* (Paris: Presses Universitaires de France, 1958), I, 83–99, presents one overview.

77. His openness to new ideas was shown in articles there on Max Weber's work and changing ecological patterns of Chicago.

Goguel and Georges Dupeux conducted studies of political geography that had roots in the Le Playists. Alfred Sauvy, Alain Girard, and their associates maintained certain activities that came down from the social statisticians. These few names are mentioned, for to some degree they functioned as cluster leaders in the postwar period. Many others could be added, but most other examples would illustrate even greater discontinuity. More than continuous traditions mantained by a professional community, the social sciences in France, since entering the university, have been characterized by discontinuous successions of clusters. As the clusters overlapped in some areas while ignoring others, their disagreements led potential followers to be skeptical of professional standards and insecure about their careers.[78] In this respect the immediate postwar period saw few structural changes from earlier years. But in the late 1950's and 1960's continuing economic prosperity, political stability, and other factors led to considerable growth in financial support. The CNRS and the Sixth Section of the EPHE increased the number of posts for research and teaching, and with other sources provided research funds in quantities considerably greater than ever before. More chairs were added to existing universities and new universities were created.[79]

Initially these new resources were channeled to support traditional cluster patterns, but as the number of researchers, laboratories, and activities increased, the clusters grew so unwieldy that the system became fragmented. Increased resources, ceteris paribus, lead to decentralization of authority; this tendency seems to have been accentuated by the increasing number of sources (especially for applied research) as well as a greater tendency to award contracts directly to younger persons.[80]

With sufficient increase in size and certain structural changes, the system might have evolved toward a German or American pattern, including relatively autonomous centers for research and training united through various professional activities. Many

78. Cf. François Bourricaud, "La sociologie française," *Transactions of the Fourth World Congress of Sociology* (London: International Sociological Association, 1959), pp. 23–32.

79. See the time series in Chapter 1.

80. Cf. my "Institutionalization of Innovations in Higher Education: Four Models," *Administrative Science Quarterly*, III (1968), 1–25.

ardently desired such a pattern, which was seriously considered at the Caen colloquia and in the early stages of "reform" proposals after May 1968.[81] But despite discussions over many years, such a pattern seems to have been scarcely adopted in the humanities or social sciences, and only slightly more in the natural sciences. Persons in most basic disciplines, and in many professional schools, have offered the same essential criticisms of the system and the same proposals for change. With the exceptions of history and geography, the social sciences have not been fully incorporated in the secondary school curriculum, and have remained excluded from the licence-agrégation sequence. Sociologists, anthropologists, and psychologists thus would generally prepare the philosophy agrégation even though licences were created for these three fields after 1945. Economics in the Faculties of Law and political science in the Institutes of Political Studies have continued training largely for nonacademic careers. None has developed strong disciplinary communities.

While the agrégation also was an obstacle to research training in the natural sciences, they were apparently more successful than other fields in establishing contacts abroad — through research and teaching exchanges, international congresses, journals, and so forth. These contacts seem to have derived both from more universalistic standards in the natural sciences and their less intimate association with French national culture. Citizens of a country that once dominated the civilized world in intellectual, economic, and military matters find egalitarian international relationships difficult to accept. Imposed cognizance of military inferiority in two World Wars, and additional colonial losses, led to considerable emphasis on cultural superiority — and correspondingly generous subsidies. The impact which international relationships might have had in stimulating French intellectual life was thus diminished.

Still, many problems for France are similar to those of other middle-sized countries, such as Germany or England: small enough that self-sufficiency invites stultification, their national

81. See, among other sources, "L'université face à sa réforme," *Revue de l'enseignement supérieur*, IV (1966); the issues of *Le Monde* subsequent to May 1968; and the last sections of *Minerva* after 1966.

traditions are still so rich as to hinder international cooperation.[82] Internationalist tendencies in France also suffer from the brilliance of Paris — not only the artistic, architectural, and gastronomical attractions — but also the presence of leading writers and scholars from all disciplines. Any one university abroad pales by comparison. The whole of Paris is more of a multiversity than any single American center, and such Latin Quarter institutions as the café, the bookshop, and the little magazine link the specialized fields with French general culture. National cultural factors aside, it is much easier to leave a small European university, or even a minor European capital, than it is to leave Paris, especially if one is French.

One means of attaining excellence is to build on the best work abroad; but to do so necessitates international contacts. Such contacts in the social sciences have been most frequent in those areas least associated with French national culture, such as mathematical models and research methods, and in those substantive fields — such as ethnology or parts of history — which are particularly strong in France. Outstanding individuals from less advanced fields also tend to have a wide range of international ties. Thus it is the less advanced substantive fields and the less qualified individuals — precisely those who most need the challenge and support of extensive professional ties — that often rely on immersion in French civilization and Parisian intellectual life as a substitute for a professional community.

This situation is aggravated of course by the structural incompatibility of the entire system with distinct disciplinary communities. Even in the natural sciences, the national professional community is seldom large enough, especially near the top, to foster the universalistic standards that are less difficult for a larger system. Given the cultural barriers to integration with American professional communities, many French natural scientists, and at least some social scientists, have sought greater association with fellow professionals in other European coun-

82. Joseph Ben-David, "Scientific Endeavor in Israel and the United States," *American Behavioral Scientist*, VI (December 1962), 12–16; Ben-David, *Fundamental Research and the Universities* (Paris: Organization for Economic Cooperation and Development, 1968).

tries. Extensive relationships with intellectually underdeveloped countries have continued as in earlier years, but these have seldom provided serious professional criticism.

An alternative to international contacts is ties with adjoining disciplines, especially those of greater stature. A third possibility is closer integration into the general intellectual community — by reading and writing in unspecialized journals, participating in Latin Quarter intellectual life, and so forth. Finally, one can turn to governmental, political, or industrial groups, and participate in the many clubs, colloquia, and applied research projects they have supported. These last three choices, however, imply contacts channeling activities away from basic disciplinary research — the principal foundation for international standing. The choice among local and cosmopolitan reference groups therefore is crucial in establishing standards to guide development of a field. These four choices, each of which was followed to some degree through the 1960's, were affected by a broad range of factors, but, as in earlier years, some of the most important were shifts in temper of the Latin Quarter, funding policies, and the position of the individual in the national system. Each will be considered briefly.

The period after 1945 was marked by a somewhat spontaneous Marxism. Then, in the late 1950's, a more cartesian reaction followed, including "technocratic" consultation, applied research, and structuralist interpretations of culture. In the late 1960s Maoist and other radical "groupuscules" remained in a strained but symbiotic relationship with a vaguely defined structuralism.

Financial support for social science seems to have come increasingly from governmental and industrial sources demanding applied work. But pressures toward applied research often were delicately counterbalanced by Latin Quarter ideology.[83] Individuals could seek to avoid role-conflict through role-segmentation, but with increased pressures from student demands, many

83. At least one observer perceived that "le sociologue français d'aujourd'hui s'efforce de garder le contact à la fois avec le Commissariat au Plan et avec les *'Temps Modernes'*." Alain Touraine, "Unité et diversité de la sociologie," *Transactions of the Sixth World Congress of Sociology* (Louvain: International Sociological Association, 1967), p. 130.

delicate balances gave way. Considerable role-differentiation has persisted within the system, but individuals seem to have narrowed their range of roles.

The many potential reference groups have appealed differently according to an individual's location in the system, a first obvious distinction being between graduates of the Grandes Ecoles and those of other institutions.[84] Ecole Polytechnique graduates, often in economics and statistical institutes, have established linkages with governmental and industrial groups; but despite rigorous training in mathematics, a weak background in economic or other social science theory narrowed the impact of much of their work. Including more social science instruction in the Polytechnique curriculum, or that of other Grandes Ecoles, could effect dramatic changes in this regard.

The Ecole Normale graduates have remained for many the major source of hope. In history there have constantly been internationally eminent *normaliens*. Most others in the social sciences have prepared the agrégation in philosophy, and thus have been largely social scientific "autodidacts." This lack of systematic social science training, coupled with the strain toward system building expected of patrons, provided a major source of intellectual discontinuity. Abolition of the agrégation requirement for *normaliens,* declining importance of the lycée as a career base, new training possibilities at the EPHE Sixth Section and elsewhere, and the broad choice of apprenticeships in small research institutes seemed, in the late 1960's, to be leading some *normaliens* toward more cumulative development.

The possibilities for innovation created by a certain marginality also should not be ignored.[85] The ambition for grand-scale contributions inculcated at the Ecole Normale, combined with the creativity of Latin Quarter intellectuals, but still grounded in the rigor of an international professional community, could potentially lead to path-breaking work. Many have no

84. Cf. Alain Touraine, *Le mouvement de mai ou le communisme utopique* (Paris: Seuil, 1968); Pierre Bourdieu, Yvette Delsaut, Monique de Saint Martin, "Les fonctions du système d'enseignement"; and Bourdieu, "Reproduction culturelle et reproduction sociale," unpublished papers, Centre de Sociologie Européenne, 1970.

85. Cf. my "Marginality, Eclecticism, and Innovation," *R.I.S.,* III (1967), 12–27.

doubt sensed this opportunity, but to achieve the optimal combination of reference groups is no easy task. General intellectual capacity is clearly essential, but by no means sufficient; more than one capable mind has been crippled by the French system. On the other hand, just a single brilliant example can exercise enormous influence. While individual genius can emerge anywhere, the operation of the American system does not provide the same strains toward brilliance as found at the top of the French system.

To date, the Ecole Normale has in principle provided training for this sort of leadership. But without strong professional norms inside the national system, leading patrons have sometimes deviated considerably from international standards. In such instances, the level of private discontent has often been so high but that of public criticism so low that patrons and observers, especially younger observers, have seen their own standards erode. Essential for assuring the informed evaluation and criticism of supposedly original contributions, and for allocating proper rewards, are a minimal number of reasonably advanced and institutionally autonomous individuals. In their research such persons also can provide a sort of middle-level consolidation of ideas. Precisely such middle-level persons, however, have often been absent from the French system (and, on the other hand, produced in large numbers by the American system). The recent growth of posts with the CNRS, EPHE, and other organizations would seem to correspond to this middle-level category. But in fact many researchers in them have become integrated into existing clusters, or if isolated, would tend not to criticize others publicly. There seem to have been recent changes in this respect, although responsible criticism deriving neither from other clusters nor from spontaneous outsiders has not become an important tradition. The absence of such middle-level persons and the lack of clear criteria for professional evaluation have derived largely from the importance of clusters.

Both the structural supports for the cartesianism-spontaneity dichotomy and organization of the university system into clusters depend, as has been pointed out, on certain traditional elements of French society. Demands for change, however, and actual changes in the political system and, even more, the economy, have been so great that the university and associated structures have experienced considerable pressure. If scientific achievement depended simply on the number and quality of researchers, the prospects of French social science would be excellent. One can only hope that structural arrangements can be adapted to make effective use of these talents.

Chapter 8

Conclusion

For most new fields to develop, three fundamental elements are essential: good ideas to build on, talented individuals, and adequate institutional support. A solid core of ideas, some sort of paradigm, must be sufficiently original by institutionalized criteria to command respect from persons in adjoining fields. In France several tentative paradigms for the social sciences were advanced during the nineteenth century, of which few were associated with the other two fundamental elements. Most often such paradigms were created by a single individual (Auguste Comte, Frédéric Le Play) who could not attract enough talented followers or support them in a manner to sustain development of the ideas. The usual tendency was toward closure into sects.

Talent may derive from many social origins, but as most societies have had few talented persons of financial independence, retention of talent in an area generally requires the third element, some sort of institutionalization. The normal locus for central intellectual fields has been the university, or occasionally the academy or research institute. But even such institutionalization may be far from adequate. A sizable critical mass to evaluate research, advance careers, and award grants is essential if universalistic values are to become operating institutional norms. Doubtless no system has ever attained absolute universalism, but the greater the deviations, ceteris paribus, the less talent will enter and remain in a field, and the less rapidly it will advance.

The development of the social sciences in France was inextricably linked with entry into the university and its associated structures. For this reason much attention in this work has focused on patterns of institutionalization in and around the university. At this stage it is perhaps useful to outline schematically the basic structure of the analysis presented above. Figure 8 summarizes the basic variables which have been used, and their most important interrelationships. Each of the basic variables will be discussed in turn.

1. *National Economic and Political Factors.* Changes on the national level are treated solely to establish a context for other developments. Progressive industrialization, the Franco-Prussian War and creation of the Third Republic, the Dreyfus Affair, and the political and economic crises of the 1930's are introduced only briefly and mainly for their impacts on the Latin Quarter climate and on institutions of higher education.

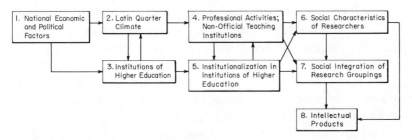

Figure 8.   Basic Variables of the Study

The ideas of the emerging social sciences are, however, related to more general patterns of French culture and social structure. Two traditions of thought, and two configurations of culture — cartesianism and spontaneity — are distinguished as fundamental outlooks rooted in different sectors of French society. In analyzing the oppositions between these two configurations, the history of French social thought has been reinterpreted with certain concepts deriving in part from cultural anthropology and organization theory. Some might designate the perspective as structuralist, but given current terminological confusion it seemed best to avoid this overused adjective.

2. *The Latin Quarter Climate.* Shifts in the climate of the Latin Quarter are considered mainly for their impact on potential supporters of social science. The popularity of certain individuals in the Latin Quarter helped them to establish activities outside the institutions of higher education, to influence the institutions themselves, and to attract capable students and followers; with shifts in climate they would lose support. Still, the Latin

Quarter climate, like national economic and political changes, is treated mainly as setting limiting conditions.

3. *Institutions of Higher Education.* In contrast, the national educational system, especially the university, is one of the central variables. Outside factors often influenced financial support and the quality and number of students entering a field. But directions of expansion of the system and patterns of relationships among scholars were heavily influenced by the structure of the system itself. Its remarkable centralization, and the corresponding linkage of the Sorbonne with the lycées, made feasible only very limited patterns of innovation.

4. *Professional Activities; Nonofficial Teaching Institutions.* When official institutions were unresponsive to changes in Latin Quarter climate, however, new centers of activity frequently emerged. New artistic currents or modes of literary criticism might lead to a new journal or appropriation of a café, but new scholarly approaches also often became institutionalized in new professional organizations, journals, and teaching institutions. In the social sciences such developments occurred many times during the nineteenth century. When supported by a favorable Latin Quarter climate, they would attract capable persons, including the best university students, and in this way exert pressure on official structures. In such nonofficial institutions ideas could be sharpened and diffused — although their success depended on continuing support from the Latin Quarter climate and the inflexibility of official institutions, neither of which was likely to endure. Nevertheless, certain activities of the social statisticians and international sociologists were long nurtured in such private institutions, and thus helped prepare the way for official support for social science.

5. *Institutionalization in Institutions of Higher Education.* Pressures from the Latin Quarter and competing institutions could provide an impetus to expand official institutions; but expansion was sharply circumscribed by the structures of the system. For new candidates to be named to existing chairs, or for new chairs to be created, it was not sufficient that the individual be competent and his ideas original. Support by members of an established field was virtually essential, and a complex network

of relationships among leading members of the system had to be activated. Differentiation from existing subjects was also curtailed by the need to justify the innovation in terms of the lycée curriculum, since the majority of students in Faculties of Letters and Sciences became lycée teachers. Nevertheless, geography gradually differentiated from history, and psychology, sociology, and ethnology emerged from philosophy. In the same way economics, political science, and statistics differentiated from law in the Faculties of Law. All of these new fields received a distinctive emphasis from their particular institutional settings.

6. *Social Characteristics of Researchers.* One source of such distinctiveness was associated with social characteristics of the persons entering a particular field. Fundamental in this regard was whether or not a field was housed in the university, and if not, by the type and strength of the private institutions from which it drew support. University entrance for a field implied many things, but one of the most important was the possibility for almost full-time research by at least a few persons. The need for would-be social scientists to support themselves by other activities hindered the work of persons around Auguste Comte, Frédéric Le Play, Paul Broca, and later René Worms. The social statisticians were recruited from persons in civil service careers, primarily directors of statistical bureaus in various ministries. The Durkheimians were the first important cluster of social scientists to enter the university; their backgrounds were typical of leading *universitaires* of the day: generally petty bourgeois in social origin, they attended the Ecole Normale Supérieure and completed the licence-agrégation examination sequence and Doctorat d'Etat while following careers in the university system.

7. *Social Integration of Research Groupings.* To develop a set of ideas beyond the formulations of a single individual, a *Nachwuchs* with a density and cohesion sufficient to elaborate the ideas systematically is normally essential: the research grouping must achieve minimal social integration. Such integration could occur in professional organizations, journals, and private teaching institutions; through such institutions the followers of Comte, Le Play, and Broca were moderately successful in achieving integration. Considerably more enduring, however, were the structures

245

of the national educational system; they were also conducive to the formation of clusters of scholars around a single patron. The Durkheimians thus formed an integrated cluster. For continuity beyond the career of a single patron, however, succession of leadership was essential. Succession was facilitated in established fields by the existence of examination series preparing students in the subject. But for the Durkheimians, with minimal support from the examination system, succession depended on more fragile relationships and a few key individuals.

8. *Intellectual Products.* Outside the official institutions, fragmentation of intellectual efforts was the general rule — certainly this was the case for the international sociologists. In their major journal, the *Revue internationale de sociologie,* and in communications to the Société de Sociologie de Paris and the Institut International de Sociologie, their research efforts remained largely fragmented, superficial, and noncumulative.

The social statisticians from an early date had a model for their intellectual efforts in the descriptive administrative report. Clear, carefully organized, self-critical with regard to the sources and processing of data, the bulk of their research eschewed generalization. Habituated to leaving policy-judgments to administrative superiors, they were similarly reticent to link their work with substantive theories.

In contrast, the impressive talents, commitment, and social integration of the Durkheimians led them to considerable intellectual achievements. The Durkheimians developed their ideas coherently and articulated them with one another and with more general concepts. Such coherence derived in part from the cluster organization of the grouping, which, following the normal division of labor in the French university, tended toward grand theory on the one hand and quite specific empirical efforts on the other; the structure of the university system discouraged middle-range theory. Horizontal differentiation, on the other hand, depended largely on the number of positions which could be occupied in the national educational system by members of the cluster. The broad Durkheimian definition of sociology facilitated such horizontal differentiation. Durkheim's ideas were thus taken up and extended by many persons throughout the system. Their efforts were most impressive — for a time. But the cluster remained too

246

closed to incorporate new talent, and it subsequently was displaced.

Since World War II the cluster pattern has diminished in importance, but no clear alternatives to it have emerged. Ambiguities, institutional and intellectual, thus continue to plague much of French social science.

Appendixes

Social Recruitment and Traditions of Research

Appendix 1

Social Characteristics and Institutional Affiliations

The appendixes focus on the journals of the three basic groupings, the *Année sociologique (A.S.)*, *Revue internationale de sociologie (R.I.S.)*, and the *Journal de la Société de Statistique de Paris (J.S.S.P.)*. Appendix III contains technical details.[1]

Occupation. The *Année* collaborators were overwhelmingly professors; the statisticians were governmental officials; the international sociologists were mixed,[2] (see Table 7). Differences among journals appear even larger when teaching institutions are compared. The percentage of professors at official institutions — Faculties of Letters and of Law, Collège de France, EPHE — was 84 for the *A.S.*, but only 19 for the *R.I.S.*, and 2 for the *J.S.S.P.* Twenty-five percent of *R.I.S.* contributions came from lycée professors.

Eduational Background. Clearly the *A.S.* collaborators were traditional *universitaires*: 78 percent attended the Ecole Normale Supérieure and 57 percent studied philosophy. Eight percent studied history and 6 percent law; the other subjects were scattered.

Contributors to the *R.I.S.* were much more diverse. There were a few with traditional academic backgrounds — 12 percent attended the ENS. More had attended a Faculty of Law — 24

1. These appendixes report only a small sample of the quantitative materials collected and analyzed for the present study. Restrictions on space prohibit more detail here, but additional information may be obtained from the author.

2. Throughout the unit is the contribution, not the author, and the base for computing percentages and the total number of articles published in each journal. In most cases information was missing for some contributors. But more than one piece of information (e.g., occupation) was sometimes recorded for a single contribution.

The leading statisticians were more frequently governmental officials than the average *J.S.S.P.* contributor shown in Table 7.

251

Appendix 1

Table 7. Occupations of Journal Contributors

| | Journal | | |
Occupation	Année sociologique	Revue internationale de sociologie	Journal de la Société de Statistique de Paris
Professor	137	81	39
Governmental Official	38	69	54
Businessman	0	1	10
Learned Profession	0	17	10
Total	175%	168%	113%
(N)	(395)	(297)	(95)

Source: See Appendix III.
See footnote 2 for explanation of percentages.

percent — but 2 to 5 percent also attended the Ecole Polytechnique, Faculty of Letters, or Faculty of Medicine. No doubt others completed less formal education, but this fact was left unmentioned by the sources used.

Mean Ages

	A.S.	R.I.S.	J.S.S.P.
1893	–	31	49
1898	29	45	54
1906	32	43	62
1914	36[a]	41	65
1925	50		

[a] 1912

Backgrounds of the social statisticians reflected training for governmental careers. The most ambitious (13 percent) studied at the Ecole Polytechnique. Others studied subjects more directly related to administration: history (14 percent), law (6 percent), and economics (2 percent), often at the Ecole Libre des Sciences Politiques.

Age. Three distinct age patterns emerge.[3] *A.S.* collaborators were quite young throughout the prewar period; but by 1925 the mean age had increased to fifty as few new associates were

3. Here in contrast to other sections the unit was the contributor, not the contribution.

attracted. *R.I.S.* contributors were consistently in their forties. *J.S.S.P.* contributors, older to begin with, aged continually.

Father's Occupation. Little precise data is available here. The most complete information was obtained for the Durkheimians, using mainly their birth certificates and the archives of the ENS. As Table 8 indicates, they were largely sons of petty bourgeois.

Table 8. Occupation of Father of Journal Contributors

	Journal		
Occupation of Father	*Année sociologique*	*Revue internationale de sociologie*	*Journal de la Société de Statistique de Paris*
Rentier or landowner	8	1	5
Well-to-do manufacturer or banker	3	0	0
Government official	3	0	3
Professor, university level	1	10	0
Professional (doctor, lawyer, clergyman, military officer)	18	1	4
Primary or secondary school teacher	22	0	0
Small businessman, merchant, etc.	26	2	2
Laborer—agricultural, industrial, domestic	5	0	0
Other	1	0	0
Total	87%	14%	14%
(N)	(395)	(297)	(95)

Source: See Appendix III.
See footnote 2 for explanation of percentages.

Much less information for the other journal contributors suggests variety compared to the Durkheimians.

Other studies suggest slightly greater representation of sons of workers and peasants.[4] This is the case for Gerbod's study of

4. Paul Gerbod, *La condition universitaire en France au XIXe siècle* (Paris: Presses Universitaires de France, 1965), p. 581; Alain Girard, *La réussite sociale en France* (Paris: Presses Universitaires de France, 1961), pp. 94, 193; Christian von Ferber, *Die Entwicklung des Lehrokörpers der deutschen Universitäten und Hochschulen 1864–1954* (Göttingen: Vandenhoeck & Ruprecht, 1956), p. 177; "A Survey of College Teachers," *Bulletin of American Association of University Professors,* XXIV (1938), 249–262.

teachers in secondary schools between 1842 and 1880, and more recent samples of French institutional elites reported by Girard. German faculty members habilitated near the turn of the century were higher in background. But social origins of American professors born before 1885 were much lower: 31 percent were sons of farmers and 12 percent of manual workers. It is obvious from the sparse character of these data, however, and their inconsistent bases, that all comparisons remain highly tentative.[5]

5. See Neil J. Smelser and Seymour Martin Lipset, eds., *Social Structure and Mobility in Economic Development* (Chicago: Aldine, 1966) on methodological dangers.

Appendix 2

Three Approaches to Research: Descriptive, Impressionistic, and Systematic

Mémoires in the *A.S.* were closer in format to the modern scientific article than articles in the other two journals. They regularly reviewed previous ideas and findings central to the topic, then formulated one or more original hypotheses. Third, they evaluated evidence bearing on these hypotheses. Finally, they discussed implications for subsequent research.

The *A.S.* appeared annually for the first ten volumes; the last two prewar issues covered three-year periods. Even by nineteenth-century standards each issue thus emerged only after extended gestation. Consequently, Durkheim (or Mauss or Simiand) had time to reread contributions, to suggest considerable revisions, and, if need be, to start over again. Each volume contained 500 to 800 pages. The first ten volumes began with two or three *mémoires originaux* of some 30 to 150 pages, followed by *analyses* of published works grouped into the classical *Année* categories. As each collaborator covered a series of publications in an area, generally year after year, the 30 to 100 page section he contributed annually permitted detailed interpretation and the elaboration of unifying themes on law, religion, kinship, and other topics. These partial syntheses became further codified in the *mémoires,* and subsequently formed the core of the Durkheimians' monographs. This cumulativeness of their research efforts was most impressive.

The contrast with the *R.I.S.* was marked. The dominant *R.I.S.* model was not the scientific article, but the essay: an informal, loosely organized form of expression more characteristic of the man of letters. Long issues of 70 to 100 pages came out monthly, a mean of 920 pages each year. About one-third of each issue was devoted to original articles, one-third to the monthly meeting of the Société de Sociologie de Paris, and one-third to reviews of books and short notes. The reviews were very brief (about a page compared to the three or more pages in the *A.S.*) and normally did little beyond serve notice of publication. The longer and more frequent issues of the *R.I.S.* implied less concern for editing; some issues appeared to have been almost thrown together. Observers have commented that the *A.S.* collaborators may have overinvested in the journal to the detriment of their own work; the opposite was the case for the *R.I.S.*

Like the *R.I.S.* the *J.S.S.P.* appeared monthly, but it was much more selective in what it published. Except in summer, the Société de Statistique de Paris held monthly meetings where two or three papers would be presented and discussed. While the *J.S.S.P.* included principally these papers and discussions, there were also comments on current events and short research notes. The editing was done largely by officers of the Société, especially the *secrétaire général,* but since officers changed frequently it is difficult to generalize about editorial procedures. The *J.S.S.P.* model was the descriptive statistical report. *R.I.S.* articles often did not consider sufficient evidence to test their assertions; those in the *J.S.S.P.* were so crammed with tables as to preclude systematic interpretation, not to mention linking them with a coherent theory. When social statisticians moved toward either more substantive social science or formal statistics, they did so largely outside their established organizations and journals.

Data Sources. The journals varied considerably in their concern with empirical materials. Although the *R.I.S.* included numerous programmatic articles, these almost never contained any careful empirical support. Simultaneously, however, the *R.I.S.* also carried a continuous flow of articles presenting undigested facts never really intended to be integrated into any theory. Journalistic reports on strikes, cabinet changes, and professions were presented, especially at the Société de Sociologie de Paris meetings. Such crude materials might have been refined into social science, but they almost never were; the Société rushed too soon on to another "relevant" topic.

In contrast, virtually all original *Année* articles carefully considered empirical evidence related to their hypotheses. The evidence varied considerably, but it was generally the best available. François Simiand used statistical time series of economic data. Durkheim used legal codes several times. Most frequent in *A.S. mémoires,* however, were ethnographic materials from preliterate societies.

The *J.S.S.P.* devoted far more explicit attention than the other two journals to securing and presenting empirical materials. Some 80 percent of these were from quantitative documentary sources (this was true for only 10 to 14 percent of *A.S.* and *R.I.S.* articles), about half the time from governmental agencies.

Methods of Analysis. As one would expect, it was the *J.S.S.P.* that included the most diverse methods of analysis, but compared with statisticians in other countries these still remained quite elementary. Only 2 to 3 percent of *J.S.S.P.* articles presented analyses with more than two variables in a table — the minimal criterion used here for "precursors of multi-variate analysis." Such unsophisticated analysis was, of course, consistent with the *J.S.S.P.*'s descriptive orientation; more specific hypotheses would have called for more sophisticated analysis. The standard procedure was to present time series for a given phenomenon — strikes, homicides, migration, and so forth — with regional breakdowns for France and comparisons with a few other European countries. Beyond this, precious little — as Table 9 starkly demonstrates. The other two journals generally lagged behind the *J.S.S.P.* in methods of analysis. Where the *A.S.* excelled, of course, was in sophisticated selection and interpretation of basic empirical materials.

Independent and Dependent Variables. If, as Léon Brunschvicg once observed,[1] the "darling vice" of the nineteenth century was constructing grandiose panoramas of human existence, the remark must be considered in context: the bulk of works at the time entertained far more modest ambitions. Most studies reviewed in the *A.S.* or published in the *R.I.S.* were descriptive ethnographic reports, histories of legal and economic institutions, and geographical descriptions of particular regions. The R.I.S. also included articles on the evils of alcohol and

1. "History and Philosophy," in *Philosophy and History—Essays Presented to E. Cassirer* (Oxford: Clarendon Press, 1936), p. 30.

Appendix 2

Table 9. Methods of Analysis

		Journal and Type of Article			
Method of Analysis	*Année sociologique* Review	*Revue internationale de sociologie* Original	Re- view	*Journal de la Société de Statistique de Paris* Original	Re- view
Quantitative data presented (with no discussion)	2	5	1	18	21
Quantitative data analyzed (some discussion of results)	9	9	5	73	61
Rates used	5	9	1	55	46
Historical (Study of one period in past)	4	1	0	9	6
Historical over time	16	15	0	71	52
Ecological analysis	10	10	3	60	52
Cross-national comparisons	8	14	5	48	27
Sophistication added to Le Playist methods	1	2	0	0	0
Precursors of sampling	1	0	0	0	0
Precursors of indices	0	0	0	0	0
Precursors of indicators	1	0	0	0	3
Questionnaire used	1	0	0	0	0
Quantification of Qualitative Data	2	1	0	0	0
Precursors of Multivariate Analysis	1	0	0	2	3
Precursors of control group	1	0	0	0	0
Total	62%	66%	15%	327%	271%
(N)	(387)	(95)	(202)	(62)	(33)

Source: See Appendix III.
See footnote 2 for explanation of percentages.

prostitution, manifestos of feminists, exhortations for economic reform, and travelers' accounts of African rituals — all side by side. The more theoretically inclined sought continually to "synthesize" this potpourri; the *R.I.S.* thus contained numerous prolegomena to the social sciences. But these attempts at synthesis were mainly after-dinner lectures which built on little previous work and remained too vague and unsystematic for others to

258

pursue. Thus, although any causal statement whatsoever was coded as indicating an independent variable, only about 30 percent of *A.S.* reviews and 20 percent of *R.I.S.* and *J.S.S.P.* articles were theoretical enough to proffer any causal explanation. There was no special preference among independent or dependent variables, but the most frequent tended to be economic, political, cultural, and geographic, in all three journals.

An effort to classify articles by theoretical models again demonstrated primarily their general absence. Organismic or functional analyses, conflict models, and social interactionist perspectives each accounted for less than 2 percent of materials in each journal. Just slightly more frequent were efforts to map evolutionary stages, but the driving elements were largely unspecified; those that were were tabulated with other independent variables.

Appendix 3

Technical Note on Content Analysis Procedures

Issues of each journal were sampled over the period from 1886 to 1914. Included were the *J.S.S.P.* for 1886, 1893, 1906, and 1914; the *R.I.S.* for 1893, 1897, 1906, and 1914; the *A.S.* for 1898–99, 1906–1909, and 1909–1912 (the last prewar issue); and *La science sociale* for 1886, 1896, 1906, and 1914. Every other article, book review, or announcement of over ten lines was analyzed, except *A.S.* mémoires, of which there were too few for quantitative study.

A code sheet of 59 entries was completed for each contribution, for the *A.S., R.I.S.,* and *J.S.S.P.* by the author, and for *La science sociale* by Mlle. Catherine Bodard (the results of which will be reported elsewhere.) Other persons were asked to code several articles and the results were then compared. The purpose was not to demonstrate interpersonal reliability so much as to make as explicit as possible the coding criteria.

The 856 contributions to the four journals came from 213 different persons. Social background data for the contributors were collected over some four months of intensive work by the author and two research assistants. A number of general biographical dictionaries were consulted first (*Dictionnaire de Biographie Française* [Paris: Letouzez, 1933 et seq.], *Qui êtes-vous?* [Paris: G. Ruffy, 1924]); then several specialized biographical dictionaries (of parliamentarians, members of the French Institute, and so forth) were used. These contained almost no information on the contributors to the journals studied, with the exceptions of Wilhelm Bernsdorf, ed., *Soziologen Lexikon* (Stuttgart: F. Enke Verlag, 1959), and Emilio Willems, *Dictionnaire de sociologie* [French version adapted by Armand

Cuvillier] (Paris: Marcel Rivière, 1961). Some additional materials were located in social science encyclopedias, especially the *Encyclopedia of the Social Sciences* (New York: Macmillan, 1930–1935). The card catalogues of the Columbia University Library, the New York Public Library, and the Bibliothèque Nationale were searched for biographical listings. Other information was collected from sources cited in the references above and in the journals themselves. Dossiers of persons holding positions in secondary or higher educational institutions under the Ministry of Education were inspected in the Archives Nationales. But as these were open for use only if the person had been dead fifty years or more, they were often unavailable. Certain unpublished files of former candidates and students of the Ecole Normale Supérieure at the Ecole and at the Archives Nationales were also used, as were the necrologies of the *Annuaire des Anciens Elèves de l'Ecole Normale Supérieure*. Finally, mayors of the towns where the Durkheimians were born were sent letters requesting that they record from the man's birth certificate the names and occupations of both parents, and the names and occupations of the two witnesses necessary by French law to obtain a birth certificate. The most useful single procedure for locating information, however, was leafing through each of the journals analyzed as well as more general journals such as the *Revue de métaphysique et de morale,* the *Revue des deux mondes,* the *Annales de l'Université de Paris,* the *Annuaire du Collège de France,* and *Bulletins et Mémoires de la Société d'Anthropologie de Paris* and recording information from the necrologies. Finally, additional information was gathered from interviews and correspondence with relatives and former associates of the contributors.

Index

Index

Index